"Filled with wisdom and insight for a culture running from God, Erwin Lutzer reveals gem after gem in *The Eclipse of God*. I burned up a highlighter reading this book!"

—**Dr. Frank Turek**, CrossExamined.org and coauthor of *I Don't Have Enough Faith to Be an Atheist*

"Erwin Lutzer writes books that beg to be read. *The Eclipse of God* is no exception. This book will make you think and invite you to believe in the one true God who alone deserves our love and lives, and equip you to engage the culture with Living Truth."

—**Dr. Jack Graham**, senior pastor, Prestonwood Baptist Church, Plano, TX

"Like a skilled physician, Erwin Lutzer not only accurately diagnoses the sickness of our culture, but also presents the only cure for what ails us—the truth of Jesus Christ. He does a wonderful job of encouraging believers to persevere and to keep the light on in an increasingly dark world!"

—**Gary Hamrick**, senior pastor, Cornerstone Chapel, Leesburg, VA

"When the noun *God* is being talked about these days, we must stop and ask, 'God who?' or 'Which god are you talking about?' This is due to the drought of sound biblical exposition that is lacking in many of America's pulpits today. Thus, many people hold to a horribly distorted view of God. These unbiblical views have had a devastating impact not only on the world but on the church as well. In *The Eclipse of God*, Erwin Lutzer masterfully lays out how we have arrived at this point and how we, as Christians, can rise above it by nurturing the correct view of God. Pastor Lutzer shows us how to engage with the culture lovingly, boldly, and effectively. This book comes at a critical hour, and I thank Lutzer for being obedient to the Lord in writing it."

—**Jack Hibbs**, president, Real Life Network; founding and senior pastor of Calvary Chapel, Chino Hills, CA

"This is perhaps Erwin Lutzer's most timely work yet. In *The Eclipse of God*, he gives crystal-clear insight into the murky pond of modern radical secularism. More than that, he shows us the appropriate response, calling us to a higher level of fighting darkness with the bright light of the Christian gospel. Most books that take a peek into our cultural quagmire cast a shadow of despair that rarely breeds optimism. Not this book! I found myself filling with hope with the turning of each page. This is Lutzer at his best!"

—**Skip Heitzig**, senior pastor of
Calvary Church, Albuquerque, NM;
author of *The Bible from 30,000 Feet*

"I can't think of a better book to quickly bring Christians up to speed on the key forces that have led to our culture's disastrous attempt to redefine and abandon God. Pastor Lutzer will take you on an enlightening journey that will not only open your eyes to the spiritual battles we face, but will also equip you to confidently proclaim the truth of who God *really* is in a culture that imagines Him to be someone very different."

—**Natasha Crain**, speaker, podcaster, author of
four books, including *Faithfully Different*

"Erwin Lutzer has provided a great gift to the body of Christ. In *The Eclipse of God*, he combines sound biblical scholarship with an awareness of current culture. Thankfully, he has the courage to identify our departures from truth and direct us toward a path of restoration. In a world of confusion and deception, this is a must read."

—**Allen Jackson**, senior pastor,
World Outreach Church, Murfreesboro, TN

"It takes a unique Christian scholarship to insightfully diagnose our crumbling Western culture and to weigh all the underlying causes and claims against the standard of God's Word. Yet I am very grateful that this book was written by one who is not only a scholar but also a lifelong pastor. He possesses the gifts to skillfully inform twenty-first-century Christians about what's really going on in our day, and at the same time, he is ably equipped to carefully shepherd his readers to respond with Christ-honoring thoughts and strategic actions. I am so encouraged that pastor Lutzer has drawn from his scholarly mind and his pastoral heart to give us this tremendously helpful work. Read it, respond to it, and pass it on."

—**Mike Fabarez**, pastor, Compass Bible Church, Aliso Viejo, CA

"Our crumbling culture has forced Christians to walk on a tightrope, and many are falling off. On the one hand, Christians are to make the most of every opportunity to share the great news that Jesus died for sinners. On the other hand, we are called to love our enemies and do what is within our power to enhance human flourishing via whatever non-sinful method possible. Walking that tightrope requires an experienced and steady hand to help us find our balance. *The Eclipse of God* will help you walk that tightrope and impact your world, both now and for eternity."

—**Todd Friel**, host, *Wretched TV* and *Radio*

"In this masterful volume, Erwin Lutzer combines his inimitable style of precise thinking and theological acumen with seasoned pastoral wisdom to provide a stirring reveal of the state of our culture. Calm, biblical, but with the clarion overtones of a bold prophet, Lutzer lays out a defense of truth that is not only accessible to all but deployable for any Christian desiring to stand firm against an ever-encroaching assault on God and the faith."

—**Dr. Mark M. Yarbrough**, president, Dallas Theological Seminary

"Amidst all our cultural wreckage, the living God of the Bible remains our only hope. In *The Eclipse of God*, Erwin Lutzer issues a clarion call for the church to walk in the light of God in an ever-darkening world."

—**Philip Miller**, senior pastor, The Moody Church

"*The Eclipse of God*—containing meticulous scholarship—is an extraordinary resource for all who seek truth. In this era of denials of basic reality and institutionalized deconstruction of facts, Erwin Lutzer's careful research and insights are more needed than ever."

—**Alex McFarland**, author, educator, broadcaster

THE ECLIPSE OF GOD

ERWIN W. LUTZER

HARVEST HOUSE PUBLISHERS
EUGENE, OREGON

Cover design by Studio Gearbox

Cover image © Ron Dale / Shutterstock

Interior design by KUHN Design Group

For bulk, special sales, or ministry purchases, please call 1-800-547-8979.
Email: CustomerService@hhpbooks.com

This logo is a federally registered trademark of the Hawkins Children's LLC. Harvest House Publishers, Inc., is the exclusive licensee of this trademark.

The Eclipse of God
Copyright © 2024 by Erwin W. Lutzer
Published by Harvest House Publishers
Eugene, Oregon 97408
www.harvesthousepublishers.com

ISBN 978-0-7369-8966-4 (pbk)
ISBN 978-0-7369-8967-1 (eBook)

Library of Congress Control Number: 2024930075

Printed in the United States of America

24 25 26 27 28 29 30 31 32 / BP / 10 9 8 7 6 5 4 3 2 1

Dedicated to the church, the body of Christ, encouraging all of us to fulfill the mandate of our Lord and Savior: "You are the light of the world. A city set on a hill cannot be hidden…In the same way, let your light shine before others, so that they may see your good works and give glory to your Father who is in heaven" (Matthew 5:14, 16).

As darkness covers our land, let us boldly shine the light of the gospel no matter the cost.

Contents

The Crisis of Our Age

R. Albert Mohler Jr., President
The Southern Baptist Theological Seminary

Any Christian living in this present age knows we are facing an epic crisis. That crisis is moral, but not merely moral. It is cultural, but not merely cultural. It is ideological, but not merely ideological. At its heart, our crisis is theological.

Alexander Solzhenitsyn courageously defined this crisis when he stated, in the last century, that the fundamental and inescapable problem is that "men have forgotten God." But, as Solzhenitsyn knew from tragic personal experience, this "forgetting" of God did not happen by accident. It was the result of the deliberate undermining of theistic belief, driven by those who, from the commanding heights of the culture, sought to subvert Christian belief and displace Christian morality. In the Soviet Union, the effort was led by Communist ideologues. In the West, the same effort was led by hedonists and self-declared cultural revolutionaries.

A look across today's conservative landscape reveals a near-universal sense of cultural crisis. But far too many conservatives place their confidence in some form of cultural rescue from our crisis. Biblically minded Christians know that we bear an important moral, cultural, and political stewardship in this age. And yet, we also know that salvation will not come by means of politics. The base problem is theological, and the only rescue that matters is, first of all, a theological rescue.

Some believers seem daunted by this task. The arrival of an aggressively secular age can appear to present an insurmountable challenge. But Christians are called to understand the challenge of this age, meet the crisis, remain faithful to the gospel of Jesus Christ, and arrive on the scene with the full measure of conviction.

We do not face a set of isolated and disconnected challenges. The rebellion of this age is both comprehensive and systemic. A rebellion that started out demanding liberation from the Bible's sexual morality now denies the physical reality of male and female. We have gone from the "swingers" of the sixties to a man in a female racing suit on the women's swim team of a leading American university. Understood from a Christian perspective, this was absolutely predictable. It can seem daunting and depressing to Christians, and understandably so. And yet, we have been called to faithfulness in this generation, and that means engaging the battle and not running from it.

Where do we start?

Well, our instinct should be to start by outthinking the world by the development of a mind and heart truly grounded in God's Word and fully alert to the critical challenge of our time. We need trusted voices and tested leaders. We need a combination of biblical fidelity and intellectual perception. That's why I am so happy about the publication of this book.

Erwin Lutzer has been on the front lines of this titanic challenge for decades. He is known around the world as a master expositor of the Bible who preached for many years from the strategic and historic pulpit of The Moody Church in Chicago. His voice is faithful and trusted. So is his pen. He has written a shelf of important and timely books, combining biblical insight with keen cultural and apologetic insight. That is exactly what he delivers in *The Eclipse of God: Our Nation's Disastrous Search for a More Inclusive Deity (and What We Must Do About It)*. One of the signal virtues of this book is Dr. Lutzer's careful delineation of the issues we face, informed by history and documented with evidence. Furthermore, he brings the crisis into focus with his understanding of the many fronts of today's pervasive doctrinal confusions. He addresses the crisis of truth and confronts the academic world and its denial of absolute truth. He understands the issues, names them, and confronts confusion with biblical truth. He does so with remarkable cultural awareness.

The world of Christian books offers a long list of near misses and a short list of direct hits. By design, this volume comes as a direct hit. As those who know him expect, Erwin Lutzer aims right at the center of our cultural crisis. At heart, it is a theological crisis. That's exactly where Erwin Lutzer takes his stand. After reading this book, you will know how to take your stand for truth and make your own difference. So, start reading.

Louisville, Kentucky
February 2024

From My Heart to Yours

My dear brothers and sisters: We are in a culture war that cannot be won by superior ideas, rationality, and common sense. There are forces at work tearing our culture apart, reviling all that is good and honoring that which is perverted and evil. Sober voices of decency seldom get a respectful hearing.

There was a time when disagreements about morality, law, freedom, and politics could be discussed in an atmosphere of basic respect and common sense. We did not have to fully agree with one another to maintain cultural cohesion based upon generally accepted Judeo-Christian values and the US Constitution.

Those days are past.

What we see is the unraveling and destruction of our culture, with the loudest voices frequently winning the argument no matter how wrongheaded, divisive, and irrational. We are, in effect, being asked to believe that two plus two equals five, that men can have babies, that children in grade school should question their gender, and that drag shows be allowed in school libraries. Meanwhile, the censorship of dissenting voices continues to accelerate, and those who seek to learn from the past and improve our culture rather than destroy it are being shouted down.

We are in a spiritual battle. Behind the destruction we see around us, there are invisible forces bringing darkness to the land—a darkness bent on destroying any light that threatens to expose it. And, as someone has said, we are living in a time when saints are being vilified as sinners, while sinners are being exalted as saints.

This is not just a clash of worldviews, but a clash of spiritual forces attempting to overthrow the God of heaven. We have forgotten, or at least many of us have, that Jesus Himself called Satan "the ruler of this world" (John 12:31). And the apostle John said that "the whole world lies in the power of the evil one" (1 John 5:19). We should be grieved when we see the encroaching darkness, and not be surprised by it.

How long can we as a nation insult the God of heaven without dire consequences? All sin has some immediate judgments, but often evil nations eventually experience catastrophic judgments. And, given our widespread sexual and gender obsessions, our varied addictions, our near-astronomical national debt, and our penchant for fighting foreign wars while allowing millions of unknown people into our country, it is doubtful that such wanton recklessness can go on indefinitely. God is watching, waiting, and weighing our nation on His scale of justice.

Yet in the midst of this, we as believers cannot lose sight of our calling. But if we fight our battles only politically and rationally, we will not be strong enough to withstand the pressure. Like a tree blown over by the winds of a tornado, we will lose our footing and submit to the culture for our very survival and livelihood. We will be condemned and shamed into silence rather than speaking for Christ and eternal values, and warning against the destructive nature of chosen paths of perversity. But when we see our battle as spiritual and not just a battle of ideas, we can engage those who differ with us in a spirit of compassion and courage with a sense of understanding, knowing that many in our culture are held captive to our real enemy, Satan.

Our choice is clear. Either we as a nation, and most urgently we as a church, return wholeheartedly to the God of the Bible in repentance, or we will find ourselves worshipping the weak, impersonal, and dark gods of our culture. We will bow either to the gods that seem to satisfy our immediate desires, or to God our Creator, before whom we will give an account. Nothing less is at stake than our understanding of the nature of God and His ways in the world.

This is not a time for half measures; it is not a time when we can have "three dollars worth of God" just enough to make us look respectable. This is a time of soul searching, a time of reflection. It is a call for humility and repentance. This is not a time for revenge and anger, but a time for counting the cost of true discipleship and gladly paying that cost no matter what it requires.[1]

> The culture war has come to us; we didn't seek
> it, but win or lose, we must stand against it
> without losing our testimony for the gospel.

The purpose of this book is to help us see that first and foremost the church must return to God—we must return to the God of fire, the God who is both merciful and just, the God who redeems but also judges. We must renew our understanding of His sovereignty and holiness. We have been given boundless spiritual resources to help us withstand the headwinds of a world that has lost its way. In truth, we have at our disposal the very power of God, if only we would be humble enough to take steps to receive it.

The culture war has come to us; we didn't seek it, but win or lose, we must stand against it without losing our testimony for the gospel. The churches in Revelation, to whom Jesus personally dictated letters, did not win their culture wars, even though Jesus pled with them to repent of their sins, to remain true to Him and endure the consequences, and to receive their reward. All throughout history, Christians have been called to faithfully represent Christ in the midst of a pagan culture. I argue for faithfulness to Christ and His church above all other loyalties, whether we can stop the moral and spiritual freefall of our culture or not. We are given the privilege of standing for Christ with grace and strength, even at great personal cost. If we have faith to believe it, this is a day of great opportunity.

Let us not be weary in well-doing, for we will reap if we faint not.

> O God, our help in ages past,
> Our hope for years to come,
> Our shelter from the stormy blast,
> And our eternal home.
>
> Under the shadow of Thy throne
> Thy saints have dwelt secure;
> Sufficient is Thine arm alone,
> And our defense is sure.
>
> Before the hills in order stood,
> Or earth received her frame,
> From everlasting Thou art God,
> To endless years the same.
>
> O God, our help in ages past,
> Our hope for years to come,
> Be Thou our guard while life shall last,
> And our eternal home!
>
> —ISAAC WATTS

If not us, who? If not now, when?

PART 1

SEARCHING
FOR LIGHT IN
A WORLD OF
DARKNESS

CHAPTER 1

Life in the Shadows: The Eclipse of God

Searching for Light in Our Darkness

C.S. Lewis wrote, "I believe in Christianity as I believe that the Sun has risen, not only because I see it, but because by it I see everything else."[1]

But what happens when there is an eclipse of the sun? The moon comes between the earth and the sun, blocking the sunlight from reaching the Earth. As for the sun, it shines as brightly as ever, but its light is obscured. This doesn't mean the Earth is totally dark; there are still glimmers of light, enough to move from place to place, but probably not enough to read a book. And if it is a total eclipse, you might lose your sense of direction and be unsure of where your destination lies. Darkness can be terrifying.

Today the moon of radical secularism has obscured the light of God; God is still God, but our nation no longer sees or acknowledges Him. In the darkness, you cannot tell the difference between an ordinary brick and a piece of gold; you cannot tell whether you are holding a diamond or a chip of iron ore. In the darkness, stumbling is inevitable. Look around you, and you will find a nation groping, looking for answers in places where there are none to be found. "The way of the wicked is like deep darkness; they do not know over what they stumble" (Proverbs 4:19).

Yes, America is experiencing a near-total eclipse. Secularism continues to make gains and is coming to its conclusion in morals, law, and education. We see the increase in violence, treachery, the abuse of the law, depravity, racial conflict, sexual perversity, drug use, and suicide. Darkness is being protected and normalized while light is being vilified and criminalized. Light is seen as a threat that must be extinguished.

The speed and extent of the changes taking place in our society should shake us into reality. We have enormous challenges ahead of us.

WHEN GOD'S FACE IS HIDDEN

Ancient Israel experienced the consequences of an eclipse of God. The Old Testament prophet Isaiah describes such an eclipse and judgment that followed: "Behold the LORD's hand is not shortened, that it cannot save, or his ear dull, that it cannot hear; *but your iniquities have made a separation between you and your God, and your sins have hidden his face from you so that he does not hear*" (Isaiah 59:1-2, emphasis added).

For "God's face to be hidden" is a figure of speech meaning that His blessing and protection have been lifted. Satanically inspired evil fills the vacuum, and shadows spread over the land. In the confusion, darkness is called light, and light is called darkness. In our day, this darkness is personal. Many people are living in despair, even contemplating suicide for the simple reason that they are trying their best to manage sin without believing in a God who is actually able to forgive them. They are left on their own to deal with their emotional brokenness without the cleansing and healing of God. Try as they might, they cannot wish their guilt and self-hatred away.

When God hides His face, we are left like a rowboat without oars, like a wanderer without a map and without a purpose. And the consequences are devastating. With the God of the Bible abandoned, we have no choice but to look to ourselves for guidance and meaning. As a result, we live randomly without an ultimate purpose, waking each morning hoping to eke out whatever pleasures we can find as our lives pass in a meaningless search for significance. And because everyone worships something, we are tempted to choose gods we can control; gods that will not judge us but affirm us; gods who do not demand repentance. Such gods do not create us; *we create them.* And these gods can only lead us into greater darkness.

Millions among us are living with what someone has called *self-directed aimlessness*, searching for some self-made god to give them meaning.

The Conflict Between Light and Darkness

What is darkness?

Spiritual darkness is the exaltation of human beings to believe they can run their own lives apart from God; it is self-dominance, an emphasis on personal independence along with rampant sexuality. Darkness is the view that if there is any meaning in life, it must be self-created; it claims that "you can be whatever you want to be," and everyone should bow to who you are. It is the lie of Satan to Adam and Eve: You are worthy to be your own god, so reject God's restrictions. Your problem is not sin; it is ignorance of who you already are. Darkness is celebrating evil.

Sin, we are told, leads to liberation.

What is light? Light is the spiritual and moral illumination that comes from God; it is the biblical assessment of the bad news of human sin and the good news of the redemption God offers through Christ. "God is light, and in him is no darkness at all" (1 John 1:5). To walk in the light is to have personal fellowship with God.

The Darkness Deepens

The dark paganization of America is most clearly seen with the sexualization of our children. Depraved minds who support this satanic assault want our children to be confused, sexually exploited, and their souls destroyed. "We're here, we're queer, we're coming for your children!"[2] the activists shout. And although some might say this chant should not be taken seriously, the fact is, yes, they are coming for our children. And when sexualized leftists come for our children, we know we are in the final stages of utter moral decay.

Consider the proliferation of drag queen shows used to groom children. At first when we warned about what was coming, we were told we were spreading a conspiracy theory, but as often happens, the conspiracy theory turned out to be a reality. Matt Walsh explains:

> A few years ago, back when conservatives first started to warn about the leftist plot to sexualize children by exposing them to drag queens, the most common response from the Left was to deny that any such thing is happening, "Drag for children?" they said indignantly. "Don't be ridiculous. This is a right-wing conspiracy theory!" But these things always follow the same script. First they deny the thing, then they admit that thing is happening but only rarely and it's not anything we need to worry about, and then, very quickly, they announce that actually the thing is happening, it's happening a lot, it's good that it's happening a lot, and it should happen a lot more...but it needs to happen because people's lives depend on it.[3]

Those who protest against this debauchery are told that they are "censors" and "book burners" and suffer from "drag phobia." All this from the very people who have done a great deal to censor or de-platform those who give a conservative voice to issues of morality and politics. Thank God there are still many parents in America who are pushing back against this onslaught.

Be warned: In ancient Israel, when parents offered their children to pagan deities, this was the final evil that led to the destruction of Jerusalem (see Jeremiah 32:35-36). Let us read what God said about Israel's sacrifice of children: "You took your sons and your daughters, *whom you had borne to me,* and these you sacrificed to them to be devoured. Were your whorings so small a matter that you slaughtered *my children* and delivered them up as an offering by fire to them?" (Ezekiel 16:20-21, emphasis added).

Don't hurry over this. God said that even these children belonged to Him; the sons and daughters offered to ancient deities were "borne" to Him. These were *His* children. And remember, these were sacrifices to the dark world of demonic spirits. Here is the divinely inspired commentary on what was happening: "They served their idols, which became a snare to them. They sacrificed their sons and their daughters to the demons; they poured out innocent blood, the blood of their sons and daughters, whom they sacrificed to the idols of Canaan, and the land was polluted with blood" (Psalm 106:36-38). In our day, Baal, the ancient god of sex and child sacrifice, has returned.

Today, parents who offer their children to the goddess of sexuality are not only destroying them but are doing great wickedness before God. To cauterize a child's conscience by telling him or her that perversion is normal is an attack against a child's soul. To ask a child to question his or her gender and to deliberately enflame lust causes confusion and guilt, and thus destroys the child's sense of decency and identity. And imagine the evil of those "gender affirming" individuals who recommend irreversible surgery for children and young adults with the result that they will never have the privilege of being a biological parent. Just as in ancient Israel, children today are being offered to demons of perversion and the widespread rebellion of our culture. Children are not safe in a pagan world.

Pedophilia is the next barrier that will fall.

A TEDx talk by Mirjam Heine argued that pedophilia is a sexual orientation that is inherent and unchangeable. She emphasized that pedophiles should not be judged but accepted; this, we are told, will help them to not act on their desires, for she agreed they must be restrained.[4] But if the argument is made that the sexual orientation of pedophiles is unchangeable, are we not depriving them of the sexual pleasure they deserve?

Until now, even the progressive Left has agreed that children are too young to consent to sex. But what if "research" shows that having sex with children is important for their development? Then anyone who argues against it would not only be impeding moral progress, but withholding sex might be perpetuating "harm" to children.

Far-fetched?

In the next chapter, we will be introduced to an influential researcher who, decades ago, argued for pedophilia. We must understand how a moral revolution takes place and cultural dominoes fall. Remember, it was only several years ago when saying that a boy can become a girl and a girl can become a boy was deemed absurd. But, to use the terminology of Francis Schaeffer, in one era, the *unthinkable* becomes *thinkable*; and within time, a new *unthinkable* will become *thinkable*. Remember, when God is evicted out of the consciousness of a person or nation, demonic darkness rushes in— and this darkness has no boundaries, no limits, and no restraints.

Whatever evil can be thought can be done. Thank God that He often restrains evil!

Jesus had something to say about anyone who would cause a little one to stumble: "Whoever causes one of these little ones who believe in me to sin, it would be better for him to have a great millstone fastened around his neck and to be drowned in the depth of the sea" (Matthew 18:6).

Meanwhile, in our so-called cancel culture, we have seen how the radical Left does not tolerate disagreement. In their minds, they are so enlightened that alternate points of view are often vilified or silenced. Ideology, even if unsupported by facts and reason, must prevail. To state that the values of the West (e.g., democracy, freedom, the nuclear family, and capitalism) are better than those of many other countries is no longer met by counterevidence, but rather, vilification. Cultural Marxism insists there must be equality of outcomes among individuals and nations; this can be accomplished only by destroying personal freedom. So the Judeo-Christian values of the West that stress individualism and personal responsibility are rejected as racist and nationalistic. Thus, the goal of much in our educational system is the demoralization of the West, particularly the United States.

As Adolf Hitler predicted, with the right use of propaganda, heaven can be made to appear like hell and hell like heaven. Like an avalanche racing down a mountain and obliterating everything in its wake, so our cultural *zeitgeist* is attempting to destroy everything that is rational, reasonable, and morally upright. The Judeo-Christian influences of our country are being discarded without any sober thought as to what might be a better foundation on which to build a civilized society. When I see the deep divisions in this country, I am reminded of a sign I saw in a Muslim demonstration: "We will use the freedoms of the Constitution to destroy the

Constitution!" We are so fragmented religiously, morally, and politically that we do not know who we are.

. . . .

We should give thanks to God for the privilege of
giving hope to a confused nation that is being torn
apart by various factions and loud incriminations.

. . . .

This is a battle that reason, science, and common sense cannot
win. Irrationality has gripped our nation. And as Paul predicted in
2 Thessalonians 2:11, prior to the coming of the Antichrist, people
would experience a "strong delusion" so they would believe "what
is false." In other words, The Lie. I believe that The Lie is man substituting himself for God.

Meanwhile, we should give thanks to God for the privilege of
giving hope to a confused nation that is being torn apart by various
factions and loud incriminations. Like many countries in the world,
we are in a period of internal unrest and many are looking for solid
footing when the foundations around us are crumbling.

Let us focus more directly on what is happening here in the
United States.

AMERICA'S UNIQUE CONSTITUTION

The United States was never an explicitly Christian nation, but
our republic is an outgrowth of the Judeo-Christian influence upon
which it was founded. Historically, this nation benefited from a
Christian ethos; among the shared values were honoring the nuclear
family, respecting the law, displaying common compassion and
decency, and most importantly, permitting religious freedom. But

as these core values are being challenged, we are edging deeper into political and moral darkness.

Unfortunately, many Americans simply do not appreciate the uniqueness of our constitutional form of government. It was built upon what Os Guinness described as the "golden triangle" that gave birth to our freedoms. In short, "Freedom requires virtue, which requires faith, which requires freedom."[5]

But let's think about it: If freedom requires virtue, what happens when virtue is replaced by unrestrained self-interest and entitlement? What happens when faith—namely, a belief in God and His laws—collapses and impersonal manmade gods take His place? What follows is that virtue is soon replaced by entitlement and a quest for power, almost always resulting in the loss of individual freedom. (Of course, we know that historically, true believers have often exercised courageous faith even under the heavy hand of tyranny.)

America is far from perfect, and never will be. We must recognize our failure to live up to our ideals both historically and in the present. But our Judeo-Christian heritage has given us the ability to preserve freedoms and has led to prosperity, by which Americans have been able to fund missionary work around the world. We should not think we as a nation have earned God's favor, but we must humbly entreat Him to give us wisdom to use our hard-won freedoms for spreading the gospel.

The Founding Fathers structured a government with three branches to provide stability and the possibility of self-correction as abuses arose. Without balancing freedom and political power, a nation must either drift into unrestrained chaos or accept tyranny. America has been able to maintain that balance because of its belief in God as the foundation of ordered liberty. Yes, thankfully, the nation does not compel belief, hence atheists are also welcome. But balancing liberty and law is a delicate task.

So can the Constitution protect us from all enemies, foreign and domestic? Can it preserve our freedoms? Of course not. Our politicians and judges can swear allegiance to the Constitution and then ignore it. China's constitution is a reasonably sane document preserving the freedom of the people, but words on paper mean nothing in the hands of tyrants. When power replaces truth and self-interest replaces character, words on a page are meaningless.

As believers, we dare not back away from the challenges that are on our doorstep. The better we understand our present crisis, the better we will understand why the voice of the church is more necessary than ever in our nation. If we have the faith to believe it, these are days of new opportunities for the church to be the church. We must live and work to create the unity that only the gospel can bring. The task can appear daunting, but we must gladly accept our calling. We are called to give hope to a nation that is in disarray.

Thankfully, God is present to give guidance and blessing to His people. We should view this moment of history as an unprecedented opportunity to represent Christ in the midst of our needy nation. We were born for this hour and none other.

Let us remember that darkness never retreats on its own; only light can expose it.

WHY THIS BOOK?

No matter today's news, as believers we must not lose sight of our God, who is majestic, sovereign, and faithful to His Word. We are called to prove that while the cult of diversity might destroy our nation, it need not destroy the church. We, as God's ambassadors, welcome people from all backgrounds, races, and religions to hear our message of the gospel of peace—a gospel that reconciles us to God and to one another. The gospel brings unity in the face of diversity; it brings forgiveness in the face of revenge and peace in the midst of chaos.

The church can be growing stronger even as our culture is declining.

We dare not forget who we are: "You are a chosen race, a royal priesthood, a holy nation, a people for his own possession, that you may proclaim the excellencies of him who called you out of darkness into his marvelous light" (1 Peter 2:9). Even as darkness deepens with wars, anarchy, rampant immorality, or an economic meltdown, we must still declare the excellencies of God and His marvelous light. Or, to put it more emphatically, in war, anarchy, rampant immorality, or an economic meltdown, *it is even more urgent that we declare the excellencies of God and His marvelous light!*

· · · · · · · · · · ·

The sun still shines behind the eclipse, and not even a determined secular world can blot out the witness of God's servants who are dedicated to sharing the light.

· · · · · · · · · · ·

As the fifth-century philosopher Augustine would put it, the city of man can be in decline even as the city of God gains in strength. When Rome was destroyed, he reportedly said, "Whatever men build, men will destroy, so let's get on with the business of building the kingdom of God."

Let every fragment of bad news (of which there is plenty) be a motivation to unite with other believers to pray, witness, and be Christ's hands and feet in a broken world. Behind the bad news, there is also good news: The sun still shines behind the eclipse, and not even a determined secular world can blot out the witness of

God's servants who are dedicated to sharing the light. And behind the headlines, God is at work.

So I write with three objectives.

1. To better understand the intellectual roots of this present darkness.

Like a doctor who diagnoses a disease before he prescribes a cure, so must we understand the ideas that got us here and how we can combat them. Doctors don't begin with heart surgery until they have done a diagnosis and are certain the patient is not having a gall bladder attack or some other ailment. In order to understand the eclipse of God, we must understand the philosophers who insisted that society should jettison its belief in accountability to God and put us in place as the supreme ruler of ourselves.

Like it or not, philosophers have shaped our modern world. Behind our moral and spiritual battles are thinkers who have convincingly articulated the original lie of Eden—that man should replace God. As such, many of them have had a massive impact in reviling the Christian faith.

We will answer questions such as these: Who are those blind guides who have led millions to fall into a spiritual pit? Who are those who have shaped our culture, given us destructive values, and traded our freedoms for tyranny? Who are those who have told us that God was oppressive and that human autonomy was the epitome of progress? Who are those whose theology promised a false hope that led us to moral and spiritual bankruptcy?

So, be warned: The next chapter will introduce us to three European philosophers whose dark shadows have spread throughout the West, including, of course, the United States. We will see that we can draw a direct line to many destructive ideas in our culture by considering those towering historical figures who sent us down a wrong path. As we have all heard it said, ideas have consequences, and bad ideas have victims.

There is a second reason for this book.

2. To rejoice that God is sovereign and stands ready to give us the blessing of His presence, no matter our predicament.

If we seriously focus on God in our worship and service, we can view our culture's darkness as an opportunity, not a liability. As mentioned, our fortunes as believers are not tied to the fortunes of the culture. God stands above our cultural and political feuds ready to give us "power from on high" (Luke 24:49).

Is God a Republican or Democrat? How does He vote?

This is not unlike the question that Joshua posed when he made a reconnaissance trip around Jericho the night before he planned to capture the city. A man appeared to him with a sword drawn in his hand. Joshua, in attempting to identify him, asked, "Are you for us, or for our adversaries?" The reply: "No; but I am the commander of the army of the LORD. Now I have come" (Joshua 5:13-14).

I have not come to take sides; I have come to take over.

In the midst of our political wrangling, we must realize that God is not a Republican, a Democrat, or an Independent. He is not running for office; He actually is God, and He is not just applying for the job!

Many of us spend time complaining about the political leaders of our nation, and there is much to complain about. But we need to step back and remember they rule at God's pleasure. Nebuchadnezzar was an evil king whose armies brutally conquered the Jewish people, and yet three times, God said of this evil ruler that he—Nebuchadnezzar—is "my servant" (Jeremiah 25:9; 27:6; 43:10). *God does not wait for the news; through His divine hand of providence, He creates the news!*

How big is the moon in relation to the sun?

If the moon of secularism has obscured the light of God, we must ask: How big is the moon in relationship to the sun? To the human eye, the sun and the moon seem to be about equal in size, but of course their actual sizes are hugely disproportionate. They look the same size only because the moon is 400 times closer to Earth than the sun, and the sun is 400 times bigger than the moon. So the moon might seem to be equal in size and prominence as the sun, but in fact, it is minuscule in comparison to it.

Secularism might appear to be as big as God, but God thinks otherwise: "Behold, the nations are like a drop from a bucket, and are accounted as the dust on the scales; behold, he takes up the coastlands like fine dust" (Isaiah 40:15). Take the 193 nations of the world, and they are like fine dust in the presence of an omnipotent, omniscient, and omnipresent God.

And there is more.

The moon has no light of its own; it shines at night because it reflects the sun's light. Without the sun, the moon would go entirely dark, powerless to shed light on Earth. Just so, secularism is totally dependent on God for any power it might exercise; even the wicked could not exist without God's permission and power. When the Antichrist arises and most of the world worships him, he will still be totally dependent on God for every breath he takes. In the words attributed to Martin Luther, "Even the devil is God's devil!"

Are you distressed because of our political polarization and wrangling? When Uzziah—the king who brought stability to ancient Israel for 52 years—died, the prophet Isaiah no doubt was concerned about the nation's future. So God graciously gave him a vision: "In the year that King Uzziah died I saw the Lord sitting upon a throne, high and lifted up; and the train of his robe filled the temple" (Isaiah 6:1). Why this vision? God wanted the prophet to remember that *even when a throne on Earth is empty, the throne of heaven is occupied.*

Psalm 103:19 reads, "The LORD has established his throne in the heavens, and his kingdom rules over all." Who established God's throne? Who crowned Him Lord of the universe? The answer, of course, is no one except Himself: God has been on His throne forever; He has established Himself, and yes, His kingdom rules over all. Such promises are given to us not to make us complacent, but rather, to embolden us to stand confidently for Him in the face of adversity. We know matters are not determined by Earth but heaven. That's why a friend of John Calvin, Theodore Beza, could say to the king of Navarre, who was persecuting Christians, "May it please your Majesty to remember, that she [the church] is an anvil that hath already broken many hammers."[6]

And knowing that God is in charge, we can fight the good fight from the standpoint of victory, not the standpoint of defeat. Remember, because every detail of the past and the future is known to Him, *He has already lived our tomorrows.*[7]

God oversees the vote in every election; no one rules but by His decree. Those who worship Him with the most fervor are the ones He enables to confidently represent Him in our fallen world. Even we as fearful believers have the resources to be faithful in adversity if only we would remember who God is. We are not culture bound.

There is one more objective for this book.

3. To remind us that only a repentant and submissive church can shine the light of the gospel with confidence and strength.

We are up against those who are convinced we can easily be crushed under the weight of secularization. Dennis Peacocke warns, "One thing is certain, that virtually no one in 'the real world' expects Christians to be a significant contributing factor in the process of creating a counteraction to secularism."[8] According to him, secular-ists just turn a deaf ear to our complaints and expect us to go away. But only with God's power can we have the courage to prove them wrong; and that power comes only to the desperate, the spiritually attuned, and the repentant. The battle is fierce. But like it or not, we are writing the next page of church history.

Seeing our battle as primarily a spiritual conflict will drive us to prayer; we will realize that we cannot fight the world on its terms. Only then will we see that when we engage with those who differ, our ulti-mate goal is to point people to the light of the world. Of Jesus we read, "In him was life, and the life was the light of men. The light shines in the darkness, and the darkness has not overcome it" (John 1:4-5). And as Christ's representatives, we have been called to share His light with the world. And "a city set on a hill cannot be hidden" (Matthew 5:14).

What would most glorify Christ? The answer is a people who are distinct from the world because Jesus Christ "gave himself for us to redeem us from all lawlessness and to purify for himself a people for his own possession who are zealous for good works" (Titus 2:14). In other words: a church that is *in* the culture, but not *of* the culture; a church that is a beacon of hope in a disintegrating culture.

The church has always been called to light a path in the night. Paul challenged believers who lived in a pagan culture with these words:

> Do all things without grumbling or disputing, that you may be blameless and innocent, children of God with-out blemish in the midst of a crooked and twisted gen-eration, among whom you shine as lights in the world, holding fast to the word of life, so that in the day of Christ I may be proud that I did not run in vain or labor in vain (Philippians 2:14-16).

The deeper the darkness, the more necessary light becomes. Or, as Apollon Maykov put it, "The darker the night, the brighter the stars, the deeper the grief, the closer is God."[9]

· · · · · · · · · · · ·

> Will we face the future with pessimism because
> we see the cultural disintegration around us, or will
> we be optimistic because we believe in God and
> that history will unfold according to His plan?

· · · · · · · · · · · ·

Unless we as God's people return in humble repentance to the God of the Bible—the God of Abraham, Isaac, and Jacob—we and our children and grandchildren will be swept away by the rising tides of irrationality and sexual perversion. We cannot stand against Babylon with a Christianity that expects nothing, demands nothing, and stands for nothing. Or, to put it differently, we cannot conquer Jericho with a wilderness heart.

As a church, we are at the crossroads: Will we face the future with pessimism because we see the cultural disintegration around us, or will we be optimistic because we believe in God and that history will unfold according to His plan? Are we willing to suffer for our convictions? And do so with compassion? Remember that millions among us have no hope beyond the haphazard struggles of this world.

We must not resort to anger and retaliation. We must cling to the gospel, sharing the redemption of Christ with as many as will hear; we must point men and women to the Light of the World and be willing to suffer the consequences of our identification with the One who died that we might have life. This is a tall order, but this is the task to which we have been called.

Let me repeat: This is not just a battle of ideas, but a cosmic battle for the minds of men, women, and children. It is a spiritual conflict. Ponder the words of William Booth, the founder of the Salvation Army: "I consider that the chief dangers which confront the coming century will be religion without the Holy Ghost, Christianity without Christ, forgiveness without repentance, salvation without regeneration, politics without God and heaven without hell."[10]

Let's get over the idea that we can please everyone. Truth, no matter how lovingly presented, will illicit indifference and even hatred among those committed to secularism. Jesus said, "If the world hates you, know that it has hated me before it hated you" (John 15:18). We are called to love our enemies (and that includes our ideological enemies), but they have no such calling on their lives. In fact, as we will see, their tactics might lead to destruction; ours should be loving but courageous engagement. Let us respect everyone, even when we can't respect what they say or believe.

Be warned: Our culture seeks to use intimidation to achieve domination. Let's not think our road will be easy; Jesus was the "light of the world" and yet He was crucified. Millions of our brothers and sisters live in countries where faithfulness demands giving up their income and even their lives. They were motivated by another world.

Running throughout this book, whether stated explicitly or implicitly, are these questions: *What price are we willing to pay to do the right thing? And to declare the right message? And to live for God's glory and not our own?*

Each chapter of this book will end with a suggested "Declaration of Dependence" and an Action Step encouraging us to begin a journey that will end on our knees. Let us remember that the sun is still shining behind the eclipse. "Restore us, O LORD God of hosts! Let your face shine, that we may be saved!" (Psalm 80:19).

In the next chapter, we will discover why the cathedrals of Europe are empty, and why we are witnessing the same decline of Christian influence here in the United States. Be prepared to jump into some philosophical waters.

A DECLARATION OF DEPENDENCE

Are we personally experiencing an "eclipse of God"? That is, have we lost a sense of His presence and favor? Are there clouds in our lives that must be confessed and forsaken so God's favor can return? We need God's light to shine in our lives before we can impact the darkness around us. How can we shine His light if we ourselves are walking in moral and spiritual darkness?

Here is a rebuke we must heed: "If we say we have fellowship with him while we walk in darkness, we lie and do not practice the truth. But if we walk in the light, as he is in the light, we have fellowship with one another [that is, we have fellowship with God and He has fellowship with us], and the blood of Jesus his Son cleanses us from all sin" (1 John 1:6-7). Many Christians—when they become dead honest—will admit they are not walking in complete transparency and honesty with God. There are shadows in their lives that keep a formal distance between them and Him. They have the right words, but their heart is elsewhere. To all of us I say, "There is no substitute for repentance."

What is the most distinguishing mark of the people of God? It is what the Puritans called "the manifest presence of God." Moses asked the question, "How shall it be known that I have found favor in your sight, I and your people? Is it not in your going with us, so that we are distinct, I and your people, from every other people on the face of the earth?" (Exodus 33:16). And Paul said that when people come into our congregations, they should be able to say, "God is really among you" (1 Corinthians 14:25).

Even when a nation experiences an eclipse of God, we can personally experience the light of His presence. Let us spend time seeking His favor. John Piper writes,

> This setting of the mind is the opposite of mental coasting. It is a conscious choice to direct the heart toward God. This is what Paul prays for the church: "May the Lord direct your hearts to the love of God and to the steadfastness of Christ" (2 Thessalonians 3:5). It is a conscious effort on our part. But that effort to seek God is a gift from God.[11]

With Moses, let us pray, "The LORD bless you and keep you; the LORD make his face to shine upon you and be gracious to you; the LORD lift up his countenance upon you and give you peace" (Numbers 6:24-26). Only the light of God can dissipate the darkness.

Let us "seek the LORD while he may be found, and call upon him when he is near" (Isaiah 55:6).

ACTION STEP

In response to this opening chapter, let us resolve to pay as much attention to our soul as we do our body. Let us give attention to our own sins rather than the sins of the culture. We face a common enemy—namely, Satan—and we have to fight together with the "shield of faith" against the "cosmic powers over this present darkness, against spiritual forces of evil in heavenly places" (Ephesians 6:12). So, before we engage the war without, let us recognize the war within us—a war against various sins and unacknowledged self-righteousness. Let us resolve to be "eager to maintain the unity of the Spirit in the bond of peace" (Ephesians 4:3). Let us be united in the battle against the encroaching darkness. *United we stand; divided we fall.*

> Search me, O God, and know my heart!
>   Try me and know my thoughts!
> And see if there be any frivolous way in me,
>   and lead me in the way everlasting!
> (Psalm 139:23-24).

CHAPTER 2

Three Gravediggers Who Prepared a Coffin for God

How the Shadows of Europe
Have Come to America

G od is dead!"

The German philosopher Friedrich Nietzsche proclaimed this news to the world back in the late 1800s; with the changes brought by European Enlightenment, we should no longer see the world as having transcendent meaning; no longer should we see ourselves as created or subject to a higher being. Nietzsche worshipped human potential, saying "the noble soul has reverence for itself."[1]

He wrote in vivid terms about the demise of God:

> Do we not hear…the noise of the gravediggers who are burying God? Do we not smell anything yet of God's decomposition? Gods, too, decompose. God is dead, and we have killed him. God remains dead. And we have killed him. How shall we, the murderers of all murderers, comfort ourselves?…Who will wipe this blood off us?[2]

So who killed God? Who are the "gravediggers" who gave Nietzsche the right to perform the last rites and bury the divine corpse?

When Nietzsche wrote in the late 1800s, Europe was on the brink of secularization. Christianity was still the cultural glue that held society together, but the union of church and state meant that the church was being politicized and had lost much authority and credibility. Also, it could not withstand the cultural streams that would sweep the continent and replace God with a flawed view of human potential. Over time, the cathedrals would become empty and a mindless tolerance would eventually morph into spiritual lethargy.

God would fade into the distance and man would arise to take His place. And so, with the death of God came the darkness of plea-sure-driven secularism. And worse, violence and unrestrained evil.

THREE GRAVEDIGGERS

I'm not sure Nietzsche had anyone in particular in mind when he spoke of the "noise of the gravediggers" who were "burying God." But we can certainly identify many influential thinkers who, figu-ratively speaking, tried their best to put nails into God's coffin. All that was necessary for Nietzsche to do was to announce the com-mittal and bury the corpse.

Among the many gravediggers, this chapter introduces us to just three: Karl Marx, whose economic revolution attacked God as *ruler*; Charles Darwin, who attacked God as *creator;* and Sigmund Freud, who attacked God as *lawgiver.* These three philosophers, per-haps more than others, influenced entire nations, the United States included. They created a contagion, a debilitating virus, that has infiltrated every one of our institutions, our lives, and our families.

As mentioned in the previous chapter, the church in Europe

was totally swept off its feet by these nineteenth-century thinkers who, building on the insights of the enlightenment, began cultural streams that ended up becoming a spiritual and moral and political tsunami, destroying everything in its wake. Christianity was revised to conform to these new realities, and in becoming transformed by the culture, it had nothing of significance to say to it.

When Enlightenment thinkers thought human reason divorced from a belief in God could give us an advanced civilization, they did not realize this would eventually lead to moral anarchy, totalitarianism, and irrationality.

The European Enlightenment was a mixed blessing. On the one hand, it gave us the freedom to think outside the box regarding human freedom, progress, government, and science (Kepler, Newton, et al., believed there were physical laws because there was a lawgiver). But it also had a dark side: When Enlightenment thinkers thought human reason divorced from a belief in God could give us an advanced civilization, they did not realize this would eventually lead to moral anarchy, totalitarianism, and irrationality. The so-called superstitions of Christianity they denounced have been replaced with emptiness, and moral *progress* has become *regress,* and *tolerance* has become visceral *intolerance.*

These three philosophers wrongly believed we could replace God with man and be better off for it. Clearly, they were blinded by their own arrogance and optimistic view of human nature. They preferred darkness rather than light.

Let's consider these thinkers more carefully.

The Theology of Karl Marx: An Attack on God as Ruler

The *theology* of Marx?

Was he not a philosopher who believed in the restructuring of the economy with the goal of the state bringing about "equality" for every citizen? We might think he had no theology. But let us not divide the world between those who worship and those who don't; the question is, Do we worship God or human potential?

So even atheists must grapple with their view of God.

Yes, Marxism is an economic theory, but at its core, it is an attack on God, who was derided as irrelevant to life in the real world. Marx taught that religion had some value as a transition, but it would soon be eclipsed by the satisfaction brought about by the exaltation of the state—not just any state, but a state controlled by the proletariat, the workers of the world. In short, the state would replace God.

Religion arose, he argued, because man needed some higher purpose in life, and so man created the idea of God. In other words, *God did not create man; man created God.* As time progressed, man felt alienated from the very God he himself created; the poor saw God as a consolation prize at the end of an oppressed life.

Marx was convinced that belief in God was a fantasy soon jettisoned once man's attention turned from heaven to Earth. People would outgrow their need for religion once communism was the ruling philosophy, and utopia would exist not in the sweet by and by, but in the here and now.

Clearly, God was not setting the world aright; therefore, Marx thought it was his task to do so. His poems affirmed that he himself would take the place of God.

> With disdain I will throw my gauntlet
> Full in the face of the world,

And see the collapse of this pygmy giant
Whose fall will not stifle my ardor.

Then I will wander godlike and victorious
Through the ruins of the world
And, giving my words an active force,
I will feel equal to the creator.[3]

I will feel equal to the creator!
Marx's philosophy had serious flaws.

The Flaws in Marx's Views
Human Nature Is Basically Good

Rousseau, who preceded Marx, taught that human beings were basically good; it was society that corrupts them. Marx, building on this thesis, taught that man is indeed good, but capitalism corrupts him. Human nature could be changed if society changed; if people owned nothing but still had their needs met, they would live in harmony.

Marx's basic axiom was that satisfaction came through work, but in a world run by capitalists, the workers felt alienated; they were exploited. Something had to be done to correct this malady. To be sure, Marx was right about exploitation, but his answer became a curse that has inflicted much of the world.

In our day, cultural Marxism argues that since human nature is basically good, we need only to exchange the oppression of capitalism with a form of socialism in order to bring about an earthly utopia of sorts. It is not the human heart but the environment alone that is at fault.

And with that, our modern "defund the police" movement generally agrees. Police and jails are "oppressive" and therefore, if penalties were either removed or lessened, a better society would be the result. Too often our cultural elite see criminals as victims, not victimizers.

Just watch the news to see how that is working out.

Loyalty from God to the State

Marx believed Christianity would have to be destroyed and replaced by loyalty to the state—the loss of God would be a step forward; in fact, the state would even take the place of Christ the Redeemer. Marx wrote, "As Christ is the intermediary unto whom man unburdens all his divinity, all his religious bonds, so the state is the mediator unto which he transfers all his Godlessness, all his human liberty."[4]

So, loyalty to an imaginary Christ would be transferred to loyalty to the state. The state would do what Christ did not—namely, to meet the daily needs of its people: The state would give the people their daily bread. Marx believed the state should centralize credit by means of a national bank to make sure wealth would be equally divided among its citizens. This would put an end to capitalists, who he believed always derived their wealth on the backs of the poor. If the state would enforce equality of outcomes (which we now call "equity"), it would bring about a level playing field.

Critical to Marx's socialism is the conviction that people should own nothing; men and women would not work for themselves but work for the state, which, in turn, would serve them. Collective farms and factories would benefit everyone and contentment would replace conflict. And at last, life would be "fair." Better that everyone be equally poor than have some richer than others.

To bring this about, Marx advocated for the overthrow of society as it was in order to cause the chaos needed to bring about a revolution. Only a revolution could force owners to surrender all they had to the state. Chaos was the necessary precursor to the revolution.

Marx believed that conflict, which already existed between the bourgeois and the proletariat, had to be exacerbated and exploited. The divisions between the oppressors and the oppressed had to be the basic mantra so that oppressors could be overthrown. It was necessary to think of people as groups rather than individuals.

The Destruction of the Family

Marx called for the abolition of the family, which he saw as a threat to his socialist agenda. The created order had to be destroyed to bring about equity, which, as mentioned, refers to equality of outcomes. The family was seen as a unit of oppression. Men oppressed their wives, parents oppressed their children and took them to church, and God was the ultimate oppressor. What is more, families tended to pass along their wealth to their children, perpetuating inequality. Thus, with the restructuring of the state, the destruction of the family was inevitable. The physical needs of the children would, for a time, be cared for by the parents, but their education would be in the hands of Marxist educators who would teach them religion was evil, atheism was scientific, and socialism would bring about utopia. Education was a task too important to be left to parents.

If the proletariat (the working class) were to foment a revolution and become the ruling class, the innate goodness of man would be realized, and a classless society would emerge.

The Communist Manifesto tells us that the revolution would sweep

> away by force the old conditions of production, then it
> will, along with these conditions, have swept away the
> conditions for the existence of class antagonisms, and
> of classes generally, and will thereby have established its

own supremacy as a class. In place of the old bourgeois society, with its classes and class antagonisms, we shall have an association, in which the free development of each is the condition for the free development of all.[5]

So, once the oppressors were destroyed and the oppressed (proletariat) were in charge, laws would no longer be needed; even the state itself would wither away, and as mentioned, oppressors (such as a police force) would become obsolete.

In the conclusion of the Manifesto, the Communists

openly declare that their ends can be attained only by the forceable overthrow of all existing social conditions. Let the ruling classes tremble at a Communist revolution. The proletarians have nothing to lose but their chains. They have a world to win! Working men of all countries unite![6]

Marx was looking for professional revolutionaries, which Dave Breese defines as "the radical individual who, while disbelieving in God, soul, and eternal destiny, is still willing to hazard his life to produce revolutionary change. The professional revolutionary is possibly the world's most dangerous man."[7] Breese later comments that "Marx saw the true Communist as a person possessed with profound insight, a limitless vision for the future, a willingness to do anything to bring that future to pass, and a total loyalty to the Party."[8]

The Bitter Fruit of Marx's Theories

How did Marx's call for a revolution turn out?

Utopia didn't arise out of the Marxist state. It is a fantasy to think people will wake up in the morning excited to work "each according to his ability" so that he can give to their fellow man "each according to his need." The equality Marxists seek can be gained only by imposing laws that seek to destroy religion, controlling salaries, and exercising brutal censorship. History has proven that socialism inevitably produces *a paradise for parasites.*

Here is a paragraph in which Alexander Solzhenitsyn described what communism brought about in Russia:

> Orthodox churches were stripped of their valuables...
> Tens of thousands of churches were torn down or dese-
> crated, leaving behind a disfigured wasteland that bore
> no resemblance to Russia as such...People were con-
> demned to live in this dark and mute wilderness for
> decades, groping their way to God...15,000,000 peas-
> ants were brought to death for the purpose of destroy-
> ing our national way of life and of extirpating religion
> from the countryside...Hatred of religion is rooted in
> Communism.[9]

Solzhenitsyn is right—"men have forgotten God." And of course, they have often forgotten the biblical doctrine of inborn sin, which is evident on every page of human history. Having rejected God's cure for our sinful woes, the selfishness of man was unleashed, resulting in intimidation, exploitation, and the destruction of human freedom.

Marx holds a special place in the minds of the elite here in the Western world and by many university professors. While writers of the Enlightenment are being removed from universities because they are "dead white men," Karl Marx's place in our educational system is secure. While the radical Left scours about trying to find traces of racism from philosophers of the Enlightenment and the Founding Fathers, Marx's racist comments are forgiven.

Marx, like Darwin, whom we will look at shortly, was racist. He vilified the Jews by calling them names. In an article entitled "On the Jewish Question," he said, "What is the worldly religion of the Jew? Huckstering. What is his worldly God? Money…Money is the jealous god of Israel, in face of which no other god may exist. Money degrades all the gods of man—and turns them into commodities… The bill of exchange is the real god of the Jew. His god is only an illusory bill of exchange…The chimerical nationality of the Jew is the nationality of the merchant, of the man of money in general."[10]

But there is no danger Marx's tomb in a London cemetery or any statues of him will be toppled. He remains a darling to the radical Left, who see in his writings the need for a cultural application of his teachings for us in America. Thus, cultural Marxism plots to take over our culture on tiptoe, institution by institution. Eventually the silent slippers become boots trampling human freedom and bringing cultural enslavement.

Marx is one of the gravediggers who inspired Nietzsche to declare the death of God. After Marx, God was no longer to be seen as the ruler of the world. The rise of the state controlled by the proletariat would replace Him. Civilization had outgrown its need for Him.

Marx for the Twenty-First Century

Karl Marx had the vision of the entire world becoming a Marxist paradise. I'm sure he would be pleased with the World Economic Forum, which is carrying his vision forward with the kind of speed and the help of technology that Marx could never have imagined. They argue that in order to shape the future of the world, you first must imagine it. In an article titled "Welcome to 2030. I own nothing, have no privacy, and life has never been better," which was originally published on the WEF website, author and Danish politician Ida Auken wrote,

Welcome to the year 2030. Welcome to my city—or should I say, "our city." I don't own anything. I don't own a car. I don't own a house. I don't own any appliances or any clothes.

It might seem odd to you, but it makes perfect sense for us in this city. Everything you considered a product, has now become a service. We have access to transportation, accommodation, food and all the things we need in our daily lives. One by one all these things became free, so it ended up not making sense for us to own much…

In our city we don't pay any rent, because someone else is using our free space whenever we do not need it. My living room is used for business meetings when I am not there.[11]

The article goes on to describe this utopian view of the future and how technology will be used to bring it about. Of course, it is difficult to take this description of the future seriously, but, if you study *COVID 19: The Great Reset, The Fourth Industrial Revolution,* or *The Great Narrative,*[12] you will discover that some of the wealthiest, most influential elites who meet in places like Davos, Switzerland, are working toward a unified, tightly controlled global Marxist strategy based on the values of Diversity, Equity, and Inclusion (DEI).[13]

If you wonder whether this will eventually be achieved, read Revelation 13:5-10. In the end times there will be a one-world government, one economic system, and one religion. Those who refuse to get on board will be executed. How better to bring this about than through a global organization committed to a strict control of world economics, the food supply, the environment, and universal healthcare. This agenda can be imposed on the world in the name of "equity." And let those who refuse to accept this new reality be silenced or eliminated.

If Marx could speak, he would shout in his native German, "Ja vol!"

The Theology of Charles Darwin: An Attack on God as Creator

Charles Darwin did not deny the existence of God, but his spiritual journey took him from his Christian upbringing to agnosticism. Some scholars believe that he died a theist, but to the end, he was unsure whether God was involved as Creator in the universe. At least, he did not believe in the God of the Bible. He called himself "the devil's chaplain."

As for the God who created all things, in Darwin's words, "As soon as you realize that one species could evolve into another, the whole structure wobbles and collapses."[14]

After Darwin arrived at the conclusion that all living beings had a common ancestry, we can understand why he said, "Science has nothing to do with Christ."[15] He made it clear: "I do not believe in the Bible as a divine revelation, & therefore not in Jesus Christ as the son of God."[16]

His rejection of Christianity was clear too:

> I can indeed hardly see how anyone ought to wish Christianity to be true; for if so the plain language of the text seems to show that the men who do not believe, and this would include my Father, Brother and almost all my best friends, will be everlastingly punished. And this is a damnable doctrine.[17]

Darwin's wife was so distressed by this passage in his autobiography that she excised it from the first published edition of that work. But be that as it may, those words expressed his sentiment.

Yes, according to Darwin, man evolved through the monkey

world. He wrote, "Our descent, then, is the origin of our evil pas-sions!!—The Devil under form of Baboon is our grandfather."[18] With a baboon as our grandfather, and with "the survival of the fittest" as the engine that carries evolution forward, certain conse-quences follow. In a later chapter, we will see how this has impacted our own educational system and culture.

It didn't take long for Darwinism to be applied to society as a whole. Men like Herbert Spencer tried to show that society itself was evolving into something better. It moved from its original sub-ject to operate in the wider world. And just as there is survival of the fittest in nature, the same is true among humans and in histor-ical development.

Natural selection would weed out the weaker, more inferior peo-ple, and the fittest would survive and reproduce. After all, if the baboon was our grandfather, and we have evolved throughout the centuries, we can expect this trajectory to continue. Why not speed up the ever-upward evolutionary cycle?

The Bitter Fruit of Darwin

Darwin himself probably did not foresee how his theories would be applied, but the more one is committed to Darwinism, the more racist one will become. There are those who reason that if natural selection weeds out the weaker members of society, then why not help the process along by weeding them out ourselves?

Darwinism led to eugenics, the idea that we should decide on various characteristics we want reproduced in human beings (per-haps intelligence, appearance, etc.) and cause the elimination of inferior individuals to hasten the development of a superior civili-zation. Francis Galton, who read Darwin, promoted the view that "the more suitable races or strains of blood have a better chance of prevailing speedily over the less suitable."[19]

In his book *The Descent of Man*, Darwin wrote, "The sole object of this work is to consider, firstly, whether man, like every other species, is descended from some pre-existing form; secondly, the manner of his development; and thirdly, the value of the differences between the so-called races of man."[20]

And that was not all. Darwin said it must "be enquired whether man, like so many other animals, has given rise to varieties and sub-races, differing but slightly from each other, or to races differing so much that they must be classed as a doubtful species?"[21]

Don't hurry past this: Darwin concluded that there are some races that are "a doubtful species." He believed the human races were distinctly different, and at different stages in the evolutionary cycle, the stronger were bound to be victorious and the weak would perish.

When Darwin traveled to South America and saw the Fuegians, the indigenous inhabitants of Tierra del Fuego, run toward his boat, he wrote in his diary that "I could not have believed how wide was the difference, between savage and civilized man. It is wider than between a wild and domesticated animal, inasmuch as in man there is a greater power of improvement."[22] According to his thinking, the next reasonable step would be the extermination of the inferior so they would not interbreed with those who were superior; and thus, the superior race would be less contaminated as it evolved upward and onward. There would be an endless number of lower races that would be eliminated by the higher, more civilized races.

Nazism-Applied Darwinism

Sometimes it is said that Adolf Hitler could not have been a Darwinian because Darwin's writings in English had not been yet translated into German. But Darwin's ideas were promoted in Germany by his disciples, such as Ernst Haeckel. Hitler agreed with Darwin's statement, "In nature there is no pity for the lesser creatures when they are destroyed so that the fittest may survive."[23] Although Darwin's name is not mentioned, his ideas undergirded Hitler's philosophy, especially in chapter 4 of his book *Mein Kampf.*

Hitler, thus supported by Darwinism, used the theory of evolution to justify the need for a pure race (i.e., no racial mixing). And of course, the elimination of the inferior races was doing humanity a favor. In attempting to eliminate the Jews, Hitler was just "following the science."

- - - - - - - - - - - -

> Without God as Creator, man could develop
> into whatever direction he wanted. He could
> embark on a journey without a map, without
> a destination, and without restraints.

- - - - - - - - - - - -

As we will see later, we can draw a straight line between Darwinism and abortion, infanticide, and euthanasia. If the baboon is our grandfather, what argument can there be against devaluing human life and making us a part of the animal kingdom?

One writer said that Darwinism was the "universal acid"[24] that dissolved Christianity. Without God as Creator, man could develop into whatever direction he wanted. He could embark on a journey without a map, without a destination, and without restraints.

More later.

The Theology of Sigmund Freud: An Attack Against God as Lawgiver

Nietzsche probably was not familiar with the writings of Freud because the latter began publishing his books on psychotherapy when Nietzsche was approaching the end of his life. But I am including Freud in the pantheon of gravediggers because Freud's contribution to the eclipse of God cannot be overstated. Freud paved the way for our culture's present obsession with sexuality; God's limitations on sexual behavior would be cast aside, and humans would rewrite the rules.

Freud considered belief in God as a fantasy based on a person's infantile need for a dominant father figure, even though he saw religion as a necessity in the development of early civilization to help restrain people's violent impulses. But as humanity becomes more educated, belief in God can and must be discarded.

Freud is known for putting sex—specifically, sexual pleasure—at the center of human existence. He perpetuated "the idea that sex, in terms of sexual desire and sexual fulfillment, is the real key to human existence, to what it means to be human."[25] Sexual pleasure is, in effect, our birthright.

In his essay *Civilization and Its Discontents*, Freud wrote:

> Man's discovery that sexual (genital) love afforded him the strongest experiences of satisfaction, in fact provided him with the prototype of all happiness, must have suggested to him that he should continue to seek the satisfaction of happiness in his life along the path of sexual relations and that he should make genital eroticism the central point in his life.[26]

Thus Freud promoted the pleasure principle: A quest for pleasure focused on sexual gratification is central to being one's self. And without a belief in original sin, and because he saw no need to put limits on sexual expression, Freud argued for sexual freedom. Whatever brought you pleasure was justified, and God as lawmaker would vanish. God was a fantasy, and sexual liberation was the path to happiness.

To Freud, the repression of sexual desire is the source of many of our frustrations and neuroses. Thus, the biblical prohibitions limiting sexual relations to within a marriage of one man and one woman was an arbitrary command taught by Christianity that resulted in unnecessary and harmful guilt. Even infants can experience sexual pleasure, and this should be encouraged, not shamed.

Freud's teaching was further popularized by Alfred Kinsey of Indiana, a bisexual who interviewed convicted sex offenders, child molesters, and people who committed sexual assault. He passed his findings along as if he had interviewed average Americans, and only later was it revealed that his research was based on interviews with people who would give him the answers he wanted. Kinsey not only claimed that children can be sexual but concluded "that so called intergenerational sex—a polite euphemism for child rape—poses no serious harm to children."[27]

These ideas were widely publicized in his books during the early 1950s and were eagerly believed. As history shows, whether it is ancient Israel or modern America, mankind has always been eager to break with biblical sexual norms. Not surprisingly, Kinsey also believed that adultery did not undermine a marriage as long as neither party became emotionally involved.

To recap: Freud and his disciples despised the idea that God was a lawgiver who created us as sexual beings and then set down the rules for sexual behavior. Now that the "fantasy" of God had been exposed, mankind was free to reject the idea that sex should be confined to marriage based on a binding covenant. With this newly discovered freedom, the desires of genital pleasure could be maximized. As for guilt, it was simply a feeling that had to be unlearned.

So, freed from the commands of God regarding sexual conduct, man took the place of God and put himself firmly in place as his own lawgiver. Away with Sinai and welcome to what Aldous Huxley called the "brave new world"!

* * *

In their attempt to destroy God,
secularists ended up destroying humanity.

* * *

With repeated hammer blows, Marx, Darwin, and Freud pounded against the walls of Europe's Christian consensus—and they did so with great success. Each put a nail into the coffin of God, apparently thinking they were doing mankind a favor.

These secularists thought they were too clever to believe in God. But in their attempt to destroy God, they ended up destroying humanity. Communism, Nazism, and Fascism brought repression, brutality, and the killing of millions of victims.

These ideas contributed to the eclipse of God; the darkness deepened in Europe and throughout the West. The results were terrifying.

THE LESSONS FOR US

As is frequently said, ideas have consequences, and bad ideas have victims.

The eclipse of God in Europe helped bring about two World Wars and the rise of Communism and Nazism, teaching us that without submission to God, mankind will always drift toward cruelty, repression, rampant promiscuity, and the quest for dominance and power. Secularism, no matter where it is found, can never tolerate dissent. It expects conformity to its ideology; freedom of speech will be denied, and dissent will be punished. And power will become a substitute for truth.

The prophets warned about exchanging the true God for fake gods that could not satisfy:

> Has a nation changed its gods,
>   even though they are no gods?
> But my people have changed their glory
>   for that which does not profit.
> Be appalled, O heavens, at this;
>   be shocked, be utterly desolate,
> declares the LORD,
> for my people have committed two evils:
> they have forsaken me,
>   the fountain of living waters,
> and hewed out cisterns for themselves,
>   *broken cisterns that can hold no water*
> (Jeremiah 2:11-13, emphasis added).

Europe soon learned the hard way that the wells of secularism were dry. But in the meantime, these three gravediggers prepared the coffin, though someone else performed the burial and declared that a requiem must be sung for the Almighty.

And the cathedrals of Europe bear testimony to God's influence. He was not just presumed to be dead, He was *declared* dead, and the church succumbed under the weight of the news.

In the next chapter, we will look at how God was deemed worthy of a respectful funeral. But the Lord Himself is in attendance, not mourning, but laughing. And, as we will see in the next chapter, the darkness deepens.

OUR DECLARATION OF DEPENDENCE

Pollsters tell us most Westerners believe in God, but so what? Their belief has little or no effect on the way they live and the values they adopt. In other words, they tell us they believe in God, but that belief makes no special demand on their lives.

Dr. David F. Wells, senior research professor at Gordon-Conwell Seminary, believes that we as evangelicals must come to grips with "the weightlessness of God." Read every word:

> It is one of the defining marks of Our Time that God is now weightless. I do not mean by this that he is ethereal but rather that he has become unimportant. He rests upon the world so lightly, so inconsequentially as not to be noticeable. He has lost his saliency for human life. Those who assure the pollsters of their belief in God's existence may nonetheless consider him less interesting than television, his commands less authoritative than their appetites for affluence and influence, his judgment is no more awe-inspiring than the evening news, and his truth less compelling than the advertisers' sweet fog of flattery and lies. That is weightlessness.[28]

When you attend church this Sunday, ask yourself: Do you and the congregation believe that God is weighty, majestic, and awe-inspiring? Or is He *weightless*? To paraphrase A.W. Tozer, just as water cannot rise above its source, so a nation cannot rise higher than its conception of God. So what is our conception of God?

This weightlessness of God has weakened us, just as it weakened the people of Israel in Jeremiah's day: "They have healed the wound of my people *lightly*, saying, 'Peace, peace,' when there is no peace"

(6:14, emphasis added). A weightless God means endless tolerance and man-made cures for serious sins.

Someday the likes of Marx, Darwin, and Freud—along with billions of others—will confess that Jesus Christ is Lord to the glory of God the Father. We who claim to be already doing just that must examine whether we have allowed ourselves to become content with an unworthy concept of God.

Only a "weighty God" can heal our wounds.

ACTION STEP

This chapter is about those who influenced future generations. We must resolve to be positive influencers, building bridges with those around us with prayer and interaction. "One generation shall commend your works to another, and shall declare your mighty acts" (Psalm 145:4). Howard Hendricks told us, "You can impress people at a distance, but you can impact them only up close."[29] Who will you influence God-ward today? And the day after?

CHAPTER 3

God Is Given a Respectful Burial, but He Is in Attendance

*How the Cathedrals of Europe
Became the Tombs of God*

Only reluctantly did Friedrich Nietzsche (1844–1900) come to the conclusion that God was dead. He was brought up in a Lutheran home in Germany and was familiar with the basic truths of Christianity. He saw more clearly than most where atheism would lead, and therefore foresaw a troublesome future and the collapse of European morality.

Nietzsche was most likely well acquainted with two of the three gravediggers discussed in the preceding chapter. He was born in 1844 and would have been four years old when Marx published his *Communist Manifesto* and a teenager when Darwin's *On the Origin of Species* was released to the public. Freud was just beginning his influential work toward the end of Nietzsche's life, but even early on, his books were widely read, and the populace was eager to believe what he said. God was becoming increasingly irrelevant and unnecessary.

Nietzsche, no doubt influenced by Darwin, dehumanized the human race. Speaking of all of us, he wrote, "You have made your way from worm to man, and much in you is still worm. Once you were apes, and even now, too, man is more ape than any ape."[1]

Yet despite all this, Nietzsche professed a great respect for religion. He did not make his pronouncement of the death of God without weighing the consequences. He saw the value of religion. He acknowledged that European morality was built upon it; it represented centuries of traditions that gave Europe a common culture.

Nietzsche agonized, believing he was the reluctant prophet who would have to declare the death of God to the world. He predicted it would introduce a period of *nihilism*—a period of absurdity during which people have no order, no truth, and no goals nor ideals to pursue. Meaninglessness would have to be accepted as a fact of life. It is he who predicted that the cathedrals of Europe would become the tombs of God.

Let us feel his emotional agony as he faced the task before him. "How shall we, the murderers of all murderers, comfort ourselves?... Who will wipe the blood off of us? What water is there for us to clean ourselves?"[2] So man has killed God, and there is no one left to wipe the blood from our hands!

Stephen R.C. Hicks says Nietzsche believed we are like a teenager who wakes up in the middle of the night and is told his parents have died and he will have to fend for himself.[3] Just so, people in the nineteenth century had awakened to the fact that the old supports of religion were gone. They were now on their own, facing a cruel, relentless world, and they had to make the best of it. Nietzsche proposed a new way of life—one in which we create our own values in a life-affirming manner.

Nature was very important to Nietzsche. Without God, we might ask, Who is left to take care of us? He agreed with the atheism of Karl Marx but disagreed with Marx's emphasis on the state imposing equality. Nature, Nietzsche argued, is not equal; *in*equality among men and nations must be accepted as a fact of life. It comes down to these questions: "Where are the men of courage? Who is willing to stare into the abyss? Who can stand alone on the icy mountaintop? Who can look a tiger in the eye without flinching?"[4]

Morality, said Nietzsche, is based on nature; human nature determines who we are and what we do. Therefore, there is no objective morality; life is as we find it, cruel and unrelenting, and the future belongs to the strong.

In writing about Nietzsche, Hicks invites us to consider the difference between sheep and wolves. What seems good to a sheep? To graze peacefully, sticking close to other sheep. What seems bad? A wolf. His nature is one of strength, cruelty, and contempt for sheep. A wolf delights in ripping a sheep's body apart and gorging himself with its flesh. There is nothing that the sheep and the wolves can agree on morally; their natures are different. No sheep could convince a wolf to think differently, and no wolf could convince a sheep to value aggression, ravenous attacks, and the exploitation of other animals.

Imagine trying to set up a peace conference with wolves and sheep coming to the table to see if they can find common ground and sign an accord. It's utterly impossible and foolish. Nature is what it is. And, reluctant atheist that he was, Nietzsche believed that human nature could not be changed. Christianity, of course, teaches that God does indeed change human nature, but such a change, Nietzsche would say, is for the worse, not the better.

Nietzsche believed that Christians are trying to teach wolves to behave like sheep. They (Christians and Jews) put emphasis on being humble, forgiving, and, as Jesus put it, "turning the other cheek" (see Matthew 5:39). But doing this is futile; wolves will never behave like sheep. The meek will not inherit the earth; the strong, the brutal, and those who are hungry for power will win in the end. Indeed, it is Christianity's emphasis on humility and submission that has produced a slave mentality.

Christianity promises that if we obediently give ourselves to the need of others, we will be rewarded in heaven. But with the death of God, such reasoning is a vain hope. This makes Christianity a threat to human flourishing and development. Humility and forgiveness get us nowhere. Only the strong and the ruthless can face reality and become great.

Listen to Nietzsche vent: "Christianity was from the beginning, essentially and fundamentally, life's nausea and disgust with life, merely concealed behind, masked by, and dressed up as, faith in 'another' or 'better' life."[5] It was the promise of heaven that motivated Christians to accept slavery here on earth.

Nietzsche looked back in history and believed that humanity's most glorious moments were ones of strength and brutality; compassionate people never achieve greatness. Greatness comes through cruelty, or to put it more daintily, "nice guys finish last."

Nietzsche taught that we need a superman, an *Übermensch*, who can achieve, and if necessary, destroy and conquer. Now that the gravediggers have buried God, the future is in our hands, not in the hands of some mythical imaginary deity. We must not be ashamed of brutality, for it alone is the path to greatness.

Is it any wonder that Hitler kept a copy of Nietzsche's writings next to his bed and gave a complete set of them to Mussolini for his birthday?[6] He also visited the Nietzsche Haus in Weimar and had his picture taken next to a Nietzsche bust.[7] Hitler asked a question that, no doubt, was inspired by Nietzsche: "Why cannot we be as cruel as nature?"[8] In a world of conflict, why cannot we be the wolves among the sheep? Victory belongs to the wolves.

Without a God to console us, guide us, or direct us, Nietzsche said that when you gaze into the abyss, the abyss stares back at you. And yet here we are, and only the fittest and cruelest will survive. He understood with clarity that if there is no God, there is no authority above the Superman who is free to do as he wishes. Might makes right.

Was there any hope to be found?

WHERE WAS THE CHURCH?

Often the greatest damage to a church comes from within, not without.

With one hammer blow after another, the church began to weaken under the political and cultural currents that atheistic philosophers had put in motion. But the sad fact is, for the most part, the core of Christianity had already been eaten away by the termites within the church that weakened the structure and made a near-total collapse inevitable. The churches—both Catholic and Protestant—had already capitulated to those within their midst who reduced the faith to superficial platitudes devoid of life-changing doctrinal content.

Consider the German Lutheran theologian Friedrich Schleiermacher (1768–1834), who did more than anyone else to proclaim that the Bible was not a revelation from God; the Bible was a human book, a collection of views about God, interesting to historians, but not a lifeline from a God who rescues us from our sins.

Welcome to liberal Christianity.

Schleiermacher, and others like him, believed there was no objective religious truth, and that the locus of religion had to be transferred from theological content to personal feelings. He is famous for defining religion as a "feeling of absolute dependence."[9] (In which case, I've heard it said that dogs must be very religious!)

The seeds of contemporary spirituality were now planted. Because religion is not what you *believe* but how you *feel*, we are now in charge of our religious experience. Doctrines that inform the mind were deemed largely unimportant; it's how you *felt* that mattered. Thus arose a group of influential scholars who agreed that the Bible was to be treated as a purely human book. It had to be "demythologized"—that is, its myths (miracles) had to be expunged from the text. The skeptic David Hume had already argued that miracles could not occur, so modern man should not believe that Moses parted the Red Sea, or that Jesus walked on water or multiplied bread and fish to feed a multitude.

- - - - - - - - - - - -

People were sold a brand of Christianity that
was not worth living for, much less dying for.

- - - - - - - - - - - -

These secular ideas infiltrating the church had a ready audience. The writers of the Enlightenment had paved the way for a liberal brand of Christianity that kept the shell but destroyed the kernel. Those who had one foot in the skepticism of the Enlightenment and the other in the church were pulled apart. *The people were sold a brand of Christianity that was not worth living for, much less dying for.*

These views swept Europe and are also firmly entrenched here in America. And so arose the idea that you can claim spirituality without doctrine and have a spiritual experience without believing in objective truth. All that was needed was "a feeling of dependence." If religion is what I feel, it is not based on truth that exists outside of me, but what I feel *within* me.

Gone was the courage of Martin Luther, who, under the sentence of death, proclaimed, "My conscience is captive to the Word of God. I cannot and I will not recant!"[10] Gone was the bravery of the martyr John Hus, who patiently succumbed to the flames before he prayed, "Lord, into thy hands I commend my spirit."[11]

In 1986, my wife, Rebecca, and I joined a group of other Christians and visited China. We had the privilege of spending several days with bishop Ding, who at that time was the head of the Three-Self Patriotic Movement; he was the government liaison to the churches of China. In the course of our discussion, he made this amazing statement: "I know that you are Bible-believing Christians, and if you go through the length and breadth of China, you will meet many people who believe like you do…there are no theological liberals in China…*persecution wiped out theological liberalism.*"

Well, of course!

What so-called Christian who believes that the faith is but "a feeling of dependence" would be willing to lay down his or her life for Jesus? What congregation schooled on theological pablum, which teaches that you have all the spiritual resources you need just by looking within yourself, can withstand the cultural currents of our time? Who would be willing to suffer for a woke, politically correct Christ who helps us but doesn't redeem us?

Have you heard of Operation Grief? Hitler came up with an idea: Nazis soldiers would dress themselves in the uniforms of captured British and US soldiers and then infiltrate Allied battalions to spread confusion. The undercover Nazis spread false rumors, reversed road signs, and gave conflicting orders among the troops. These efforts were not very successful because no matter how well the Germans spoke English, their accent revealed who they were. But conceptually, it was a brilliant idea: Wear the uniform of your enemy, then spread your lies, deceit, and false hopes.

Yes, as Peter the apostle predicted, there will be false teachers who "secretly bring in destructive heresies" (2 Peter 2:1). They proudly wear the Christian uniform, but when you talk with them, their "accent" (their inability to articulate the gospel, and their lack of true love for and worship of Christ) betrays them. What false teachers tout as light is actually darkness. Jesus warned, "Be careful lest the light that is in you be darkness" (Luke 11:35).

The liberal European churches had the uniform of Christianity but the heart of its enemy, secularism. For the most part, gone was the call for repentance and accountability to a holy, all-knowing God. Having stood for nothing, the churches fell for anything. They did not take seriously these words from Jesus: "Behold, I am sending you out as sheep in the midst of wolves, so be wise as serpents and innocent as doves. Beware of men, for they will deliver you over to courts and flog you in their synagogues, and you will be dragged before governors and kings for my sake" (Matthew 10:16-18). Few people were willing to risk their lives for a Christ they thought was just an extraordinary teacher.

With some notable exceptions, the pastors in Europe had no message about a supernatural gospel that would save sinners. Weary of the religious wars, the people were already disappointed with the apparent silence of God. If God was not dead, He certainly was eclipsed and could not be seen amid the cultural rubble. Churches were no longer centers of redemption, but centers of self-improvement.

. . . .

Two doctrines have always destroyed the church:
belief in the essential goodness of man, and the
endless tolerance of a nonjudgmental deity.

. . . .

This liberalism crossed the ocean, came to America, and has had a continuing impact on the major denominations of our country. In 1937, H. Richard Niebuhr described the gospel of liberalism as "a God without wrath brought men without sin into a kingdom without judgment through the ministrations of a Christ without a cross."[12] Two doctrines have always destroyed the church: belief in the essential goodness of man, and the endless tolerance of a non-judgmental deity.

I caught a glimpse of the effects of this kind of Christianity in Europe firsthand. On many occasions, I have had the privilege of leading tours to the sites of the Reformation; I have lectured in Wittenberg, Erfurt, and Eisleben, tracing the life and impact of Martin Luther. Several years ago, while visiting the great Castle Church in Wittenberg (where Luther nailed his *Ninety-Five Theses*), our tour group was asked to leave because the church announced the beginning of a brief service (the German word is *gottesdeinst*) at the noon hour. But because I understand some German, I stayed.

Imagine the scene: The pastor read from the Old Testament in honor of Judaism; he read from the New Testament in the honor of Christianity; and had a reading from the Qur'an in honor of Islam. Then he said, "In this church we honor all three of the world's religions."

All that was said while he was standing next to the grave of Martin Luther!

The wrecking balls directed at Christianity from the eighteenth century onward were successful, and a weakened church could hardly protest. Buried under the rubble of philosophical and theological attacks, fearing the charge of being hateful or insensitive to the cultural and religious currents, the God of the Bible was eclipsed, and various forms of darkness took His place. Tragically, even those who understood what was happening feared the price they would have to pay to stand for truth. As is so often the case, even devoted men and women lost their courage when the price of faithfulness became too high. *Congregations were misled in churches led by good men who surrendered to political and cultural pressure.*

Thus, Friedrich Nietzsche felt an obligation to finish the task. He believed it was his duty to preside over the funeral for God. He believed God was worthy of a respectful eulogy.

GIVING GOD A RESPECTFUL BURIAL

Nietzsche could no longer tiptoe around the reality: The grave-diggers had done their work; God was dead, and Nietzsche was on hand to announce the committal. His eulogy was brief and to the point: "We have killed God!"

In his book titled *The Madman*, Nietzsche described a madman entering various churches to sing a *requiem aeterman deo*—that is, a requiem for God. And then he called out, "What are these churches now if they are not the tombs and sepulchers of God?"[13]

The churches are now the tombs of God!

Chilling, but all too true. And so, yes, go throughout Europe today, and you will find the empty cathedrals converted into libraries, mosques, restaurants. The Cathedral of John Bunyan in Bedford, England, is now a nightclub. Blasphemy, which is speaking about God with contempt, no longer exists; after all, there is no God whom one can offend.

GOD ATTENDS HIS OWN FUNERAL
NOT MOURNING BUT LAUGHING

So what did God think of Nietzsche's bold proclamation? Reportedly, when a newspaper asked Mark Twain whether he was still alive, he said, "Rumors about my death have been greatly exaggerated." God, of course, has His own commentary on the reports of His demise: "The fool says in his heart, 'There is no God'" (Psalm 14:1). As for those kinds of fools, "The Lord laughs at the wicked, for he sees that his day is coming" (Psalm 37:13).

As you read the following verses, note that, even thousands of years ago, there were gravediggers who organized together to do away with God. The kings "set themselves" against the Lord, and they took "counsel together" to cast God out of their lives and their nations. God was neither surprised, fearful, or worried. He laughed.

> Why do the nations rage
>   and the peoples plot in vain?
> The kings of the earth set themselves,
>   and the rulers take counsel together,
>   against the LORD and against his Anointed, saying,
> "Let us burst their bonds apart
>   and cast away their cords from us."
> *He who sits in the heavens laughs;*
>   the Lord holds them in derision.
> Then he will speak to them in his wrath,
>   and terrify them in his fury
> (Psalm 2:1-5, emphasis added).

The rest of the psalm speaks about the exaltation of Christ and the coming judgment of God on those who despise the Almighty. I am reminded of the T-shirt I saw at a festival. On the front it read, "God is dead—*Nietzsche*." The back read, "Nietzsche is dead—*God*."

To recap: Marx attacked God as *Ruler* of the world. Darwin attacked God as *Creator,* Freud attacked God as *Lawgiver,* and Schleiermacher attacked God as the *Redeemer* of the world. For all intents and purposes, God was dead.

LESSONS WE HAD BETTER LEARN

Like the radical Left in America, the three secular gravedig-gers, along with religious men such as Schleiermacher, could only destroy; they could not build. When God was banished, Satan occupied the empty spaces. Two World Wars brutally destroyed millions of people; the Communist revolutions with their devotion to Marx and the unthinkable torture and brutality of the Nazi Holocaust killed many more, showing what happens when man abandons God.

The wolves would run loose, wantonly devouring the sheep.

Despite the terrifying consequences of treating God as if He were dead, for the most part, Europe has not returned to God. Even now, the victory of secularism in Europe is so complete that there is no culture war such as we still have in America. Yes, there are individual churches, pastors, and congregations who are living faithfully and witnessing for Christ, but they are relatively few and remain isolated from the culture at large.

Douglas Murray writes, "Europe today has little desire to reproduce itself, fight for itself or even to take its side in an argument."[14] Even defending freedom is considered by some to be bigotry and intolerance. It may well be that Europe has led the way for our own cultural moment. The shadows of Europe have long since reached our shores, and the darkness deepens.

We had better pay attention; there is much we need to remember.

First, we dare not take the continued future of our churches for granted. Communism turned churches into libraries, storage facilities, factories, and in some instances, museums dedicated to the memory of God, pointing back to a time when people were primitive enough to believe in a fantastical deity.

As for Islam, its armies wiped out the church almost completely throughout North Africa and Turkey, turning churches into mosques that still exist centuries later. My wife, Rebecca, and I visited the ancient church in Nicaea, Turkey, where the seventh Ecumenical Council was held in AD 787. The church has been a mosque for six centuries. Even here in America, hundreds of churches close their doors for one reason or another each year.

We cannot simply quote the words of Jesus, "On this rock I will build my church, and the gates of hell [Hades] shall not prevail against it" (Matthew 16:18) as if we can do church as usual and all will be well. Clearly, these words are not a guarantee that any individual church or the churches in a given nation will never be closed. I believe that the phrase "gates of hell" refers first and foremost to Jesus' own death (see Isaiah 38:10; Job 38:17; and similar passages where the phrases "gates of Sheol" and "gates of death" is used to speak of individual death). This explains why Jesus immediately goes on to say He must go to Jerusalem to be crucified; He is saying that His death will not hinder the establishment of the church (indeed, His death was necessary to bring it about). And the church to which He referred can also be spoken of as the "invisible church"—that is, a body of believers worldwide that often exists in unknown places and countries. History has shown that when Christianity has been stamped out in one country, it often flourishes in another. But complacency about our own future is not an option.

A second lesson is that any nation or Christian ministry can end up in a dark place gradually, one compromise after another. Some European countries did not accept the implications of secularism overnight; step by step, hammer blow by hammer blow, they were crushed beneath the weight of the political, economic, and religious realities they believed were forced upon them. Entire denominations both here and abroad have become apostate one small concession after another.

But sometimes change comes quickly, as in the case of a national crisis or revolution. We as the church should ask: How will we be able to survive a chaotic economic, social, and political tsunami, perhaps enflamed by a cyberattack? What preparations should we be making now for when the America we once knew collapses and we are left to pick up the pieces?

Third, we must remember that good people can be intimidated into silence. Those who know better often seek the shaky middle ground instead of standing firm. Soon they discover there is no safe place; and the threat of exposure, isolation, and persecution is too great to bear. When their children or other members of their family are threatened, they eventually surrender rather than face the humiliation that awaits them.

Interestingly, when Rebecca and I visited the Czech Republic a few years ago, a pastor told us that under Communism, believers depended on each other for prayer and even sharing food. They were determined to be faithful in attending church, even in small groups. But when Communism collapsed and the country was set free, the younger generation, giddy with their new freedoms and with the help of technology (especially the cell phone!), is, for the most part, lost to the world. What persecution could not do, the secular values of materialism and pleasure accomplished. I remember Howard Hendricks saying that it is almost impossible to develop worshippers in an affluent society.

As our own culture closes in, we can expect spiritual hemorrhaging among those who seek to find a "middle path." But they will soon discover that there is no middle path to be found. To give but one example, consider that in Oxford, England, churches are now being rated on the basis of LGBTQ acceptance as a "trigger warning" for those who are so disposed. A report published in *The Times of London* explains the grading system is like that of traffic lights. *Red* means that a church is supposedly homophobic, meaning that the church calls homosexuals to repentance. *Amber* means that the church officially believes that homosexual relationships are sinful but is quiet about it. *Green* means that the church is fully on board with the homosexual agenda, and in many instances, it becomes their identity. (I encourage you to read the full report.)[15]

Standing in the mushy middle is no longer possible. We must thoughtfully and prayerfully make up our minds now where we stand. When we are called upon to declare ourselves, it might be too late. History has shown that often, only a remnant survives.

After these sobering thoughts, we need some good news, and we are heartened when we realize that God is not dead. He is not intimidated by the Nietzsches of this world. G.K. Chesterton understood this when he wrote, "Christianity has died many times and risen again, for it had a God who knew the way out of the grave."[16] Chesterton is also quoted as saying, "A dead thing goes with the stream, but only a living thing can go against it."[17] Thanks to Christ, we are "a living thing."

God continues to hold the bride of Christ in His hands.

Meanwhile our Western culture is not yet brave enough to stare with Nietzsche into the abyss. Oh yes, we have the rise of the new atheists with their lofty claims of living without God. But lip service to God is still expected of our politicians and the cultural elite, who are using their power to direct culture in woke directions. God is often invoked to give legitimacy to things, even to various forms of immoral behavior.

In other words, Christianity has been reinvented to suit modern sensitivities. God still exists, but He is whatever people want Him to be. He must be manageable and kept under control. Many have been willing to adopt theological liberalism without going all the way to "theological atheism."

Christianity has been reinvented to suit
modern sensitivities. God still exists, but He
is whatever people want Him to be.

With the de facto death of God, an assortment of many other gods and goddesses are available to moderns. The eclipse of God the Almighty is spreading, and the darkness is engulfing us. Spirituality has taken the place of doctrine, and feeling has replaced thoughtful investigation. The word *God* is still often used, but very selectively. And it has been emptied of serious thought and redefined to suit modern preferences.

In the next chapter, we turn to a form of religion that can be described as Nietzsche for Americans. Spirituality without truth, sin without judgment, and self-salvation without God. And in the darkness of secularism, people must now try to be content without any eternal hope. No forgiveness, no grace—just rancor, hatred, and a ruthless quest for power.

Stay tuned.

OUR DECLARATION OF DEPENDENCE

Dietrich Bonhoeffer, who was executed by Hitler's order in 1945, proved that it is not necessary to win in this life in order to win in the next. He remains famous for saying, "When Christ calls a man, he bids him come and die."[18] Pushing against the darkness might cost us our reputations, our livelihoods, and our very lives. That's what it cost Jesus.

But for now, let us spend a few moments in worship of the

sovereign God of Scripture. Let us also pray for those who are "practical atheists"—that is, those who do not call themselves atheists but live as if they are not accountable to God. Let this prayer for others also be a prayer for ourselves.

> The fool says in his heart, "There is no God."
>> They are corrupt, they do abominable deeds;
>> there is none who does good.
>
> The LORD looks down from heaven on the
>> children of man,
>> to see if there are any who understand,
>> who seek after God.
>
> They have all turned aside; together they
>> have become corrupt;
>> there is none who does good,
>> not even one.
>
> Have they no knowledge, all the evildoers
>> who eat up my people as they eat bread
>> and do not call upon the LORD?
>
> There they are in great terror,
>> for God is with the generation of the righteous.
> You would shame the plans of the poor,
>> but the LORD is his refuge.
>
> Oh, that salvation for Israel would come out of Zion!
>> When the LORD restores the fortunes of his people,
>> let Jacob rejoice, let Israel be glad (Psalm 14).

God may be dead, but only in the minds of fools whose worldview is like puffs of smoke in a hurricane.

But the LORD is the true God;
 he is the living God and the everlasting King.
At his wrath the earth quakes,
  and the nations cannot endure his indignation
  (Jeremiah 10:10, emphasis added).

He is a God who redeems us; He is a God worth dying for.

ACTION STEP

Those believers who remained faithful when the cathedrals were empty and their spiritual supports collapsed did so by meeting in small groups to pray, study the Scriptures, and encourage one another. Let us find likeminded believers with a heart to seek God for wisdom and the courage to ask: What lines will I not cross to be obedient to Christ? And what can we do to shine light in our sphere of influence?

CHAPTER 4

"Nearer My God to Me"

Worshipping at the Shrine of Self-Made Deities

Years ago, I was told that Art Linkletter (1912–2010), a well-known radio and television host and the author of *Kids Say the Darndest Things*, saw a small boy scrawling wildly on a sheet of paper.

"What are you drawing?" Linkletter asked.

"I'm drawing a picture of God."

"You can't do that because nobody knows what God looks like."

"They will when I'm finished," the boy replied confidently.

So what *does* God look like? Can we draw our own portrait of Him?

"I believe in God" is perhaps one of the most meaningless statements people make today. The word *God* has become a canvas on which each is free to paint his or her own portrait of the divine; like the boy scribbling at his desk, we can draw God according to whatever specifications we please. To say "I believe in God" might simply mean that we are seeing ourselves in a full-length mirror.

For the most part, our generation is not ready to stand with

Nietzsche and stare into an empty abyss. Many people, perhaps the majority, want to live as if God does not exist, but they are not yet ready to jettison the entire idea of God. So they need a god or gods to fill a need, as long as these deities do not interfere with who they are and what they want in life.

The Economist is one of the most influential periodicals in the world, and each year, they come out with a special issue titled "The Year Ahead." Looking into 2022, they featured an online article headlined "The Church of England's God is becoming more liberal." The print version is titled "Nearer, my God, to me." The author of the article, Catherine Nixey, is a British correspondent for *The Economist*.

Referring to God as portrayed in the Old Testament, she writes, "Smiting used to be so simple. God smote and the people trembled, and they sometimes died. He smote the rebellious Israelites (tens of thousands died)…and the Philistines (they got hemorrhoids). The Sodomites suffered a particularly striking smiting. In Genesis, the men of Sodom are 'wicked and sinners before the Lord exceedingly,' so God rained 'brimstone and fire' upon Sodom."

Her point is clear: In our day, people don't see God as a deity who would smite anyone. And she says what is sadly true: "Few in Britain celebrate a 'smitey' Almighty today. God, as the archbishop of Canterbury put it recently, 'is love.' And now fewer celebrate a homophobic God."

Which, of course, means that few people in Britain actually believe in the God of the Bible—especially a God who judges sinners.

She goes on to say that Methodists in Britain voted "after prayerful consideration" to allow same-sex marriages. She points out that this step is in contrast to the book of Leviticus, so this is proof that God is becoming "more liberal," more accepting, more inclusive.

Nixey warns, "It is possible that a deity who once stated, 'You shall not lie with a man as with a woman; it is an abomination'" is now understood as a deity who will be "used to justify same-sex blessings in the Church of England." And traditionalists, she warns, "should brace themselves for even more change."[1]

Nixey reminds us that the Lord's prayer reads, "Your will be done, on earth as it is in heaven" (Matthew 6:10), but today, in the minds of many, the prayer runs in the opposite direction—it reads, "in heaven as it is on earth." So we on earth determine what happens both here and in the heavens.

And more changes are coming.

One of those changes is that the Church of England is considering making God out to be nonbinary. That will require changes in the liturgy to make God more inclusive, both a *She* as well as a *He*. The male pronouns, we are told, is what drives discrimination and sexism against women; to use male pronouns is patriarchal and oppressive.[2] And so Reverend Joanna Stobart from the Diocese of Bath and Wells asked the church to develop "more inclusive language" in their authorized liturgy.[3] God needs to be updated.

The February 9, 2023, *New York Times* carried the headline, "Gender term used for God is considered by church," while their online edition said, "Church of England Considers Gender-Neutral Language for God."[4]

So, if God were described as female, nonbinary, or even transgender, He/She/They would be more culturally relevant and accessible to all kinds of people on the gender spectrum. This deity would be one to which/whom all could relate with a feeling of acceptance; God would be more like one of us because we get to redefine Him in accordance with who we are.

These arguments are, of course, foolish for several reasons. First, as Al Mohler has suggested, we could begin by asking, Should we not honor God's preferred pronouns? After all, He names Himself repeatedly in Scripture as a male, as a He and not a She. Should we not respect His wishes? Does He not get to name Himself? Do we really want to misgender Him?

We all agree that God is neither masculine or feminine, but He reveals Himself to us as masculine and repeatedly as "Father." Jesus told us to pray, "Our Father in heaven" (Matthew 6:9). Only a male can be a father, and Jesus Christ is the Son of God. (We might wonder whether the Church of England would have to change Jesus to "Daughter of God"?) Some are even proposing the idea that Jesus was trans.[5]

But God names Himself a Father, and we are invited to worship Him as Father. As Al Mohler says, "We have no right to tamper with God's self-revelation. We have no right to name him. We have no right to rename him."[6] God has the right to name Himself.

Mohler points out: Change the language, and you change God.

CREATING GODS THAT RESEMBLE US

Religious lies are always seductive.

Cleary as a nation, we long for a more inclusive deity, a deity that is more "sin friendly." So yes, we create a god who is just like us—affirming, inclusive, and culturally progressive. A god who can be acknowledged without demanding anything from us. A god who can give us a veneer of credibility yet accepts us just as we are.

In other words, we want Nietzsche without the stigma of atheism; we want Darwinism without explaining the origin of the universe; and we want Marxism without a bloody revolution. In short, we want a god, but one who serves us and exists for our benefit—a god we can control. Thus the voice of human desire turns out to be the voice of "God." We crown the god we have self-created. We call it *spirituality*.

This redefining of God to suit our likes and dislikes is not new. Read every word of this passage:

> These things you have done, and I have been silent;
> *you thought that I was one like yourself.*
> But now I rebuke you and lay the charge before you.
>
> Mark this, then, you who forget God,
> lest I tear you apart, and there be none to deliver!
> (Psalm 50:21-22, emphasis added).

You thought that I was one like yourself!

Meanwhile, the original lie of Satan still stands: "You will be like God, knowing good and evil." What is more, "your eyes will be opened" (Genesis 3:5). You will be attracted to darkness but call it light. Thinking will take a back seat to feeling, and irrationality will not be an impediment to your experience.

Ezekiel described the process clearly: "Son of man, these men have taken their *idols into their hearts*, and set the stumbling block of their iniquity before their faces. Should I indeed let myself be consulted by them?" (Ezekiel 14:3, emphasis added). Should God—the true God—step off of His throne and defer to deluded prophets?

Read Jeremiah's cryptic description of such idolatry:

> Their idols are like scarecrows in a cucumber field,
> and they cannot speak;
> they have to be carried,
> for they cannot walk.
> Do not be afraid of them,
> for they cannot do evil,
> neither is it in them to do good (Jeremiah 10:5).

Idolatry has its advantages.

First, an idol can be carried. An idol allows me to remain at the center of my life; my loyalties are always under my control. An idol responds to me on my terms; it never tells me I am wrong.

Second, an idol can be of some help to human beings. To use Jeremiah's illustration, a scarecrow might frighten some birds away. It might do some good (witness the number of self-help books available today). Idols can make us more optimistic about our future.

Third, we can make our idols any shape we desire, and yours can differ from mine. We can credit them with mystery, with magic, and with meanings derived from our own mind or the occult world. In the end, because we manufacture reality, we are our own god.

Imagine a god of undefined spirituality, a god whom we can invoke to justify our every longing and to approve of whatever we long to do. Millions worship at the shrine of human potential, and agree with Nietzsche that the soul should have reverence for itself. These are idols of the heart.

SPIRITUAL WARFARE

If you don't like combat language, my challenge is that you read Ephesians 6:10-20, and you will soon discover that like it or not, we are in a spiritual battle. As long as we think we don't have enemies (the world, the flesh, and the devil), we will sink into the spiritual lethargy that the church has battled throughout the centuries. As for our culture, a student told me that in her university studies, "You would be surprised at the occultism that is rampant on the campus."

How are wars fought? With the deceit of false promises.

Satan markets his ideas through the means of various forms of "spirituality"—that is, spiritual experiences cut off from objective truth and biblical doctrine. He holds out some tangible dividends without arousing fear and attention. Amid all the promotion of materialism, sexual freedom, drugs, and despair, there is still one thing that Satan longs for above all else: *worship*.

C.S. Lewis perceptively realized that the highest form of deception would be for demons to duplicate spiritual experiences. The fictional demon in *The Screwtape Letters*, in giving instructions to his underling Wormwood, says, "I have great hopes that we shall learn in due time how to emotionalize and mythologize their science to such an extent that what is, in effect, a belief in us (though not under that name) will creep in while the human mind remains closed to belief in the enemy [God]."[7]

Think of the sinister delight Satan receives when playing God in the life of an individual, even to the point of granting his client a spiritual conversion. He does it by baiting a hook—like putting a worm on a fishing pole or a piece of meat on a bear trap. The trapper remains hidden, but behind the trap is the trapper, and behind the deceit is the deceiver. And "the light" leads to darkness. "For such men are false apostles, deceitful workmen, disguising themselves as apostles of Christ. And no wonder, for even Satan disguises himself as an angel of light" (2 Corinthians 11:13-14).

The prince of darkness presents himself as an angel of light.

The great advantage of using the term *spirituality* is that people can be spiritually fluid, they can pick and choose what they believe about God from a buffet of religious options. Americans, nurtured on consumerism, go "god shopping" at a spiritual smorgasbord, trying to find a deity that is best suited to their tastes. And as each individual makes their way through the buffet, they might choose very different options than their friends, and almost certainly their spiritual menu will be different than that of their parents.

Most importantly, Satan tells his clients, "Choose your *personal* combination of delicacies; no choice is better than another. Do not judge the person ahead of you who has chosen an entirely different menu. Pick and choose, forming a concept of God that is just right for you." To quote the words of Thomas Paine, "My own mind is my own church."[8]

· · · · · · · · · · · · · ·

Spirituality is religion without God; it is
self-acceptance without confronting sin;
it is self-redemption without any need
for the blood Christ shed for sinners.

· · · · · · · · · · · · ·

We could describe it this way: If I want to improve my unholy life, I begin by believing in a god who tolerates unholiness without rebuking me. I am willing to be helped, but not transformed. I want a god who helps me manage my confusion and emptiness without making me repent of my sin.

To summarize: Spirituality is religion without God; it is self-acceptance without confronting sin; it is self-redemption without any need for the blood Christ shed for sinners. It is words without meaning and experiences without substance. And it is the pretense of religion without having to believe anything significant. In short, it is a form of atheism without the stigma, and self-exaltation hidden behind platitudes. It is Satan quoting snatches of Scripture to bolster people's belief that God is much like us.

Note the contrast:

> Our God is in the heavens;
>   he does all that he pleases.
> Their idols are silver and gold,
>   the work of human hands.
> They have mouths, but do not speak;
>   eyes, but do not see.

They have ears, but do not hear;
  noses, but do not smell.
They have hands, but do not feel;
  feet, but do not walk;
  and they do not make a sound in their throat.
Those who make them become like them;
  so do all who trust in them (Psalm 115:3-8).

Adherents of these new kinds of "faith" can go on triumphantly, constructing as many conceptions of God as there are cravings in the world. Thirty years ago, we heard, "If it feels good, *do* it." Today, people say, "If it feels good, *believe* it."

Let's take a quick tour of just two of the self-made gods of modern culture. Let's try to grasp how tempting it is to construct an idea of God based on our own desires and interests.

EXAMPLES OF
NIETZSCHE FOR AMERICANS

Like Nietzsche, many in our culture worship at the shrine of human potential. But living off the perfume of our Judeo-Christian heritage, confessing to atheism is still a bridge too far. So people have created alternate deities that will serve as a substitute for the God they inherently dislike; the God who smites and judges.

What follows are a few examples of nonjudgmental self-made gods, or idols of the heart.

The God of My Personal Self-Authentication

Several years ago, I struck up a conversation with some tourists from Germany who had a layover at the O'Hare International Airport in Chicago. Knowing a bit of German (along with a few verses of Scripture I had learned in German as a child), I engaged them in conversation, hoping for an opportunity to share the gospel. I discovered that they spoke some English, so we were able to understand each other quite well.

To my chagrin, one man had just read the book *Conversations with God* by Neale Donald Walsch, in which the author claims to have his questions answered directly by God. In fact, Walsch says that he was not so much writing the book as taking dictation. His stream-of-consciousness writing was interpreted as hearing God's voice. I was acquainted with the book, having read it a few months prior.

Don't hurry past this. He, like many authors on spirituality, admits that while he was writing his book, he felt guided by an unseen spirit, which he interpreted to be God. The same claim was made by Helen Schucman, author of *A Course in Miracles* (who died in terrifying emotional agony). This phenomenon is known as "automatic writing," which is common in occult circles. In other words, a demonic spirit dictates the words.

What does Walsch's god say? This god says we are to reject all authoritative sources, for truth comes to us through our feelings. We discover that this god derides the idea that he/she/it is some omnipotent being that answers some prayers and not others. Let me quote directly: "Your will for you is God's will for you. You are living your life the way you are living your life, and I have no preference in the matter. This is the grand illusion in which you are engaged: that God cares one way or the other what you do. I do not care what you do, and that is hard for you to hear."[9]

So what is this god's will for you? No worries. It is what *your* will is for yourself. He has no preferences. We are not to look for "the truth" about this god outside of ourselves. Instead, he says, "Listen to your feelings. Listen to your highest thoughts. Listen to your experience. Whenever any one of these differ from what you've been told by your teachers, or read in your books, forget the words. Words are the least purveyor of Truth."[10]

Walsch, however, is not clear about how we can distinguish our highest thoughts from our lower ones. And, because his god repeatedly says that there is "no such thing as right or wrong, good or bad, better or worse," at last we get to this core doctrine: "There is only what serves you, and what does not."[11]

Walsch's god is the stream of consciousness in my mind, under my control. This god, we are told, "does not speak in words but feelings," and yet this god gave Walsch a revelation of 750 pages that comprises the book *The Complete Conversations with God*, now translated into dozens of languages. Evidently contradictions are not an impediment to believing in a figment of one's imagination.

Walsch is also luring your children and grandchildren into the fellowship of occult spirits. He has written a book titled *Conversations with God for Teens*.[12] We should not be surprised that this book has been well received, for it tells teens exactly what they desire to hear. They are accountable only to themselves regarding matters of sexuality, their future, and the like. Without having a God outside of themselves to deal with, they can simply try their best to forgive themselves for any guilt they experience and move on.

To summarize: Why is Walsch's idea of God so approving of all our lifestyles, beliefs, and values? To no one's surprise, this god is exactly everything we want him/her/it to be: no sin, no reproof, no judgment. In fact, there is no right or wrong! After all, in a world without a transcendent and holy God, the word *evil* is emptied of all meaning. There is no god outside of themselves to whom they must give account; their own self-consciousness is indistinguishable from their god.

The Bible strongly condemns those who, in effect, look into a mirror and say they see God. Earlier in this book, I already referenced the verse that God gives them strong delusion "so that they may believe what is false" (2 Thessalonians 2:11)—that is, The Lie.

Nietzsche was more honest than the Neale Walschs of this world; he did not spin platitudes about spirituality, but rather, simply said, "God is dead." I think Nietzsche would tell Walsch, "Your god does not exist except in your deluded mind. Have the courage to stare into the empty abyss. Live with it."

The God of My Sexual Identity: Bow to Who I Am

In ancient times, rampant sexuality was always practiced as a ritual in pagan worship. That is why Israel was so prone to idolatry; the idols were tolerant of every form of sexual perversion.

Today, as I have already emphasized, we are confronted by a spiritual enemy—Satan. He is capturing the hearts and minds of all who are in our churches, telling them they can worship at the ancient altar of Baal, the god of child sacrifice and sexuality, and at the same time, go to church and affirm that they are also worshipping at the altar of Christ. But John the apostle reminds us that a person who loves the world does not have "the love of the Father...in him" (1 John 2:15).

We've already learned that for Freud, the basic human desire is to be happy, and what made people happy was genital pleasure. As we saw in chapter 2, Freud wrote that "man's discovery that sexual (genital) love afforded him the strongest experiences of satisfaction."[13] He believed that children are sexual from birth, and therefore, sexuality lies at the heart of our identity. The pleasure principle—the prototype of all happiness—is that sexual pleasure should be experienced at all ages. As theologian Carl Trueman observes, "But if children and infants are sexual from birth, then to be human is always to be sexual, even prior to the onset of puberty."[14]

There is no need to discuss these ideas further except to say that, in the minds of many, Freud's pleasure principle can be justified by appealing to a god of some kind. In fact, the god of spirituality can be redefined to accommodate almost every form of sexuality imaginable, as long as it is done with so-called trust, respect, and love.

In the widely read book *Shameless*, author Nadia Bolz-Weber insists that God accepts all kinds of sexuality as long as it's consensual and not with children. She makes frequent references to God, but certainly not the God of the Bible. "So if you have been told that…your sexuality is good only if it is confined to a tiny circle, then you have been lied to…God gave you your gifts and never intended for them to be buried."[15]

Only serious spiritual warfare in prayer and repentance can keep the church holy at a time when we are overwhelmed with so many opportunities to live out our desires without restraint.

So God is now redefined to conform to the idols of our culture—the god of self-authentication and the god of sexual freedom. Only serious spiritual warfare in prayer and repentance can keep the church holy at a time when we are overwhelmed with so many opportunities to live out our desires without restraint.

Years ago, I heard a fable about a kite that said to itself, "If only the string would not hold me down when I fly in the wind; if only I could be free, I could fly as high as the stars!" One day its wish came true and the string broke; the kite thought it could finally reach its potential among the clouds in the sky. But alas, it came crashing to the ground. It discovered that *the string that held it down was actually the string that held it up.* The lesson: We can only reach our potential when we let God—the God of the Scriptures—be in control.

We do ourselves no favor when we jettison the moral laws of God by redefining Him. "When the true story gets told," writes Donald McCullough, "whether in the partial light of historical perspective or in the perfect light of eternity, it may well be revealed that the worst sin of the church at the end of the twentieth century has been the trivialization of God." He continues, "We prefer the illusion of a safer deity, and so we have pared God down to more manageable proportions."[16]

The illusion of a safer deity! A God of more manageable proportions!

To summarize, C.S. Lewis said it more accurately than anyone: "The Pantheist's God does nothing, demands nothing. He is there if you wish for Him, like a book on a shelf. He will not pursue you."[17] No wonder we read of idolaters, "There is no fear of God before their eyes" (Romans 3:18).

You will hear me say it multiple times—there are two deceptions that turn churches from centers of redemption to societies for self-improvement: belief in the essential goodness of man, and belief in the endless tolerance of God, variously defined.

Because of these deceptions, we have lost our capacity to despise our sin.

Self-Made Deities Cannot Keep Their Promises

We deceive ourselves when we substitute well-meaning illusions for reality. Read these powerful words: "As when a hungry man dreams, and behold, he is eating, and awakes with his hunger not satisfied, or as when a thirsty man dreams, and behold, he is drinking, and awakes faint, with his thirst not quenched" (Isaiah 29:8). In modern spirituality, the thirsty are promised water but it is from their own inner self; in the end, they are still thirsty for forgiveness, reconciliation with God, and a future hope. And the hungry are hungry still. When critical needs arise, self-made gods leave it all up to us.

Many years ago, two friends invited me to join them for my first and only game of golf. I had by far the highest score, and they would not let me forget that I lost. But I did have an experience I will never forget. When we were next to a pond, suddenly a duck hopped up and pretending to have a broken wing and attempted to lead us away from her nest. I looked into her nest and found—to my dismay—that she was sitting on a lone golf ball!

I have often thought about that mother duck. Positive thinking, or as some would call it, possibility thinking, has its benefits, but it also has its limitations. No doubt she sat on that golf ball in faith, the faith that someday a duckling would hatch and she, as a mother, would have the privilege of providing food for her precious offspring. But alas, it was not to be. Positive thinking, a fervent faith, and the hope borne of a worthy desire could not bring about the future she longed for.

There are similarities between a duck egg and a golf ball; they are approximately the same size and the same shape. The difference is that one is dead, and the other—if fertilized—has life. We should not be surprised that the mother duck was deceived. She did not lack faith; the problem was that her faith was based on an illusion.

> The God of the Bible has revealed to us that we
> have to connect with Him on His terms, not ours.

Modern spirituality stimulates people's optimism about who they are and who they can become. It tells them that they have to look within themselves to find "the god who already resides within them" and to manage their regrets and failures. But meaning in life cannot be found where there is none; a hope for a better future cannot be realized in a fallen world headed for destruction. The introspection of self-salvation cannot bring peace into the lives of sinful human beings. Illusions remain illusions no matter how sincerely they are believed. A golf ball in a mother duck's nest cannot deliver on its promises. Optimism in our self-created gods gives us no remedy for meaninglessness and despair.

The God of the Bible has revealed to us that we have to connect with Him on His terms, not ours. In order to receive His approval we need an acceptable sacrifice and a mediator, who is a qualified redeemer who doesn't just help us, but rescues us from our sins. We don't just need a life preserver thrown in our direction; we need a lifeguard who comes into the murky water of our personal existence and lifts us into the presence of a God whose holiness cannot be compromised. Only Jesus meets those qualifications.

New Agers, those who claim spirituality without biblical doctrine, are, spiritually speaking, like the walking dead. Speaking of mankind's natural love of darkness, we read, "We grope for the wall like the blind; we grope like those who have no eyes; we stumble at noon as in the twilight, among those in full vigor we are like dead men" (Isaiah 59:10).

As we noted earlier, no man or woman can rise above his or her conception of God. With that point made, we now return to the God revealed in Scripture.

TURNING TO THE GOD WHO EXISTS, NOT THE GOD WE WANT HIM TO BE

What a fresh breath of spiritual air we enjoy when we contemplate the God of Abraham, Isaac, and Jacob! The one true God is a God who is separate from us, a God who can guide us, a God who responds to our needs, but also a God who also judges—a God who condemns but also forgives. This God is frightening, but also merciful. Angry, but loving. And unchanging.

But immediately we are forced to answer several questions about God's character. In the Old Testament, He appears to deal with Israel and the surrounding nations with harsh judgments. Why the apparent difference in the New Testament? Yes, God says He does not change, but He appears to be more tolerant now than He was back then. People often ask questions about the commands to stone people in the Old Testament era for a variety of sins, some of which are considered minor infractions today. Certainly the strong condemnation of homosexual acts in the Old Testament raises a furor in our contemporary culture. And what about the commands to Joshua to destroy the Canaanite cities and to do so without mercy? Could it be that God, who seemed so harsh in the Old Testament, is more tolerant in the New? Does the "smiting" God no longer exist?

These are questions that need to be answered, and we will respond to them in the upcoming chapters. Specifically, the next chapter takes a closer look at the God of the Old Testament, the "smiting God," to use Nixey's expression. We will learn that God is not becoming more like us; in fact, the differences could not be more stark.

But before we delve into that challenging subject, let us commit ourselves to the God of Abraham, Isaac, and Jacob; let us pray against the "schemes of the devil" (Ephesians 6:11) and the false gods that surround us.

Remember, we fight with the assurance that we are already victorious; the devil has already been conquered, thanks to Christ (Colossians 2:13-15). To use the imagery of Jesus, "the strong man" (the devil) has been bound, so we can plunder his house! (see Mark 3:27).

OUR DECLARATION OF DEPENDENCE

Read Micah 7:18: "Who is a God like you, pardoning iniquity and passing over transgression for the remnant of his inheritance? He does not retain his anger forever, because he delights in steadfast love." Ask yourself: Are you worshipping the God who has revealed Himself in Christ?

Now read this experience of theologian John Stott:

> I have entered many Buddhist temples in different Asian countries and stood respectfully before the statue of the Buddha, his legs crossed, arms folded, eyes closed, the ghost of a smile playing round his mouth, a remote look on his face, detached from the agonies of the world. But each time after a while I have had to turn away. And in imagination I have turned instead to that lonely, twisted, tortured figure on the cross, nails through hands and feet, back lacerated, limbs wrenched, brow bleeding from thorn-pricks, mouth dry and intolerably thirsty, plunged in Godforsaken darkness. This is the God for me![18]

May this God have no competition for our hearts.[*]

ACTION STEP

Build bridges with people by asking them where they are on their spiritual journey. Listen to them carefully; ask questions and be genuinely curious. Point out that the God of the Scriptures can not only

---

[*] Portions of this chapter were adapted from my book *Ten Lies About God* (Grand Rapids, MI: Kregel Publications, 2009), 11-12, 40-58. Used with permission.

help them but rescue them from their sin and aimlessness. We have the same assignment that Jesus gave to Paul: "to open their eyes, so that they may turn from darkness to light and from the power of Satan to God, that they may receive forgiveness of sins and a place among those who are sanctified by faith in me" (Acts 26:18). Pray. Consider. Engage.

CHAPTER 5

Should We Still Be Worshipping the "Smitey Almighty" of the Old Testament?

Coming to Grips with the "Violent" God of Moses and the Prophets

Yes, Catherine Nixey—in her article, "The Church of England's God is becoming more liberal"[1] (referred to in the previous chapter)—was right when she says that few believe in the God of the Old Testament, the God who "smote" the Egyptians, the God who rained fire and brimstone on Sodom and Gomorrah, and the God who commanded Joshua to wipe out the Canaanites—*that* God is no more. He has been pushed off the scene to make way for a more tolerant, inclusive God.

All of us have faced the questions: What do we do with the seemingly harsh and stringent judgments of God in the Old Testament? Is God a cosmic bully, as some suggest? And has He mellowed over time, becoming His more loving self as displayed in the New Testament?

The Old Testament God has His critics.

The world's most outspoken atheist, Richard Dawkins—give him kudos for the clarity of his thoughts—heaps upon the God of the Old Testament the most damning criticism:

> The God of the Old Testament is arguably the most unpleasant character in all fiction: jealous and proud of it; a petty, unjust, unforgiving control-freak; a vindictive, bloodthirsty ethnic cleanser; a misogynistic, homophobic, racist, infanticidal, genocidal, filicidal, pestilential, megalomaniacal, sadomasochistic, capriciously malevolent bully.[2]

Paul Copan, who defends the God of the Old Testament, says he has a cartoon portraying Dawkins's distorted picture of God. He is pictured as a bearded old man at a computer ready to hit the "smite" key; woe to the person who offends Him or gets in His way. They just might experience the "smiting" of God!

Copan points out in his book *Is God a Vindictive Bully?* that the God of the Old Testament is not only attacked from those who are outside the faith, but also by some who say they are within the faith, including theologians who claim they belong under the label of evangelicalism. Whether they can claim that title is up for debate.

For example, Greg Boyd (pastor of Woodland Hills Church in Saint Paul, Minnesota, who taught at Bethel University for 16 years), in his book *The Crucifixion of the Warrior God: Interpreting the Old Testament's Violent Portraits of God in Light of the Cross,* believes that a distinction has to be made between the God who actually exists and "the textual God" as He is described in the Old Testament. The Old Testament portrait of God, he insists, must be readjusted in light of the cross, where God is portrayed as accepting and forgiving.[3]

So according to Boyd, the 415 mentions of "Thus says the LORD" often don't come from the actual God, but the "textual God." And who is this textual God? Copan summarizes it this way: "This is the literary depiction of God by a fallen, violence-prone, culturally conditioned ancient Near Eastern biblical narrator or prophet."[4] To clarify, according to Boyd, this textual God is a fictitious and flawed representation of God. The textual God we read about in the Old Testament simply does not exist.

What about Moses? Boyd suggests he apparently was demonically influenced when he commanded the Israelites to drive out the Canaanites and massacre them. Boyd goes on to say that such commands violate the message of the cross and that we should place Moses' command "under God's curse."[5] Boyd calls God's commands to kill the Canaanites "ghoulish" and contrary to the Jesus who said, "Father, forgive them, for they know not what they do" (Luke 23:34).

But, as we all know, nowhere in Scripture are we given to believe that Moses was vindictive or demonically inspired. We are led to believe that the Moses portrayed in the Old Testament really did exist as he is described. According to multiple New Testament references, Moses was not speaking on behalf of some textual God, but rather, knew God face to face (Exodus 33:11) and so is honored throughout Scripture: "Moses also was faithful in all God's house" (Hebrews 3:2). There is no hint that what he wrote was not to be taken at face value.

There is no doubt that the law under Moses was given in a culture of paganism, lawlessness, warfare, and servitude. At times, it did not represent the ideal, but rather, what had to be moderated and humanized. For example, as for slavery, God laid down stipulations, such as slaves should be given the option of leaving their master after six years of service (Exodus 21:2). We also know that God prohibited the enslavement of another person: "Whoever steals a man and sells him, and anyone found in possession of him, shall be put to death" (verse 16). We struggle with the various details about the Old Testament's teachings about slavery, but these regulations were more humane than those found in any of the surrounding cultures.[6]

Once you choose to dismiss the seemingly harsh commands of the Old Testament, it affects your understanding of the New Testament.

Jesus routinely saw the law as good; indeed, not one jot or tittle would pass away until all was fulfilled (Matthew 5:17). Once you choose to dismiss the seemingly harsh commands of the Old Testament, it affects your understanding of the New Testament.

What do we do with Paul's strong warning that when Jesus is revealed, He will "repay with affliction those who afflict you...when the Lord Jesus is revealed from heaven with his mighty angels in flaming fire, inflicting vengeance on those who do not know God and on those who do not obey the gospel of our Lord Jesus. They will suffer the punishment of eternal destruction, away from the presence of the Lord and from the glory of his might" (2 Thessalonians 1:6-9)?

Boyd thinks Paul got it wrong: "He [Paul] rather seems to be satisfying the Thessalonians' and/or his own fallen thirst for vengeance to come upon their enemies...To be frank, would it not have been more loving and more Christlike for Paul to at this point remind the Thessalonians to 'love your enemies and pray for those who persecute you'?"[7]

Boyd continues, "I consider it beyond question that some of Paul's language about opponents reflects a hostile and mean-spirited attitude." And again, "I certainly cannot deny that Paul's occasional nasty name-calling is inconsistent with his teaching that followers of Jesus are to 'do everything in love' (1 Corinthians 16:14)."[8] And so, Boyd dismisses the wrathful God of both the Old and New Testament.

When Boyd sits in judgment of Moses and Paul, he gets to decide when they were speaking on behalf of God and when they were just venting their prejudice and anger. This, of course, raises huge questions about the validity of other passages of Scripture, but we must move on.

> God is a complex being, and we must consider
> His character, His actions, and His revelations
> holistically, without sacrificing one for the other.

Pastor and author Andy Stanley, in his book *Irresistible*, claims that the New Testament has to be "unhitched" from the Old Testament. After all, he claims, the Old Testament advocates misogyny (disrespect of women and treating them as property). The Old Testament portrays God as angry, but in the New Testament, He is depicted as "brokenhearted." So if we don't unhitch the Old Testament from the New, according to Stanley, we will end up with terrible things such as "the prosperity gospel, the crusades, anti-Semitism, legalism, exclusivism, [and] judgementalism."[9]

Let's pause and reflect.

What if the God of the Old Testament and the God of the New Testament is a God of vengeance, anger, and severe judgment? What if He is also loving, forgiving, and merciful? God is a complex being, and we must consider His character, His actions, and His revelations holistically, without sacrificing one for the other. It is dangerous for us to adjust our view of God based on our preferences.

Our age wants to replace the wrathful God of the Old Testament with an "endlessly tolerant and indulgent Jesus."[10] But we are told that "all Scripture is breathed out by God" (2 Timothy 3:16), and when Paul wrote those words, only the Old Testament existed. Think of the passages we would have to delete based on our own inclinations and understanding of what we think love requires.

Anyone who views Jesus merely as "meek and mild" has to dismiss Old Testament passages such as Psalm 2:9, which predicted the coming of Jesus, the Messiah: "You shall break them with a rod of iron and dash them in pieces like a potter's vessel." This doesn't sound like Boyd or even Stanley's view of what a loving Jesus should be doing. Some New Testament passages about the judgment Jesus will bring in the future are even more terrifying. We will look at these passages in the next chapter.

Alexander Pope wrote a poem that appears to apply to those who would dismiss the hard teachings about God in both Testaments and replace them with portrayals of a more loving, tolerant, and inclusive God. He wrote that they

> Snatch from his hand the balance and the rod,
> Rejudge his justice, be the God of God.[11]

If we believe the Bible is the Word of God "from cover to cover," as the saying goes, then as someone has warned, we dare not treat it as if it is a cafeteria in which we are free to select only chocolates and our other favorite delicacies. We must deal with those troubling passages that seem to count against a loving God.

JUDGMENT IN THE OLD TESTAMENT

The Genesis Flood

Was the sending of the flood an overreaction by a hot-tempered God?

Several years ago on an episode of a PBS program hosted by Bill Moyers, the participants agreed that there was development in God. He sent the flood to the world, but then, like a child who builds a sandcastle only to destroy it in anger, God regretted what He had done. He felt duly chastised and so gave the rainbow with a promise to never do that again. Most of the panelists agreed that Noah's flood was evil; it had no redeemable value. Choose almost any human being at random, and they would have been more benevolent than God.[12]

The panel assumed, of course, that the Bible is only a record of what ancient people thought about God. So as they evolved to become more tolerant, their conception of God becomes more tolerant. Thus in the New Testament, with its emphasis on love, we see a more mature, gracious representation of God. According to this scenario, the way we view God is simply a reflection of our culture. And further, it is believed that this surely explains the apparent discrepancy between the God of the Old Testament and the God of the New Testament.

But let's consider the flood more closely. This event not only depicts the anger of God, but also the sorrow of God. He looked upon mankind's evil and violence and was greatly distressed (Genesis 6:5, 11); He grieved in His heart. And as Daniel Hawk observes, "Divine anger...must be understood against the backdrop of divine sorrow."[13] The "wickedness in the human heart affects the heart of God."[14] As a consequence, men, women, and children were drowned.

Let us never forget that because God is the giver of life, He is also the taker of life. Furthermore, as Copan says, "God simply

finished off the ruination and disintegration that humans began."[15]
The fall in Eden sent mankind in a godless direction, but of course
there were, most probably, men and women who were exceptions,
like Noah and Enoch, who "walked with God" (see Genesis 5:22
and 6:9).

God's hatred for sin is incomprehensible to us; He hates those
who resort to violence and unrestrained immorality and rampant
idolatry. The flood did not increase the number of people who died;
everyone who drowned would eventually have died. Their deaths
must have been terrifying, and if some cried to God for mercy and
forgiveness even when they were about to drown, God would have
granted it.

And, in the middle of this judgment, God showed grace by spar-
ing Noah and his family. Noah's descendants would continue awaiting the promised seed of the woman (Genesis 3:15). The thread of
redemption runs through the Old Testament, and God preserved a
family to perpetuate the human race.

We face a choice: We can turn away from God in anger, or we
can turn toward Him in repentance and faith based on Old Testament texts such as this: "For as high as the heavens are above the
earth, so great is his steadfast love toward those who fear him; as far
as the east is from the west, so far does he remove our transgressions
from us" (Psalm 103:11-12).

God's anger is never out of control. He expresses a righteous and
merciful anger. It should drive us to His loving-kindness and His
grace. And let us remember: Noah's ark represents the safety of all
who flee to God for refuge.

Wiping Out the Canaanites

During a visit to the country of Jordan, I asked a Muslim guide,
"If you had the military might, would you invade the United States

and force the US to become Muslim, killing those who refuse?" His answer? "We would have no choice...but we would give you a chance to convert to Islam first." This, of course, sounds much like what Joshua was commanded to do when God chose him to conquer the Promised Land for the Israelites.

Several questions come to mind. Was the command given to Joshua a case of ethnic cleansing? Were the Canaanites to be exterminated because they did not believe in Yahweh, the true and living God? Was God merely acting as a cruel, vindictive, and ethnocentric bully?

The Chilling Command

"Show them no mercy!"

Those were the words of the Lord to Joshua as the Israelites were about to enter into the land of Canaan. Speaking of the various nations, God warned,

> You must devote them to complete destruction. You shall make no covenant with them and show no mercy to them. You shall not intermarry with them, giving your daughters to their sons or taking their daughters for your sons, for they would turn away your sons from following me, to serve other gods...you shall break down their altars and dash in pieces their pillars and chop down their Asherim and burn their carved images with fire (Deuteronomy 7:2-5).

The Canaanites were to be completely destroyed.

In context, we must remember that the Canaanites had been warned that the Israelites were coming and judgment was imminent. We have good reason to believe that the leaders of the various

Canaanite tribes knew at least as much about Israel as the prostitute Rahab. When Israel's spies came to the city of Jericho, here's what she told them:

> I know that the LORD has given you the land, and that the fear of you has fallen upon us, and that all the inhabitants of the land melt away before you. For we have heard how the LORD dried up the water of the Red Sea before you when you came out of Egypt, and what you did to the two kings of the Amorites who were beyond the Jordan, to Sihon and Og, whom you devoted to destruction. And as soon as we heard it, our hearts melted, and there was no spirit left in any man because of you, for the LORD your God, he is God in the heavens above and on the earth beneath (Joshua 2:9-11).

If a prostitute had that much knowledge about Israel's history and was aware that the people worshipped the true and living God, you can be sure that the news of God's victories was widely known. And yet with that knowledge, the various Canaanite tribes kept worshipping their pagan deities and sacrificing their children to demons.

But still, questions remain.

Not a Matter of Ethnicity

The command to wipe out the Canaanites was not motivated by ethnic hatred. God was not advocating ethnic cleansing. We know this for two reasons. First, the Israelites themselves had the same ancestors as the Canaanites. Of the Israelites we read, from Ezekiel, "Your origin and your birth are of the land of the Canaanites; your father was an Amorite and your mother a Hittite" (16:3). Yes, because the Israelites were in Egypt for 400 years, they had developed their own culture. But when God called Abraham, it was out of the paganism of Ur of the Chaldees. The Israelites were hardly in a position to punish others because they were of a different ethnicity.

Furthermore, the harlot Rahab, as we have learned, was a Canaanite. Not only was she spared when the walls of Jericho collapsed (because she accepted the God of the Israelites), but she even became an ancestress of Jesus Christ (Matthew 1:5). Think of it: In His family genealogy, Jesus had a Canaanite woman—a prostitute—as a distant grandmother. God was not against the Canaanites because of their ethnicity.

When it came to harsh judgments, God often did not discriminate. Achan, an Israelite, was stoned to death under God's direction because he had disobeyed an order to totally destroy certain goods after the destruction of Jericho. He saw a Babylonian garment and some silver and gold and took them. Later, he confessed that he had coveted the items. Despite his confession, God commanded that he be put to death (Joshua 7:10-26). When it came to smiting, God did not limit Himself to the Canaanites; disobedient Israelites also came under severe judgment.

Not Simply a Matter of the Wrong Religion

For hundreds of years, God tolerated the Canaanites worshipping their pagan gods. This was a sign of God's patience toward them, but the time would come when "the iniquity of the Amorites" would be complete (Genesis 15:16). Their religion had disintegrated into the wanton worship of demons. This was combined with horrid cruelty and unimaginable forms of sexual deviancy, including incest and bestiality. Their satanic worship even led to the sacrificing of children to pagan deities.

The Israelites had nothing to brag about because God made it clear that they had done nothing special to be chosen to end the Canaanite rule. It wasn't because they were by nature more holy, but because of God's sovereign mercy and purpose. The land didn't inherently belong to the Israelites, nor for that matter, the Canaanites. It belonged to God, and He was giving it to a people He had chosen for it:

> Do not say in your heart, after the Lord your God has thrust them out before you, "It is because of my righteousness that the Lord has brought me in to possess this land," whereas it is because of the wickedness of these nations that the Lord is driving them out before you. Not because of your righteousness or the uprightness of your heart are you going in to possess their land, but because of the wickedness of these nations the Lord your God is driving them out from before you, and that he may confirm the word that the Lord swore to your fathers, to Abraham, to Isaac, and to Jacob. "Know, therefore, that the Lord your God is not giving you this good land to possess because of your righteousness, for you are a stubborn people" (Deuteronomy 9:4-6).

The land had become so unclean, so morally polluted, that in vivid imagery, God said, "I punished its iniquity, and the land vomited out its inhabitants" (Leviticus 18:25). God had given the Israelites the title deed to the land back in the days of Abraham, and now they came to claim it. God patiently waited for 400 years before the Canaanites were judged (Genesis 15:13). And God did not want the Israelites to be influenced by their degrading practices.

Now they were to be destroyed.

Why do we find this so difficult to accept? Apologist Clay Jones says it is because we do not hate sin. In his words,

> Could it be that because our culture today commits
> the same Canaanite sins, we are inoculated against the
> seriousness of these sins so that we think that God's
> judgment is unfair?...In short, most of our problems
> regarding God's ordering the destruction of the Canaan-
> ites comes from the fact that God hates sin and we don't.[16]

We superficially use words such as *bestiality, incest,* and *child sacrifice* and read about the horrific sexual attachment of the people to
demonically energized idols, yet we do not (and are unable to) see
these evils from God's point of view. In ordering the destruction
of the Canaanites, God was, in effect, asking Israel to bring about
a similar destruction as happened during the flood, except that in
this case, only a specific group within the human race was subjected
to death.

In short, the God who gave human beings life now used Israel
to take the lives of these demon-worshipping military men together
with their families. Eventually, God would bring much the same
destruction to Israel by using the Assyrians and the Babylonians,
though a remnant of the Israelites would be spared.

And let us remember that the God who asked Joshua to destroy
the Canaanites is the same God who will one day eternally punish
all those who have not found protection from His wrath though the
gracious redemption He provided. As Clay Jones said, God views
sin very differently than we do. Thankfully, He is a God who gives
grace to those who seek it. (This will be explained more fully in
chapter 11 of this book.)

I remain unconvinced of the view of some evangelicals who
attempt to soften the clear command of Scripture and teach that
when God gave these commands to Joshua, He emphasized the
judgment was directed only toward the cities and the military

outposts. John Walton, a professor of Old Testament studies, compared it to what the Allies set out to do during World War II. They were on a mission to end the Nazi regime, but that didn't mean they sought to kill every German.[17]

Pastor James Emery White agrees with Walton. In the culture of the Ancient Near East, most people lived in outlying areas, not the cities. White writes,

> The cities were military fortifications for soldiers and military officers. It's not where the women and children, farmers and laborers lived. So, in terms of warfare, this was not about civilians. Also, in terms of the ancient language of the day, even destroying everyone in the city was common hyperbole. It wasn't about literally taking every life, but ensuring that the war was won.[18]

We know from the biblical accounts that even if a city or region was to be taken, most often, its inhabitants were not totally destroyed. For example, there were cities the Israelites conquered where we're told that no Canaanites survived. But just a few chapters later, when other Israelites go to these cities, there are still Canaanite people living there (compare Joshua 11:21 and 15:13-15). How do we explain this apparent discrepancy? Again, some interpreters do not ascribe this to the disobedience of Joshua, but refer to how the Allies might have referred to "killing all the Nazis," and yet that didn't mean the entire population. And we do know that in the case of the Gibeonites, they were to be spared because of Joshua's promise to them (Joshua 9:15).

Finally, God also laid out the rules of warfare for the Israelite nation with parameters and limitations. He instructed Israel to offer terms of peace to their enemies before a battle (Joshua 20:10). The book of Joshua doesn't include detailed accounts of the offers of peace, but Joshua indicates that offers were made and were almost always refused. "There was not a city that made peace with the people of Israel except the Hivites, the inhabitants of Gibeon" (11:19).

To recap: Even as we personally wrestle with these difficult commands, let's not assume God wiped out innocent people in Canaan; there were no innocent people in the land. For that matter, there were no innocent people among the Israelites. It was not as if God destroyed a wicked people for the sake of a righteous people. Rather, He destroyed a wicked people because of their wickedness. They would be replaced with a different tribe of people whom He chose to draw to Himself and use to prepare the world for the coming of the Messiah. In other words, God brought justice to the Canaanites but showed mercy to the Israelites—at least for a time. God does not treat everyone alike.

Let us face a reality that we, in our modern day, find difficult to hear: God does not owe us mercy; He owes everyone justice, and not everyone receives mercy. As R.C. Sproul put it, "Suppose ten people sin and sin equally. Suppose God punishes five of them and is merciful to the other five. Is this injustice? No! In this situation five people get justice and five get mercy. No one gets injustice."[19]

As mentioned, God did not overlook the iniquity of the Israelites. Remember the terrible judgments that came upon them when the Assyrians invaded the land and carried off ten tribes. Later the Babylonians destroyed Jerusalem and took thousands of inhabitants to Babylon, and 70 years later, only a remnant returned. They had experienced much of the same death and destruction as they had heaped upon the Canaanites centuries earlier. God hates sin no matter who does it.

Interestingly, when the Israelites were taken to Babylon, despite their number, God did not expect them to set up a theocratic state;

the Israelites had to live in the land as best they could under a pagan government, with its pagan gods and allegiances. In fact, Daniel, Shadrach, Meshach, and Abednego served the wicked pagan king Nebuchadnezzar. It was only when Nebuchadnezzar demanded they worship a false god that they disobeyed and were thrown into the fiery furnace (Daniel 3:8-30). Jehovah's command for warfare applied only to the Israelites when conquering the land of Canaan.

Can a so-called holy war be justified today? No, it cannot. Israel was in a unique position as a theocracy chosen and directed by God (that this is not true of us today will be clarified in the next chapter). And displacing the people of the land applied only to what today we call the land of Israel. No nation or religion today can claim that specific revelation.

We must live with the tension of both the severe judgments of God and His divine, undeserved mercy. We must, in the end, appeal to God's holiness, wisdom, sovereignty, and eternal purposes.

No matter what unanswered questions we have about these commands, we must live with the tension of both the severe judgments of God and His divine, undeserved mercy. We must, in the end, appeal to God's holiness, wisdom, sovereignty, and eternal purposes. And we must give Him thanks that He is gracious and merciful to all who call upon Him. As we will see, the Old Testament is dotted with pronouncements about God's patience, mercy, and loving-kindness.

The next holy war will take place when Jesus returns in power and glory and judges His enemies both on Earth and at the Great White Throne Judgment (see Revelation 19–20).

The Stoning for Adultery, Homosexuality, and Other Sins

In the book *Shameless* (referred to in the previous chapter), the author tells the story of a young woman named Cindy, a lesbian who was deeply hurt by the church. Eventually, filled with shame and guilt, she simply confessed who she was to God as she understood Him. One weekend she stood outside a lodge with a couple of close friends, their faces focused on the flames of a campfire before them.

We read, "Cindy reached into her bag and took out her Bible." And then, "Slowly, without words, she tore out eight very specific pages from her Bible—namely, those that mentioned homosexuality—and burned them one by one." Then Cindy "tore out the Gospels: Matthew, Mark, Luke, and John. The story of Jesus had never hurt her; Jesus had not asked her to split. So, with her right hand she clutched the pages of the Gospels over her heart, and with the left she tossed in the rest to burn."[20]

Before I go further, it is important for us to pause and to feel the depth of the pain that Cindy was experiencing. We don't know, but perhaps she was a victim of abuse and painful rejection. She represents many others who have felt condemned by their sexual identity without experiencing the grace that God extends to all sinners. Without this balance, the Scriptures can only be a means of condemnation, not transformation and hope.

Although we are not told what passages Cindy tore out of her Bible, we don't have to guess. Among them would have been the command that homosexuality, whether practiced by a man or a woman, should be punished by death. In the Old Testament, there are numerous commands stating that the punishment for various kinds of sins is stoning. Yet it is interesting that apart from two or three instances of stoning in the Old Testament, we have no other examples in Jewish history. In other words, as far as we know, this command was seldom carried out.

Why?

It is clear that this penalty was up for negotiation; there was a ransom that could be paid in lieu of being stoned to death. Murder was the only crime in which a settlement could not be negotiated. The key text is Numbers 35:31: "You shall accept no ransom [substitute] for the life of a murderer, who is guilty of death, but he shall be put to death."

The availability of ransom seems to have been so prevalent that little is said about it. Old Testament scholar Walter Kaiser draws the same conclusion, indicating that there were some 16 crimes that called for the death penalty, but only in the case of premediated murder did the text say that the officials of Israel were forbidden to take a ransom or substitute. Kaiser comments, "This has widely been interpreted to imply that in all the other fifteen cases the judges could commute the crimes deserving of capital punishment by designating a 'ransom' or 'substitute.' In that case the death penalty served to mark the seriousness of the crime."[21]

According to R.C. Sproul, the late Hans Küng, the deceased controversial Roman Catholic theologian, writing about the seemingly harsh judgments of sin in the Old Testament, said the most mysterious aspect of the mystery of sin is not that the sinner deserves to die, but rather, that other sinners continue to live.

Sproul said Küng asked the right question. "The issue is not why does God punish sin but why does He permit the ongoing human rebellion? What prince, what king, what ruler would display so much patience with a continually rebellious people?"[22] In other words, we should not ask, Why did God punish people so harshly? Rather, we should ask, Why does God not punish everyone with that same harshness?

God is more patient and tolerant than we often realize. His patience is designed to lead us to repentance, to give us time to be redeemed. The supreme folly we make is thinking we can get by endlessly with our revolt.

MERCY, LOVE, AND FORGIVENESS
IN THE OLD TESTAMENT

The neat division people sometimes make between the Old Testament with its wrath and the New Testament with its mercy is not a fair reading of the text. Yes, there were strict penalties in the Old Testament, but there also was grace. In fact, looked at in one way, God appeared tolerant. Read these Old Testament passages thoughtfully:

> The LORD is merciful and gracious,
>   slow to anger and abounding in steadfast love.
> He will not always chide,
>   nor will he keep his anger forever.
> He does not deal with us according to our sins,
>   nor repay us according to our iniquities.
> For as high as the heavens are above the earth,
>   so great is his steadfast love toward those who
>   fear him;
> as far as the east is from the west,
>   so far does he remove our transgressions from us
>   (Psalm 103:8-12).

> The steadfast love of the LORD never ceases;
> his mercies never come to an end
> (Lamentations 3:22).

> Rend your hearts and not your garments.
> Return to the LORD your God,
>   for he is gracious and merciful,

> slow to anger, and abounding in steadfast love;
>   and he relents over disaster (Joel 2:13).

> Who is a God like you, pardoning iniquity
>   and passing over transgression
>   for the remnant of his inheritance?
> He does not retain his anger forever,
>   because he delights in steadfast love.
> He will again have compassion on us;
>   he will tread our iniquities underfoot.
> You will cast all our sins
>   into the depths of the sea.
> You will show faithfulness to Jacob
>   and steadfast love to Abraham,
> as you have sworn to our fathers
>   from the days of old (Micah 7:18-20).

Finally,

> Let the wicked forsake his way,
>   and the unrighteous man his thoughts;
> let him return to the LORD, that he may have
>   compassion on him,
> and to our God, for he will abundantly pardon
> (Isaiah 55:7).

We can respond to God's actions in the Old Testament in one of two ways: We can turn away from God in anger and disgust, or we can turn to Him in humility, knowing He deals ruthlessly with sin but also extends grace to all who come to Him in faith and repentance. We do not have to understand the complexity of God's dealings with the humans He created in order to bow in reverence and worship.

. . . .

In all of history, God only once punished an innocent person. We can rejoice that Jesus, though innocent, bore the sin of all who believe on Him.

. . . .

Second, and most importantly, keep in mind that in all of history, God only once punished an innocent person. We can rejoice that Jesus, though innocent, bore the sin of all who believe on Him. He got what He didn't deserve—namely, our sin; and believers get what we don't deserve—His mercy. For "the LORD has laid on him the iniquity of us all" (Isaiah 53:6).

Clearly, there are radical changes in the New Testament, and we turn to this topic in the next chapter. But for now, let us again repent of our anger and our judgments about the God revealed in the Old Testament.

OUR DECLARATION OF DEPENDENCE

God, from all of eternity, has had the attributes He possesses. When He told Moses, "I AM WHO I AM" (Exodus 3:14), He was saying, in effect, "I Am Who I am and not who you want Me to be." Our privilege is to submit to His judgment knowing that we do not have to understand all His ways to accept that He does all things well. As Abraham put it, "Shall not the judge of all the earth do what is just?" (Genesis 18:25).

For those who despise the actions of God, let us obey the command of Jude: "You, beloved, building yourselves up in your most holy faith and praying in the Holy Spirit, keep yourselves in the love of God, waiting for the mercy of our Lord Jesus Christ that leads to eternal life. *And have mercy on those who doubt*" (Jude 20-22, emphasis added).

Let our truth always be presented with compassion, and our witness tempered with grace. Ponder carefully the words of the prophet Nahum, who balanced God's judgment and His mercy.

> Who can stand before his indignation?
>   Who can endure the heat of his anger?
> His wrath is poured out like fire,
>   and the rocks are broken into pieces by him.
> The LORD is good,
>   a stronghold in the day of trouble;
> he knows those who take refuge in him.
>   But with an overflowing flood
> he will make a complete end of the adversaries,
>   and will pursue his enemies into darkness
> (Nahum 1:6-8).

Like the prophet Habakkuk, let us pray, "In wrath remember mercy" (Habakkuk 3:2).

ACTION STEP

When you encounter those who reject God because of His apparent harshness or indifference, remind them that if we are angry with God, we negate the comfort He gives to those who submit to Him. God's ways are not our ways. Become a worshipper, and you will trust God's heart even if you cannot understand His hand. With the seemingly purposeless death of his ten children, Job still bowed and worshipped, even without explanations. And God honored his faith. In every perplexing circumstance, let us do likewise.

CHAPTER 6

Is God More Tolerant Than He Used to Be?

Are the Abominations of the Old Testament Still Abominable?

'm glad no one really believes the Bible anymore, or they'd stone us!" Those are the words of a gay activist, replying to a Christian who was using the Bible to show that God condemns homosexuality. The homosexual's argument was clear: Since the penalty for homosexuality in the Old Testament was death (a penalty Bible believers do not think should be applied today), you should be stoning us. And if you don't agree with that, then don't use that command to argue against homosexuality!

How do we answer those who insist that God is more tolerant today than He was in the days of the Old Testament? Back then, homosexuals could be stoned to death along with adulterers, children who cursed their father and mother, witches, and blasphemers (although as we pointed out in the previous chapter, some penalties could be ransomed or substituted).

Today, everything has changed.

No more stories of Nadab and Abihu, struck dead for offering "unauthorized fire" (Leviticus 10:1-2). No more documented accounts like that of Uzzah, who touched the ark (contrary to God's instructions) and was instantly killed (2 Samuel 6:6-7). People today can be as irreverent or blasphemous as they wish and live to see old age.

Is God more tolerant than He used to be?

We need to answer this question for two reasons. First, we want to know whether we are free to sin with a minimum of consequences. Can we now live as we please with the assurance we will be treated with compassion and not judgment?

A young Christian woman confided to me that she chose a life of immorality in part because she was sure "God would forgive her anyway." She had no reason to fear His wrath, for Christ had borne it all for her. Of course, she did later confess her sin, she said, but only when the defilement and the full regret of what she had done weighed upon her conscience. But still, conduct that received a strong rebuke in Old Testament times—if not the possibility of the death penalty—can now be carried out with the sure knowledge that God is forgiving, showering us with what some call "unconditional love."

At one time, Christians in Western nations (including the United States) might have been described as legalists for adhering to the letter of the law. But few would say that's true today. We are free: free to ski in Colorado and romp on the beach in Hawaii; but also free to watch risqué movies and gamble, free to be as greedy and immoral as the world in which we work and live, *free to sin*.

Is it safer for us to sin in this age than in the days of the Old Testament? The question begs for an answer.

There is a second reason we want an answer: We want to know whether it is safer for *others* to do wrong today. If you have been sinned against, you want to know whether you can depend on God to "even the score." The girl who has been raped, the child who has been abused, the person who was cheated out of his life's savings by an unscrupulous relative—all these victims and many others like them want to know whether God is so loving that these infractions and crimes will be overlooked. What are the odds that these perpetrators will be brought to justice? We want God to judge us with tolerance; yet at the same time, we hope He will severely punish those who have wronged us. So will God be lenient or harsh? Merciful or condemning?

That God appears to be silent today in the face of our own sin and that of others seems clear enough. The question is, How should this silence be interpreted?

We must first affirm that God has not changed. His standards are the same, but He has chosen to interact with people differently— at least for a time. In fact, in this chapter, we will discover that the attributes of God revealed in the Old Testament are affirmed in the New. In the Old Testament, we see the severity of God, but also His goodness; just so in the New Testament, we see His strict judgments, but also His undeserved grace.

The same expression of attributes is found in both Testaments. There are compelling reasons to believe God has not lowered His standards revealed in the Old Testament. The New Testament might reveal a fuller expression of grace, but throughout the Bible, God reveals Himself with amazing consistency.

We should remind ourselves that the New Testament writers consistently and frequently connect the Old Testament with their New Testament writings. The unity of the Testaments is obvious.

THE UNITY OF THE TESTAMENTS

There is no rational way to "unhitch" the New Testament from the Old.

The hardening of Pharaoh's heart in Exodus 5–12 connects with Romans 9, where Paul discussed the sovereignty of God. The story of Noah and the flood was mentioned by Jesus. Israel's entire history—including the killing of the firstborn, the crossing of the Red Sea, the idolatry of the golden calf—was used by Paul as illustrations for us today (see 1 Corinthians 10:1-13). The imprecatory Psalm 69 (which is a prayer of judgment upon the wicked) is quoted to bolster the point Paul was making in Romans 11:8-10.

Of course, such examples could be multiplied. The unity of the Testaments is found on almost every page of both Testaments. Imagine what would happen to the genealogy of Jesus if we were to unhitch the New Testament from the Old, or if we were to delete all passages in the New Testament where God is described with Old Testament references. Or what about all the places where writers of the New Testament quote the Old and say, "It is written…"? Do any of these things, and the New Testament would collapse into a short, disjointed narrative.

We should not think the Old Testament was Plan A, then when that didn't work, God switched to Plan B. Be assured, all of God's plans are Plan A. God works all things after the counsel of His own will. And Christ was the Lamb slain from before the foundation of the world (see 1 Peter 1:19-20; Revelation 13:8). In other words, redemption was in God's plan even before creation.

Yes, there are clear distinctions between the Old Testament and the New. In the Old Testament, there were severe punishments for many transgressions, many abominations. In fact, there are eight Hebrew words in the Bible translated as "abomination" or a form of that word. Some of the definitions used to describe these Hebrew words are disgusting, abhorrent, filthy, offensive, to detest, to pollute, to enrage, to stink. In the Old Testament, God called dozens of things an abomination.

For example, eating the carcasses of sea creatures that don't have fins or scales is an abomination. Eating certain unclean birds is forbidden (see Leviticus 11). Along with other prohibitions as to what should not be eaten, there are 14 verses that regulate sexual relations, and various forms of sex outside of marriage are all called abominations (Leviticus 18:6-26, 29-30).

So why do we accept the Old Testament teaching about sexuality but fail to observe all the other rules, commandments, and prohibitions?

THE CONTROVERSIAL ISSUES OF SEXUALITY

I repeat: Why do we observe some regulations of the Old Testament but not others? On what biblical grounds can we say that sins such as homosexuality and other sex acts outside of the man-woman covenant relationship are regarded as sinful, but not eating birds or fish deemed unclean in Old Testament times?

Christians are sometimes ridiculed when they quote Old Testament texts regarding sexual sins. "Are you sure you are not mixing wool and linen?" (In Leviticus 19:19, there are instructions that forbid the wearing of blended fabrics.) Or we are asked, "Do you know for sure you are not eating food that has been contaminated because of different seeds?" (In Deuteronomy 22:9-11, planting two different seeds on a field was forbidden. And the list goes on.)

On what basis do we accept or reject certain Old Testament teachings? (I have been helped to understand this more clearly from a lecture by Voddie Baucham Jr.)[1]

How should we respond?

Before we answer that question, let's point out that the book of Leviticus, with its harsh penalties for various sins, also has passages that everyone can agree on. Below are some excerpts:

> You shall not steal…You shall not oppress your neighbor
> or rob him…You shall do no injustice in court. You shall
> not be partial to the poor or defer to the great, but in
> righteousness shall you judge your neighbor…love your
> neighbor as yourself: I am the LORD (Leviticus 19:11-18).

Love your neighbor as yourself! Yes, that is in the book of Leviticus!

But back to the question: Why do we quote Leviticus regarding sexual prohibitions, but not regarding many other matters that were also prohibited?

We must distinguish between three different kinds of law in the Old Testament. First, there is the *civil* law, which had to do with life in the desert. These laws cannot apply to us directly. For example, if your neighbor's ox comes onto your property, how do you handle it? How should various disputes be resolved? Some of the admonitions about the mixing of various kinds of fabric have to do with making a distinction between Israel and the pagan nations around it. And the distinctions between the different foods that should or should not be eaten are clearly abolished in the New Testament. These civil laws cannot and do not apply today.

Then there is the *ceremonial* law, which has to do with offering sacrifices. These laws, of course, were done away with when Christ made His perfect sacrifice on the cross. To insist we should carry out the kind of temple worship prescribed in the Old Testament would be an insult to the work of Christ. Several chapters of the book of Hebrews are dedicated to making that crystal clear.

But the *moral* code, and sins of the heart, do have application for today. Consider this:

> There are six things that the LORD hates,
>   seven that are an abomination to him:

haughty eyes, a lying tongue,
    and hands that shed innocent blood,
a heart that devises wicked plans,
    feet that make haste to run to evil,
a false witness who breathes out lies,
    and one who sows discord among brothers
(Proverbs 6:16-19).

Are these still abominations in God's sight? Yes, because they are violations of the basic commandments of character: We are to be truthful and humble, loving one's neighbor as one's self. And to God, the purity of our hearts is more important than our deeds.

Let's return to the matter of sexuality, which occupies so much discussion in our society. In the same list that mentions homosexuality, the book of Leviticus also condemns incest, offering your children to pagan gods, and bestiality, all of which are recognized as evils in most of Western culture.

But—and this is very important—we also know that such commands carry over into our era because they are repeated—either implicitly or explicitly—in the New Testament.

Read this carefully from the New Testament:

> Now we know that the law is good, if one uses it lawfully, understanding this, that the law is not laid down for the just but for the lawless and disobedient, for the ungodly and sinners, for the unholy and profane, for those who strike their fathers and mothers, for murderers, the sexually immoral, men who practice homosexuality, enslavers, liars, perjurers, and whatever else is contrary to sound doctrine, in accordance with the gospel of the glory of the blessed God with which I have been entrusted (1 Timothy 1:8-11).

This list covers the gamut of the moral sins mentioned in the Old Testament. The most controversial sin on this list is homosexuality. Why has this behavior been opposed by the church for 2,000 years, and why does it receive more condemnation than at least a few of the other sins on the list? Why among Christians is same-sex marriage singled out as perhaps more grievous than even adultery or divorce?

We need to respond to a question posed by E.J. Dionne in a *Washington Post* article titled "A question to conservative Christians on gay marriage: Why draw the line here?" His point: Christians view adultery and even divorce as sins, but these sins do not spark a great deal of controversy. He writes, "But unless I'm missing something, we do not see court cases from website designers or florists or bakers about refusing to do business with people in their second or third marriages. We don't see the same ferocious response to adultery as we do to same-sex marriage."[2]

That is a fair question that deserves an answer. Al Mohler responds, agreeing that yes, adultery and divorce are serious sins that destroy marriages, harm children, and incur the judgment of God. But in answer to the question "Why draw the line here?," Mohler writes, "It is because unlike divorce and adultery, which after all accept a definition of marriage, you have what is called same-sex marriage, a rejection of any stable objective definition of marriage. Marriage is no longer the union of a man and a woman, it is declared to be what marriage is not and cannot be."

Mohler continues,

> A same-sex relationship, to use the historic language of Christianity, lacks many of the capacities and many of the dignities of marriage. Most importantly, it lacks the procreative possibility. A man and a man and a woman

and a woman cannot on their own, alone, the two of them together create a baby. It can't happen…

But we have to take this one step further, what is the biblical basis for drawing the line here? It has to do with the fact that according to scripture, same-sex sexual relationships are not merely contrary to scripture, but contrary to nature. That is what is different.[3]

So homosexual marriage is a misnomer; you can have two men or two women cohabiting, but you cannot call that marriage. These relationships destroy the very concept of marriage and are contrary to natural law. The very fact that every homosexual has a father and a mother illustrates that the created order cannot be ignored in the discussion of marriage and the family.

Attempts have been made to teach that the Bible doesn't really mean what it seems to mean about homosexuality. There are those who say all references to it in Scripture are actually references to pedophilia or pederasty (the sexual relationship between a man and a boy). The argument is that the biblical writers did not know what we moderns do—namely, that homosexuality is actually an orientation. Thus, the Bible does not truly condemn same-sex acts as we know them today.[4]

* * *

We must help our generation understand
that we must interpret the culture through
the lens of Scripture, and not Scripture
through the lens of contemporary culture.

But think about it: If we say that the writers of Scripture did not really know what we now know, we are saying that the God who inspired them to write the Bible was less informed than we are today. This is a serious charge against Spirit-inspired Scripture. We must help our generation understand that we must interpret the culture through the lens of Scripture, and not Scripture through the lens of contemporary culture.

I want to emphasize that we must approach these matters sympathetically, with compassion. We must lovingly assure those who are hurting that although God has not changed His mind nor become more lenient about sin, He has made redemption possible for all who will repent and believe the gospel (1 Corinthians 6:9-11).

But why do Christians believe that homosexuals, adulterers, and other immoral actors should not be stoned? Why the apparent leniency regarding penalties in the New Testament compared to Old Testament times? That brings us back to our original question: Is God more tolerant than He used to be?

In the upcoming pages, we will see that the New Testament does not represent a change in God, but a change in the way He deals with us.

GOD'S ADMINISTRATION
HAS CHANGED

So to recap the question: How do we account for the difference between the consequences of disobedience in the Old and the New Testaments? Why does it appear to be so safe to sin today?

We will discover that God's opinions have not changed; His penalties, if anything, are more severe. There is, however, a change in the timetable and method of punishment. The more carefully we look at the Scriptures, the more we become aware of the unwavering consistency of God and His intention to punish sin. He hates it just as much today as He ever did. Thankfully, He offers us a remedy.

In Hebrews 12:18-29, we see the unity of God reflected in both Mount Sinai and Mount Calvary. Here, like a diamond, the fuller range of God's attributes are on display. We see that God has not lowered His standards; He will, in the end, prove He has not mellowed with age. Those who are unprepared to meet Him will face a future of unimaginable horror. No, He has not changed.

But His management has changed, and this is represented in three ways. Stay with me as I try to develop the above passage (Hebrews 12:18-29) step by step. The contrast between Sinai and Calvary will give us the answers we seek.

From the Earthly to the Heavenly

Let's reread this as if for the first time:

> You have not come to what may be touched, a blazing fire and darkness and gloom and a tempest and the sound of a trumpet and a voice whose words made the hearers beg that no further messages be spoken to them. For they could not endure the order that was given, "If even a beast touches the mountain, it shall be stoned." Indeed, so terrifying was the sight that Moses said, "I tremble with fear." But you have come to Mount Zion and to the city of the living God, the heavenly Jerusalem (Hebrews 12:18-22).

On Mount Sinai, Moses and Aaron were brought low before the Almighty in silence and worship. If so much as an animal or man touched the mountain, they were not to be retrieved but to be shot with an arrow. Moses was called to the top of the mountain to see the fire, lightning, and smoke. He then returned to tell the people they would be struck down if they came too close to the mountain.

The physical distance between the people and the mountain symbolized the moral distance between God and us. Not even Moses was able to see God directly, though he was given special privileges. The warning to the people was "Stay back or be killed!"

Imagine the power needed to shake a mountain! Even today we see the power of God in tornadoes, hurricanes, and earthquakes. God wanted this special revelation to be accompanied by a physical act that would remind the people of His power and judgment. They were to step back because He is holy.

There was also a vertical distance between God and man. God came down out of heaven as a reminder that we are from below, creatures of the earth. He is separated; He is from above and exceeds the limits. To quote Sproul, "When we meet the Infinite, we become acutely conscious that we are finite. When we meet the Eternal, we know we are temporal. To meet God is a powerful study in contrasts."[5] Imagine a progressive Christian standing at Mount Sinai engulfed in bellows of fire and smoke, saying, "I will come to God on my own terms; we can all come in our own way!"

Sinai was God's presence without an atonement, without a mediator. This was sinful man standing within range of God's holiness. Here was the unworthy creature in the presence of his most worthy Creator. Here was a revelation of the God who will not tolerate disobedience, the God who is to be "feared above all gods" (Psalm 96:4).

Now comes an important contrast: "But you have come to Mount Zion and to the city of the living God, the heavenly Jerusalem" (Hebrews 12:22). When David conquered Jerusalem and placed the ark on Mount Zion, this mountain was considered the earthly dwelling place of God. Later, the word *Zion* was applied to the entire city. Centuries passed, and Christ came and died outside of its walls, fulfilling the prophecies that salvation would come from Zion.

Mount Zion represents the opening of heaven; and now we are invited to come to enjoy the privileges of the "heavenly Jerusalem" (verses 22-24). As believers, we are already citizens of heaven (Philippians 3:20). As such we are invited into the Most Holy Place by the blood of Jesus. Think of it: Today we are invited into the very place where, in Old Testament times, only the high priest could enter; unauthorized entry would have been met by death.

And supremely, we come to "Jesus, the mediator of a new covenant, and to the sprinkled blood that speaks a better word than the blood of Abel" (Hebrews 12:24). Abel's sacrifice was accepted by God, but his shed blood could not atone for his sin, much less for the sin of his brother. Jesus' blood, however, was sufficient for us all.

The contrast is clear. Sinai was covered with clouds; Zion is filled with light. Sinai is symbolic of judgment and death; Zion is symbolic of life and forgiveness. The message of Sinai was "Stand back!" The message of Zion is "Come near!"

Look at a calendar, and you will agree that Christ splits history in two; we have BC (before Christ) and AD (*anno Domini,* the year of our Lord). But Jesus also splits salvation history in two, even as the veil of the temple was torn from top to bottom. Now that His blood is shed, we can come to God in confidence.

Does this mean that God's hatred for sin has been taken away? Has Christ's coming made the Almighty more tolerant? Let's continue to study the passage to have our questions answered.

There is a second way to describe this change of administration.

The Old Covenant vs. the New Covenant

Jesus, we have learned, is the mediator of "a new covenant" (Hebrews 12:24). What does this mean? If He gave us a new covenant, what was the *old* covenant?

In Old Testament times, God made a covenant with the entire nation of Israel. He chose to rule directly through kings and prophets, revealing His will step by step, expecting them to follow His instructions. The prophets would say, "The Word of the Lord came to me," and told the kings what God's will was. There was no separation between religion and the state as we know it; the state existed to implement the divine will of God.

Obviously, there was no freedom of religion in the Old Testament era. Idolatry was punishable by death. "You shall have no other gods before me" (Exodus 20:3) was the first of the Ten Commandments given to the nation Israel. If the people did not obey, the penalties were immediate and, from our standpoint, severe.

Jesus brought with Him the radical teaching that His followers could live acceptably under a pagan government. He did not come to overthrow the Roman occupation of Israel; indeed, His kingdom was not of this world. When faced with the question of whether taxes should be paid to the pagan Romans, Christ replied, "Render to Caesar the things that are Caesar's, and to God the things that are God's" (Luke 20:25). Yes, they could pay taxes to a corrupt government, and yes, they could fulfill their obligations to God as well.

There are two major changes from the old covenant. First, God would no longer deal with one nation, but with individuals from all nations. He would now call out from among the nations a transnational group of people from every tribe, tongue, and people to form a new gathering, called the church. These people would live, for the most part, in political regimes hostile to them. We who are a part of this program are to continue as salt and light, representing Christ wherever we find ourselves.

· · · · · · · · · · · ·

Christians should be involved in government
as good citizens, but our primary message
is the transformation of nations through
the transformation of individuals.

· · · · · · · · · · · ·

In our era, we are to submit, as much as possible, to worldly authorities; we are to do their bidding unless such obligations conflict with our conscience. Indeed, Paul, writing from a prison cell in Rome, said we must submit to the governing authorities (in his case, Nero) because they were "instituted by God" (Romans 13:1).

Our agenda as a church is not to take over nations, politically speaking. Of course, Christians should be involved in government as good citizens, but our primary message is the transformation of nations through the transformation of individuals. The early disciples had all of our national woes times ten, and yet without a political base. Without a voting bloc in the Roman senate, they changed their world, turning it "upside down" as Luke the historian put it (Acts 17:6).

When Paul came to the immoral city of Corinth, he taught what surely must have appeared as a novel idea—namely, that it was not the responsibility of the church to try to punish the unbelieving world, even with regard to people's sexual behavior. But as for the church, some sins that merited the death penalty in the Old Testament should, in this era, be a matter of church discipline. For example, the man who was having sex with his "father's wife," which was most probably his stepmother, was to be removed from the congregation (1 Corinthians 5:1-2).

The church, the body of Christ, should not keep on its rolls a member in good standing who is living in wanton sin, but the church does not have the right or the authority to imprison or execute an offender. This explains why, in our churches today, when there is a criminal charge brought against a church member, the church leadership has the responsibility of working with the secular authorities (the police and the courts) to administer penalties.

Then to clarify, Paul helped believers to understand that they are not called to separate themselves from the immoral people in the world (1 Corinthians 5:9-12). Paul said we are not called to judge them; rather, we are called to judge those within the church ranks. "Is it not those inside the church whom you are to judge?" he asks (verse 12).

In fact, Paul taught that if a Christian is admonished but continues to live in wanton sin and we have fellowship with him over a meal, or if we enjoy his company, we are, in some sense, approving of his sin. To help such believers see the error of their ways, Paul said "not even to eat with such a one" (verse 11).

Now we are ready to understand why we as a church do not sentence people to death today as Israel did in the Old Testament. The church is not a theocracy, and we have no authority to judge those who "are without." The state is to penalize those who commit certain crimes, and those laws must be upheld. Although we as the church do not have the right to take a life, we can announce spiritual death to those who persist in their sins. The immoral man in the congregation of Corinth was not to be put to death, but was to be put out of the congregation (1 Corinthians 5:2-5). Such discipline is our duty.

Needless to say, the matter of church discipline is controversial, especially today, when SOGI laws (Sexual Orientation and Gender Identity) are applied in the wider culture. Churches today dare not allow the state to dictate to them what their standards should be. This is why constitutions and church covenants should be clear to members, and they must know in advance what conduct will be deemed worthy of expulsion.

My experience as a pastor has taught me that consistency in church discipline is difficult because sometimes the issues are unclear and the information sketchy, and knowing exactly where the lines should be drawn is most controversial. My only caution is this: Be sure that offenders are given ample time to repent of their ways before they are removed from the church rolls. The goal should always be forgiveness and the restoration of the offender.

It is foolish for us to think we can sin with impunity just because Christ has come. The purpose of redemption was to make it possible for us to live holy lives. It is blessedly true, of course, that God does forgive, but our sin, particularly deliberate sin, always invites the discipline of God. We are to pursue holiness, for "without which no one will see the Lord" (Hebrews 12:14). God has not revised His list of moral offenses.

There is a final important way to describe the contrast between Sinai and Calvary, and at last, we will specifically answer the question of whether God is more tolerant than He used to be.

Thanks for staying with me.

Immediate (Physical) Judgment vs. Future, Eternal Judgment

In Hebrews 12:25-27, we are reintroduced to the absolute holiness and justice of God. As you read this breathtaking passage, ask yourself if God is more tolerant today than he was in Old Testament times:

> See that you do not refuse him who is speaking. For if
> they did not escape when they refused him who warned

them on earth, much less will we escape if we reject him who warns from heaven. At that time his voice shook the earth, but now he has promised, "Yet once more I will shake not only the earth but also the heavens." This phrase, "Yet once more," indicates the removal of things that are shaken—that is, things that have been made—in order that the things that cannot be shaken may remain.

We can't miss it: If God judged the people for turning away from Him when He spoke at Sinai, just think of the greater judgment that will come to those who turn away from the voice that comes out of heaven, from Mount Zion! The unbelieving Jews who heard God speak at Sinai did not get to enter the land—they died in the wilderness. Their primary punishment was physical death, though for the unrepentant there was eternal, spiritual death as well. Today, God does not usually judge people with immediate physical death (though it might happen on occasion), but the judgment of spiritual death remains, with even greater condemnation.

In an earlier chapter in Hebrews, we are given a statement that ends with a chilling question:

> Anyone who has set aside the law of Moses dies without mercy on the evidence of two or three witnesses. How much worse punishment, do you think, will be deserved by the one who has trampled underfoot the Son of God, and has profaned the blood of the covenant by which he was sanctified, and has outraged the Spirit of grace? (Hebrews 10:28-29).

So how much worse do you think the punishment will be for those who have heard the gospel and rejected it? The answer is given two verses later: *"It is a fearful thing to fall into the hands of the living God"* (verse 31).

If God judged the Jews who had a limited understanding of redemption, think of what He will do to those who have heard about the coming of Christ, His death, and His resurrection! If Israel by its disobedience did not enter the Promised Land, those today who reject Christ will forfeit spiritual blessings in this life and will most assuredly be severely judged by an eternal, conscious form of death in hell. Imagine their fate!

At Sinai, God shook the earth. From Zion, He is going to shake the whole universe. "At that time his voice shook the earth, but now he has promised, 'Yet once more I will shake not only the earth but also the heavens'" (Hebrews 12:26). The phrase is borrowed from Haggai 2:6, where the prediction is made that God will judge the earth (cf. Revelation 6:12-14). Everything that can be shaken, which denotes the entire physical order, will be destroyed, and only eternal things will remain (cf. 2 Peter 3:10).

Don't miss this basic principle: *The greater the grace, the greater the judgment for refusing it.* The more of God we know, the greater our responsibility to accept it. The judgment of the Old Testament was largely physical, and for the unrepentant, eternal judgment. In the New Testament, judgment is, for the most part, postponed until the end of life on earth, but eternity awaits. That endless punishment is more severe because more light has come, as the passage above teaches.

In a sense, we can say that the harsh penalties of the Old Testament also demonstrated an overabundance of grace. By seeing these punishments immediately applied, the people had a visual demonstration of why they should fear God. In our day, these penalties are frequently postponed, and as a result, people feel free to misinterpret the patience of God as laxity or indifference.

Today, sins are allowed to accumulate, and the judgment of the unrepentant is delayed. Paul, writing to those who had hardened their hearts against God, wrote, "Because of your hard and impenitent heart you are storing up wrath for yourself on the day of wrath when God's righteous judgment will be revealed" (Romans 2:5). Retribution and justice have not escaped God's attention.

. . . .

We should never interpret the silence
of God as the indifference of God.

. . . .

Grace gives the illusion of tolerance, and if not properly interpreted, can be construed as a license to sin. Indeed, the New Testament writer Jude warned of "ungodly people, who pervert the grace of our God into sensuality and deny our only Master and Lord, Jesus Christ" (Jude 4). They confuse the patience of God with the leniency of God.

I've said it before: *We should never interpret the silence of God as the indifference of God.*

God's long-suffering is not a sign of weakness or indifference; it is intended to bring us to repentance. "The Lord is not slow to fulfill his promise as some count slowness, but is patient toward you, not wishing that any should perish, but that all should reach repentance" (2 Peter 3:9). It would be a mistake to think that His "slowness" means He is letting us skip our day of judgment. In Ecclesiastes, Solomon warned that God's supposed slowness encourages wrongdoing. "Because the sentence against an evil deed is not executed speedily, the heart of the children of man is fully set to do evil" (Ecclesiastes 8:11). How easily we misinterpret divine patience as divine tolerance!

In the end, all penalties will be exacted; retribution will be demanded; nothing will be overlooked. At the Great White Throne Judgment, unbelievers of all ages will be called to account and meticulously judged. Visualize the scene:

> The sea gave up the dead who were in it, Death and Hades gave up the dead who were in them, and they were judged, each one of them, according to what they had done. Then Death and Hades were thrown into the lake of fire. This is the second death, the lake of fire. And if anyone's name was not found written in the book of life, he was thrown into the lake of fire (Revelation 20:13-15).

Nothing that terrifying occurs in the Old Testament.

IS IT SAFE TO SIN?

In C.S. Lewis's *The Lion, the Witch and the Wardrobe*, we read the story of three children who are about to meet Aslan, the golden lion (Christ). Some talking beavers are describing the lion to Lucy, Susan, and Peter, who are newcomers to Narnia, and they fear meeting Aslan. The children ask questions that reveal their fears.

> "Ooh!" said Susan, "I'd thought he was a man. Is he— quite safe? I shall feel rather nervous about meeting a lion."

> "That you will, dearie, and no mistake," said Mrs. Beaver, "if there's anyone who can appear before Aslan without their knees knocking, they're either braver than most or else just silly."

"Then he isn't safe?" said Lucy.

"Safe?" said Mr. Beaver. "Don't you hear what Mrs. Beaver tells you? Who said anything about safe? 'Course he isn't safe. But he's good. He's the King, I tell you."[6]

Is God safe? Of course not.

If we still think God is more tolerant of sin in the New Testament than in the Old, let us look at what His Son endured at Calvary; see Him as He languishes under the weight of our sin. Our only hope is to come under the shelter of His gracious protection. Paul says in the New Testament that He "delivers us from the wrath to come" (1 Thessalonians 1:10).

Is it true that justice delayed is justice denied? For human courts, this is so; for as time passes, evidence is often lost, and the offender is set free. But this does not apply to the Supreme Court of heaven. For God, no facts are lost, no circumstances are capable of misinterpretation. The whole earthly scenario can be recreated so that scrupulous justice can be satisfied. Judicial integrity will prevail, and we shall sing forever, "Salvation and glory and power belong to our God, for his judgments are true and just" (see Revelation 19:1-2).

In the same C.S. Lewis story quoted above, the children meet Aslan the lion. Lucy observed that his paws were potentially very soft or very terrible. They could be as soft as velvet with his claws drawn in, or sharp as knives with his claws extended. Christ is both meek and lowly, but also fierce and just.

Have you ever heard a sermon about "the wrath of the Lamb"? We read that a day is coming when those on the earth will shout to the mountains and rocks, "Fall on us and hide us from the face of him who is seated on the throne, and from *the wrath of the Lamb*, for the great day of their wrath has come, and who can stand?" (Revelation 6:16-17, emphasis added). The wrath of the Lamb!

No wonder people will want to hide from His coming as judge:

In righteousness he judges and makes war. His eyes are like a flame of fire, and on his head are many diadems, and he has a name written that no one knows but himself. He is clothed in a robe dipped in blood, and the name by which he is called is The Word of God. And the armies of heaven, arrayed in fine linen, white and pure, were following him on white horses. From his mouth comes a sharp sword with which to strike down the nations, and he will rule them with a rod of iron. He will tread the winepress of the fury of the wrath of God the Almighty. On his robe and on his thigh he has a name written, King of kings and Lord of lords (Revelation 19:11-16).

What follows is an unbelievable description of the carnage that will take place after Jesus executes His judgment. With sword in hand, He will smite His enemies and leave them dying on the battlefield. Even if we grant that the account is symbolic, it can mean nothing less than the revelation of the vengeance of God Almighty.

Terrifying.

But this makes God's mercy and undeserved grace more wonderful.

A PLEA TO COME TO
BOTH SINAI AND CALVARY

Don't despair!

"Do homosexuals go to hell?" I have been asked. To ask the question is to misunderstand the gospel. Yes, of course they go to hell along with heterosexuals, faithful husbands and wives, those who run food pantries and give their lives in the service of others. Sin is found in every human heart, and even self-righteous sins merit the just judgment of God. Hell is in the future for everyone who does not find shelter in Christ. But the good news is that "where sin increased, grace abounded all the more" (Romans 5:20).

The news is better than we could ever hope or imagine.

Finally, *figuratively speaking, we must come to Sinai before we come to Zion*. We must see our sin before we can appreciate grace. In the allegory called *The Pilgrim's Progress*, a man named Christian is seen traveling with the weight of sin on his shoulders, but the burden of the law is too much for him. Thankfully, he comes to Calvary, and there, his load is rolled unto the shoulders of the One who is able to carry it. To his delight, the terrors of Sinai are borne by the Son at Calvary. What a tragedy to meet people who are comfortable with who they are and managing their sin as best they can—people who have lost their capacity to grieve over their sin and accept God's mercy.

To those aware of their need, we say, "Come!" Stand at Mount Sinai to see your sin; then come to linger at Calvary to see your pardon. "Therefore let us be grateful for receiving a kingdom that cannot be shaken, and thus let us offer to God acceptable worship, with reverence and awe, for our God is a consuming fire" (Hebrews 12:28-29). There was fire at Sinai, and there will also be fire at the final judgment. *A consuming fire!*

Donald McCullough writes:

> Fire demands respect…With one spark it can condemn
> a forest to ashes and a home to a memory as ghostly as
> the smoke rising from the charred remains of the family
> album. Or with a single flame it can crown a candle with

power to warm a romance and set to dancing a fireplace blaze that defends against the cold. Fire is dangerous to be sure, but we cannot live without it; fire destroys but it also sustains life.[7]

There is a story that comes to us from the days when home-steaders built homes on the open fields. Fearing the possibility of being engulfed by the flames of a prairie fire, when the wind was favorable, farmers would light a "controlled burn" around their homestead. They would burn one patch of grass after another in an ever-widening circle. Then when a distant prairie fire came near, they were safe from its flames because they were living where the fire had already been.

When we come to Mount Zion, we come to where the fire of Sinai has already struck. We come to the only place of safety; we come to the place where we are welcome. There, we are sheltered from terrifying judgment.

> Jehovah bade His sword awake,
> *O Christ, it woke 'gainst Thee!*
> Thy open bosom was my ward,
> It braved the storm for me.[8]

God's Son endured the fire that was headed in our direction. Only those who believe in Him are exempt from the flames. Let us ponder the cross, and with the centurion, say, "Truly this was the Son of God!" (Matthew 27:54).*

---

* Portions of this chapter were adapted from my book *Ten Lies About God* (Grand Rapids, MI: Kregel Publications, 2009). Used with permission.

OUR DECLARATION OF DEPENDENCE

The author of Hebrews asks: "How shall we escape if we neglect such a great salvation?" (2:3). The writer comes to this conclusion because God proved in Israel's history that "every transgression or disobedience received a just retribution" (verse 2).

When I taught a seminary course in homiletics (preaching), I would take the students to a local cemetery and challenge them to choose a tombstone and preach to the dead. Sometimes I could almost see the color drain from their faces. But I was making a point: When we share the gospel, we are speaking to people who are, by nature, "dead in…trespasses and sins" (Ephesians 2:1). But the message of the gospel does what we can't: It causes the spiritually blind to see, the spiritually deaf to hear, and the spiritually dead to be raised. In the gospel, God does what we cannot; we point the way, He does the miracle.

Let us urge people to join us on the winning side: Calvary.

ACTION STEP

Let's not be combative in our witness for Christ. The more aware we are of our sin, the more understanding we will have for those who are relying on their own goodness to save them. Martin Luther is quoted as saying, "I am more concerned about the sin in my own heart than I am about the Pope." With a humble awareness of your own need, reach out to others and help them to see the urgency of trusting in Christ.

RETURNING TO THE GOD OF OUR FATHERS

CHAPTER 7

Returning to the God of Truth, Not "Truthiness"

Speaking the Truth in a World of Lies

Anything can be true, even a lie, if enough people believe in it."[1]

The college student who said those words was simply echoing the modern notion that objective truth does not exist, but rather, truth is a path to power. In other words, truth is socially and personally constructed to get from Point A to Point B. Truth is based on individual perceptions—*my* wishes and *my* desires. Or perhaps *your* wishes and *your* desires.

The people at Merriam-Webster, a dictionary-publishing company, always choose a Word of the Year, generally, a relatively new word, but one that is most searched for on their websites. In 2006, the word was *truthiness*—that is, "a truthful or seemingly truthful quality that is claimed for something not because of supporting facts or evidence but because of a feeling that it is true or a desire for it to be true," or something that "refers to the quality of seeming to be true but not necessarily or actually true according to known facts."[2]

But we have moved beyond truthiness to a more dangerous form of disinformation. More recently, in 2022, Merriam-Webster's Word of the Year was *gaslighting*, which it defines as "psychological manipulation of a person usually over an extended period of time that causes the victim to question the validity of their own thoughts, perception of reality, or memories and typically leads to confusion, loss of confidence and self-esteem, uncertainty of one's emotional or mental stability, and a dependency on the perpetrator."[3]

"Truth," pastor H.B. Charles said in a sermon, "is not safe in a pagan world."

WELCOME TO DOUBLETHINK:
WHEN TWO PLUS TWO IS FIVE

Imagine, for a moment, that your name is Winston, and you are taken into a room named the Ministry of Truth. There, a man named O'Brien insists that two plus two is actually five; but sometimes it's three and sometimes it's both. If you are finding it difficult to believe that two plus two equals five, you are introduced to *doublethink*—that is, to be willing to believe two contradictory things simultaneously. Doublethink is taught by Big Brother, and Big Brother demands your absolute obedience. Whatever he tells you, you must believe. Absurdity is no grounds for dismissing what he has to say.

I've just described one of the scenes in George Orwell's novel *Nineteen Eighty-Four*, a dystopian depiction of the totalitarian state—a state in which everything is meticulously controlled for the purpose of maintaining power. The book describes the manipulation and control exercised by a totalitarian government and how people are conditioned to accept whatever they are told, even to live with obvious and provable lies.

Winston, who initially hates Big Brother, is taken to the Ministry of Love so he can be indoctrinated to not only *obey* Big Brother, but even learn to *love* him. The manipulation continues, and as the book ends, it is frightful to read that Winston "had won the victory over himself. He loved Big Brother."[4]

Lies, manipulation, and conditioning had destroyed Winston's common sense and values. Today, our media, in lockstep with our politicians and elites, subject us to the same mental and emotional distortions of reality. Don't ever think gaslighting does not work. How else can people believe men can have babies and women can be fathers? And how else can children be urged, for the good of their health, to question their gender and switch if they wish and even mutilate their bodies to do so?

With the collapse of belief in God and the radical Left's quest for power, we are invited to accept *doublethink*—that is, to be comfortable believing contradictions or lies. The argument is that there cannot be any objective truth in a random world created by impersonal forces, so truth is individualized. "Your truth" would differ from "my truth," but if I have enough power, I can use "my truth" to crush "your truth."

As Karl Marx taught, truth must be seen as a tool of interest groups who promote their agenda using political and cultural power. Truth is not discovered; it is fabricated. Even laws are not based on any objective criteria but are created by people in power, shaped for their benefit. Every country can have their own laws based on the elites who control the populace. As long as words are not connected to reality, haphazard and contradictory ideas can triumph. (We will return to the topic of law in a future chapter.)

Darwin, who said the baboon was our grandfather, wondered if you can actually trust the mind of a baboon; and if you can't trust the mind of our "grandfather," we might well question whether we can trust our own. Maybe two plus two does equal five!

With incredible insight, G.K. Chesterton, who understood

where culture was headed in his day, predicted, "We shall soon be in a world in which a man may be howled down for saying that two and two make four...in which people will persecute the heresy of calling a triangle a three-sided figure, and hang a man for maddening a mob with the news that the grass is green."[5]

That world has arrived.

Once you derive your view of truth from Karl Marx, who said that "rational thought is the product of people's interaction with their socioeconomic environment,"[6] there can be no objective truth claims. But I must point out that this is held to be "objectively" true.

Meanwhile our culture has rejected reason and accepted the ambiguities of truthiness and even gaslighting.

WHERE TRUTHINESS LEADS US

What might your children be taught in our universities and colleges?

There was a time in America when there was a belief that truth existed objectively; there was a consensus that God existed even if views about Him differed. There was disagreement as to how to find and prove the truth, and whether we had found it or not, but at least we knew that objective reality did exist. We knew truth existed outside of us; we knew something wasn't true just because we believed it. We told people they could have their own opinions, but they could not have their own truth.

With the eclipse of God, all that has changed.

Postmoderns have moved the source of truth from objectivity to whatever an individual determines it to be. Therefore, an opinion, no matter how irrational, is now called "*my* truth." Truth, we are told, is culture-bound, dependent on a person's experiences and personal history. Truth is what a person *feels* to be true.

Scripture expects us to begin with facts and
doctrines and then our emotions are to fall wherever
they may. To repeat a cliché, feelings are not facts.

To summarize the difference between so-called progressive post-moderns and traditional education, we can say this: The progressives begin with their feelings, and then adjust "facts" to conform with how they feel. In contrast, traditional education and certainly Scripture expects us to begin with facts and doctrines and then our emotions are to fall wherever they may. To repeat a cliché, feelings are not facts.

For example, the LGBTQ+ agenda has been driven largely by feelings of compassion, not the teaching of Scripture nor the supporting facts of physiology and the created order of the family and children. Although compassion is a worthy motive—indeed, we should be sensitive and compassionate—this should not be used as an excuse to upend obvious facts, realities and revealed doctrines.

I wish I could shout the words of Omar Bradley from the house-tops, "Set your course by the stars and not the lights of every passing ship!"[7]

But let's consider how the modern theory of "truthiness" largely based on the "your truth and my truth" philosophy is being applied. What happens when we set our course by every passing ship?

Truthiness in Historical Studies

So where does truthiness lead when applied to history? Students today are taught that all texts are propaganda; therefore, they must be deconstructed, meaning we can only speculate about the motive of the writer and how what was written contributed to their quest for power. Remember, "deconstruction is a tool used to identify arbitrary hierarchies, presuppositions, exclusions, and contradictions in a text."[8] So the reader has to identify a meaning that makes sense to him or her or they.

Because it is said that there is no stable meaning in a text, the reader is given the opportunity to invent personal interpretations that are meaningful to him or her or they. And every interpretation is equally valid. With this understanding, the intent of the author becomes irrelevant. "According to postmodern critics, deconstruction empowers readers and liberates them from the oppressive authority of the text and author."[9] Each reader is free to create their own meanings. Words are said to be a prison house that the reader must get beyond; knowledge is not found "out there," but constructed in the mind of the learner. *The reader, not the text, is in charge of its meaning.*

Obviously, radical Leftists believe that the Bible cannot be considered as an authoritative book; they say we must be liberated from its dogmatism, its commands and assertions that purport to describe reality. They strongly reject the biblical teaching that we should accept instruction and reproof (see Proverbs 15:32); such statements are obsolete. They reason, "There is no authority above myself; therefore, I am fully in charge of what I believe and what I reject. In fact, I am actually in charge of who I am; if I don't like who I am, I can rebrand myself according to my liking. What I believe about myself need not correspond to the reality that exists outside of me." In a world of irrationality, there is no final bar of appeal. And this is not where our culture is going; this is where our culture already *is.*

I read a story about a person who was asked, "If, when you die, you discover yourself standing before God to be judged, what would you say to Him?" The answer: "I will tell Him He has no right to judge me because I did not acknowledge Him; I was not under His authority."

Take note: Even in the final judgment, the individual is deemed to be in charge.

Carl Trueman summarizes much of modern education in a few sentences:

> ...institutions cease to be places for the formation of individuals via their schooling in the various practices and disciplines that allow them to take their place in society. Instead, they become platforms for performance, where individuals are allowed to be their authentic selves precisely because they are able to give their expression to who they are "inside."[10]

So, forget objectivity, and let me express who I am "inside." History is no longer a search for some verified "facts." Rather, it is an "an opportunity for formerly excluded and silenced groups in society such as gays and lesbians to finally be heard."[11] The writings of the Enlightenment are to be discarded because they represent a European cultural construct intended to keep power in the hands of the reigning elite. As already stated, Western culture cannot be seen as better than other cultures, for this would be contrary to the ideology of equality of outcomes—and keep in mind that this ideology is absolute. History is about social control and serves as a mirror in which each student gets a better understanding as to who they really are.

Some educational theories say no student should ever be told they are wrong. One educator's advice to teachers who are responding to students' comments (presumably, no matter how irrational) is that teachers must remember a student's self-esteem is uppermost.

The goal of learning is not so much about knowledge as it is a tool for enhancing one's own well-being. Opinions are being passed off as facts. The study of history has been turned into an exercise in therapy.

As Gary DeLashmutt and Roger Braund write, "When self-esteem becomes the be-all and end-all of education, teachers are no longer in a position to insist on performance."[12] If a student is told their answer is wrong, it might damage their self-esteem. Rather than telling a student they are wrong, teachers are instructed to have alternative responses.

Here are some substitutes that have been suggested:

> "'Um-humm,' 'That's a thought,' 'That's one possibil-ity,' 'That's one idea,' 'That's another way to look at it,' 'I hear you,' and eleven other ways not to tell a student the answer was...wrong."[13]

Is it any wonder that I heard one educator say that many (though not all) students today are incapable of listening to different points of view? Just witness the riots that break out on a university campus when a conservative speaker is advertised to speak. Because for some students truth is essentially irrational, the thought of a different point of view—especially if it claims objectivity—is too much for them to handle. And if by chance they hear something that offends them, they must retreat to a "safe place" where they can process their wounded feelings.

Pastors, parents, and educators: We all must help young people build resilience, teaching them that they must learn to listen to ideas that might offend them. If we listen only to what we agree with, we will never learn to interact, to discuss, and even debate the conflicting ideas that bombard us each day. There is a good form of tolerance, a tolerance that gives others their space even as we insist on ours.

Unfortunately, à la Karl Marx, the purpose of some courses is to needlessly divide people against each other. It is a search for oppressors; it is to seek blame for the sins of the past without the student having to confront their own sins. The sum is, "The whole world is sexually oppressive, racist, bigoted, and intolerant, but thankfully, I am just fine." To use the words of Jesus, they see the speck in other people's eyes, but do not see the log in their own eye (see Matthew 7:3-5). They do not realize that the seeds of sin—terrible sins—exist in us all. We are born with a highly developed capacity for self-justification; we all intuitively argue, "It is them but not us; it is society but not me."

The result? We are left with many in our culture who cope with what some have called self-directed aimlessness; we are left with spokes but no hub; petals with no flowers, and leaves without trees. We are left with plenty of takers, and few givers.

Big Brother indoctrinated them well.

Truthiness in Our Culture

In a 1946 essay titled "Politics and the English Language," George Orwell wrote, "If thought corrupts language, language can also corrupt thought," and "the present political chaos is connected with the decay of language."[14] And yes, the decay of our language and the redefinition of words does indeed lead to political chaos. It also leads to moral chaos (which we'll discuss in a future chapter).

If you want to see an example of the decay of language, consider the recently published speech code at Michigan State University. It discourages using words such as *tribe*, *minorities*, and *America*—yes, you read correctly, *America* shouldn't be used. We also read, "In winter and spring avoid references to majority religious imagery and

language such as the word 'merry' or 'Christmas trees,' 'wreaths'..."
The code continues with suggesting alternates like "wishing you a
wonderful winter/spring break..."[15] We could also point out that the
University of Southern California School of Social Work decided to
remove the word *field* from its communications due to is perceived
ties to slavery."[16] And so on.

What is next? No one knows, and that is the point.

Far from elevating the discussion, the purpose is to silence the
discussion. Elsewhere I have written extensively about how language is used to censor and confuse the public, and to promote propaganda that corrupts a civilization—proving that Orwell was right,
that thought corrupts language and language corrupts thought.[17]

In our angry, polarized culture, accusations are traded between
the so-called Left and the so-called Right. Let's consider the use
of the phrase *white Christian nationalism*. Someone has pointed
out how in this phrase, the word *white* divides the racial ethnicities, *Christian* vilifies Christianity, and *nationalism* often is a broad-
side against patriotism. The goal of phrases like this is to act as if
white conservative Christians (judging people by the color of their
skin, not the content of their character) should not be involved in
the political process and that Christianity is inherently oppressive.
Let me give an example from a political consultant who said that
"Christian nationalists are 'a bigger threat than al-Qaeda.'"[18] Such
statements are not only wrong but inflammatory, like throwing a
can of kerosene on our overheated political rhetoric. Let's not reply
in kind.

Yes, sadly, there are historical examples of the evils of white Christian nationalists who have dishonored the gospel by uniting it with
political agendas, but most Christian conservatives in America do
not fit that description. What many forget is that Christian influence in this country gave rise to the freedoms that radical Leftists

use to try to destroy Christianity. Let us gladly affirm the separation of church and state, but we cannot separate the state from morality. Lobbying for Christian morals and influencing laws is our privilege and responsibility.

> We must never forget that our ultimate aim
> is always advancing the gospel, not winning
> politically, however important that might be.

Meanwhile, I do want to warn Christians that there is a danger of giving first-rate attention to second-rate causes. We must never forget that our ultimate aim is always advancing the gospel, not winning politically, however important that might be. Fighting for a political cause is not the same as fighting for the gospel.

Though all of us have biases, the media is especially adept at cherry-picking stories and "facts" to support their biases, whether it comes from the so-called Right or the so-called Left. Want to do a story about why we should have open borders? Send someone to write a story about a mother with a baby in her arms, but ignore the drugs, the sex trafficking, and the millions being made by the drug cartels; ignore the hundreds of thousands of "got aways" that could include criminals and even terrorists. Want to promote a conservative politician? Carefully amplify the positives and ignore the negatives. Want to shame a church or Bible college? Find a disgruntled trans student who complains about not being treated fairly.

What about conspiracy theories? Yes, there are many of them floating around on social media. However, sometimes yesterday's conspiracy theory is today's settled "truth." We need to carefully evaluate the evidence; we do not need to have a settled opinion about everything. As Christians, we hold tenaciously to the promises of the Bible and to Christ our Lord and Savior. But when it comes to the daily news, we pray for wisdom and discernment, separating truths, half-truths, and lies. Somewhere I read that we must wisely exercise "strategic hesitancy." There are two sides to every story, but only one truth; let us work diligently to come as close as possible to the *one* truth.

The tenuous nature of truthiness is illustrated in a story I heard years ago about a man who was being tried for negligence for failing to warn a train of impending danger. When the trial was over, he said to a friend, "The judge asked me if I waved my lantern, and I truthfully answered yes. I'm just glad he didn't ask me if it was lit."

We should appreciate the word *tolerance*; to be tolerant of others who disagree with us is a positive response that enables us to live civilly despite our differences. But there is a form of "intolerant tolerance"—you can walk through a door with a sign that says *Tolerance*, but once inside, you discover it locks behind you, forcing you onto a narrow ideological path. Choosing to leave might cost you your career, your voice on social media, your reputation. Tolerance can be used as bait on the Leftists' hook.

GOD, LOGIC, AND ABSOLUTES

Can we show that everyone actually believes in what Francis Schaeffer used to call "true truth?"[19] "True truth" is objective truth, it's universal and not subject to revision. We are not talking about people's personal preferences or the changing of airline schedules; we are talking about truth that is stable—true today, true tomorrow, and true for all of eternity.

Many years ago, a college student told me she was sitting across the aisle from a student who wrote a one-page paper on why he did not believe truth existed. Truth, he said, lacked coherence; nothing was objectively true. I read the paper and wrote a short note saying, "If there is no truth, you have just written a full page of lies…and if you ever open your mouth to speak, we know in advance you are speaking lies." She gave him my note. Later she told me he never spoke to her again. I commend him for his consistency; there are many people who tell us truth is relative yet go on arguing why they are right, unaware they are assuming some objective standard. They don't notice the inconsistency.

Yes, even atheists must admit truth exists; after all, they think they have "the truth" about the nature of reality. What they do not realize is that they have to assume God exists in order to express their views. Atheists deny the existence of God and all absolutes, and they deny them absolutely. As Melanie Phillips cautions, "There can be no such thing as free-floating reason; for it to have any meaning, reason has to be grounded in a prior concept."[20]

Let me explain further: There is a universal law known as the law of noncontradiction, which means, quite simply, that two contradictory propositions cannot both be true in the same sense at the same time. You cannot both exist and also not exist in the same way and at the same time. If the world is round, it cannot also be flat; and try as you might, if you are honest, you cannot bring yourself to actually believe that two plus two equals five or that a triangle has four sides. In Orwell's novel, if Winston actually did believe that two plus two equaled five, he would be insane. He could only speak nonsense.

The reason we understand each other is because we have, in our minds, a universal law common to all of us. Everyone in every corner of the world—billions of people—who talk and think must agree that something cannot be both true and not true at the same time. If the law of noncontradiction did not exist, and in its place were random atoms without established order or uniformity, there would be only nonsense and disconnected experiences. Period.

Human beings might change, but the laws of logic do not. As Frank Turek writes, "The laws of logic provide an unchanging independent measuring stick of truth across changing time, culture, and human belief."[21] The bottom line: There is transcendent (universal) truth, but this could not exist apart from being created by a divine mind. The laws of logic cannot simply be a private human invention, different for each individual. To quote Turek again: "The laws of logic are immaterial realities that don't change. All physical things change, but the laws of logic do not. They are fixed, immaterial, eternal laws that would not exist if the purely material world of atheism were correct. While atheists use them, they cannot explain them."[22]

Laws of basic logic can only be explained by positing a Creator who created us with the ability to communicate. God made all of us with a uniform understanding of logical coherence. If thoughts were just arrangements of matter, what interest would matter have in forming intelligence? When atheists speak, they are unaware that they are pointing to God.

Christianity asserts that not even God is capable of self-contradictions. He cannot both deny and affirm the same thing in the same way at the same time. If He could, not a single one of His promises could be trusted, for their opposite might be equally true! When God speaks, He means what He says, not the opposite. Logic is rooted in God; it is an essential priority of His existence.

· · · · · · · · · · ·

Truth is always truth and error is always error.

· · · · · · · · · · ·

And, now we turn to a more detailed biblical view of truth—a view that dispels the darkness and has far-reaching applications for today. An observation often attributed to Geoge Orwell but actually written by Selwyn Duke states, "The further a society drifts from truth, the more it will hate those who speak it."[23] In our day truth is often cancelled, but culturally approved lies are mandated. Like ancient Israel, "we have made lies our refuge, and in falsehoods we have taken shelter" (Isaiah 28:15).

Truth, we will learn, does not bow to our feelings; truth is always truth and error is always error. Truth can offend, but it can also guide; it can hurt, but it can also heal.

Keep reading.

A BIBLICAL
UNDERSTANDING OF TRUTH

Truth dies in darkness; light reveals it.

The scene was dramatic.

Pilate was faced with a political decision with huge implications when the religious leaders brought Jesus to him. They were accusing Jesus of criminality and asking Pilate to sentence Him to death. But Pilate could not get a satisfying answer from them as to what Jesus had done worthy of crucifixion. So he asked Jesus whether He claimed to be King of the Jews. Jesus answered that His kingdom was not of this world; Pilate pressed Him for more details, and Jesus replied with an explanation as to why He came into the world: "You say that I am a king. For this purpose I was born and for this purpose I have come into the world—to bear witness to the truth. Everyone who is of the truth listens to my voice" (John 18:37).

Pilate replied, "What is truth?"

He did not wait for an answer, but turned away and went back to the mob and gave them what they demanded and sentenced Jesus to death. For one moment, Pilate stood eye to eye with the Truth. But under pressure, he chose to have the One who bore witness to the truth crucified. He disregarded the truth and opted to appease a mob who preferred a lie. He learned you can kill a man, but you can't kill truth.

But—let's not hurry over this. Jesus expressly said that His purpose for coming into the world was not to bring peace; it was not to make people feel better about themselves; His purpose was to "bear witness to the truth." And as best we can, we must also bear witness to the truth that Jesus brought. We bear witness in a world that does not want to hear the truth no matter how lovingly it is presented.

In a world without God, even insanity is preferred over truth.

All Truth Has Its Source in God

God's first creative act was to create light, which is used symbolically in Scripture for truth. This physical light would be symbolic of the spiritual and moral light we need to dispel our gloom and darkness; it would expose reality. God is "gracious, longsuffering, and abundant in goodness and truth" (Exodus 34:6 KJV). He is "a God of truth" (Deuteronomy 32:4 KJV). And while God revealed His truth throughout the Old Testament, it is especially seen in the person of Christ, who, with good reason, declared, "I am the light of the world" (John 8:12).

Truth is not truth unless it meets God's definition of truth. We speak truth only as we approximate the truth God has revealed. "All the paths of the LORD are mercy and truth" (Psalm 25:10 KJV). Only the gospel gives us the privilege of praying, "Into Your hand I commit my spirit; You have redeemed me, O LORD God of truth" (Psalm 31:5 NKJV).

Saint Augustine, who is known as the greatest thinker of the fourth and the beginning of the fifth centuries (354–430), argued convincingly that we can approximate God's standard of truth; and if we believe that two plus two equals four, we are doing so because God is the source of all truth. Johannes Kepler, who discovered the laws of planetary motion and is revered as the father of modern astronomy, is quoted as saying that he was "merely thinking God's thoughts after him."[24] When we read the Scriptures, we are also "thinking God's thoughts after him." The Bible is the only reliable guide to give us an entrance into understanding metaphysical truth—that is, truth beyond the senses. Truth that is invisible to the human eye but nevertheless real, objective truth. This is truth we could never discern if God had not revealed it.

All Lies Originate with Satan

Jesus, speaking to a group of religious leaders who preferred lies to truth, explained, "Why do you not understand what I say? It is because you cannot bear to hear my word. You are of your father the devil, and your will is to do your father's desires. He was a murderer from the beginning and does not stand in the truth... *When he lies, he speaks out of his own character, for he is a liar and the father of lies*" (John 8:44).

Should you ever believe the devil? Only when he tells you he is lying, or when Jesus forces him to speak the truth. And a drop of his deceitful rebellion has fallen into every human heart. Because liars don't self-report, it is difficult to get statistics on how many people tell lies each day. But deceit is everywhere.

We should ponder the words of John: "We know that we are from God, and the whole world lies in the power of the evil one" (1 John 5:19). Little wonder that the battle for truth rages on. And so often, truthiness wins.

All Truth Is Exclusive

The answer to any question is always exclusive, not inclusive. There is only one right answer to the sum of two plus two. The answer, four, excludes an almost infinite number of wrong answers. Truth does not allow for multiple answers. There is only one way to be right; there are many ways to be wrong. If someone tells you that truth is not coherent, simply ask them if they want you to respond to that statement coherently or incoherently.

Back in 1993, I attended the Parliament of World Religions here in Chicago, where 5,000 delegates met to seek to unite the religions of the world. On the first evening, a speaker announced over the sound system, "We are building a sacred place that will hold all our polarities and paradoxes." All the world's faiths were to be united under one spiritual roof, but the only common ground was that all the religions believed in some form of undefined mysticism. Objective truth was rejected.

Consider, for example, the idea of God. Hinduism has 300,000 gods; most devoted Hindus revere a few of their favorites. In contrast, Buddhists don't even believe in a god; when they go to a temple to pray, it is really to meditate. Christians believe there is only one God; these disparate points of view cannot be reconciled. So when the Parliament of World Religions drafted a Global Ethic, they did not use the word *God* because they knew that no matter what definition they had for God, it would exclude some religion or other.

There are Christians who think the religions of the world are fundamentally the same, but superficially different. Not so. The opposite is true: They are fundamentally different and only superficially the same. The teachings of the Bible—that salvation was a gift given to those who believe and repent—sets it apart from all of the other religions of the world. There can be no logical harmony between the essential message of Christianity and other religions.

When Jesus said, "I am the way, and the truth, and the life. No one comes to the Father except through me" (John 14:6), He was excluding other ways to come to the Father. He was making a universal statement. Truth always divides and excludes. And if Christ is the truth, anyone or anything that differs from Him is a lie.

Jesus came to bring us a costly redemption no other religion can offer. And yes, the path to the Father is narrow, but the good news is that all are welcomed. "Everyone who calls on the name of the Lord will be saved" (Romans 10:13).

The early Christians understood that there was an unbridgeable gap between Christianity and all other options. Any similarities between their religion and the religions of Rome were superficial and misleading. They were committed to truth, to its universality and consistency.

Once again, we learn that the laws of logic are transcultural. They must be accepted or we would go insane; communication would end. We would be living in an incomprehensible madhouse, and lunacy would prevail. To repeat, truth is very exclusive.

And, as the adage goes, "It is better to be separated by truth than to be united in error."

Truth Is Objective

Truth exists independently of us. It does not depend on whether or not you believe it. It is not found by looking within ourselves; rather, truth must be sought. The issue is not "Is this true for me?," but rather, "Does this correspond to reality?" And in the spiritual realm, as in science, we cannot create reality; we can only discover it. As Booker T. Washington is reported to have said, "A lie doesn't become truth, wrong doesn't become right, and evil doesn't become good just because it is accepted by the majority." In other words, you can have your own opinion, but you cannot have your own truth. You can ignore the truth, but that won't make it go away.

Truth Can Be Offensive

We live in what we can describe as "the offended generation." Whether it is an athlete who refuses to wear a pride-themed jersey or a church that opposes same-sex relationships, the accusation is the same: You have *offended* people! The big sin of our culture—assuming there is still sin among us—is to offend someone because of your convictions.

Jesus, however, offended people wherever He went.

"The disciples came and said to him, 'Do you not know that the Pharisees were *offended* when they heard this saying?' He answered, 'Every plant that my heavenly Father has not planted will be rooted up. Let them alone, they are blind guides'" (Matthew 15:12-14, emphasis added). In other words, He was saying that only those who are open to the truth will receive it. Our feelings are not facts.

In another context, after uttering some "hard sayings," Jesus' disciples were grumbling, so He asked them, "Do you take *offense* at this?" (John 6:61, emphasis added). Then Jesus continued with more hard sayings, such as "This is why I told you that no one can come to me unless it is granted him by the Father" (verse 65).

The response? "After this many of his disciples returned back and no longer walked with him. So Jesus said to the twelve, 'Do you want to go away as well?' Simon Peter answered him, 'Lord, to whom shall we go? You have the words of eternal life'" (verses 66-68).

· · · · · · · · · · ·

Jesus was loving, but He did not bend
the truth to make it less offensive.

· · · · · · · · · · ·

As for those disciples who departed from Jesus, their departure said more about themselves than it did about Jesus. Yes, Jesus was loving, but He did not bend the truth to make it less offensive. People who encountered Jesus were changed, either for better or worse, but Jesus remained the same. It goes without saying that we should not seek to be offensive; and if we do offend, let it be with the right attitude and for the right reasons.

A missionary told me that a Muslim came to faith in Christ after reading the above story about Jesus and His disciples. In Islam, if you walk away from the faith, you could be ostracized or even put to death. But in contrast, Jesus gave even his closest disciples the option of walking away from Him. That's the kind of leader that attracted this Muslim to come to faith in Jesus.

Truth can cause people to walk away, or it can lead them to repentance and faith. As the saying goes, "Truth hurts, but lies hurt even more." Jesus said that people "loved darkness rather than light, because their deeds were evil" (John 3:19). We might hate what God says about sexuality or the matter of salvation, but truth does not bend to our preferences, our likes and dislikes. Religion, if it is worth the name, claims to make factual statements about reality. Football coach Tony Dungy said, "To those who hate the truth it will sound like hate, but if you love the truth it will sound loving."[25]

Our day was predicted—the day when people "will turn away from listening to the truth and wander off into myths" (2 Timothy 4:4). Those days are here, and we as believers are called to expose the lies of our culture.

So, is it hateful to tell the truth? Yes, if telling the truth is done in anger or for self-glorification. But truth is not hateful if it is motivated by love, a love that wants to keep someone from disastrous consequences. Telling the truth—even painful truth—is a loving act.

Because the preaching of the cross is an offense to man's pride (Galatians 5:7-15; 1 Peter 2:7-8), churches that never offend anyone have compromised the gospel. Of course we should not be offensive, but we can expect the gospel to be hated, even as Jesus predicted (Matthew 10:22). Let us not be ashamed of "the offense of the cross."

Our motivation? The Lord's servant must not be quarrelsome but kind to everyone, able to teach, patiently enduring evil, correcting his opponents with gentleness. God may perhaps *grant them repentance leading to a knowledge of the truth, and they may come to their senses and escape from the snare of the devil, after being captured by him to do his will* (2 Timothy 2:24-26, emphasis added).

Truth Is Costly

"Buy the truth and sell it not" (Proverbs 23:23).

How much are you willing to pay for the truth? And, for what price will you sell it? Do you value the truth so highly that you are willing to pay any price to get it? And if you have it, is it for sale?

Truth can cost us our livelihood; it can cost us our lives.

Standing for truth might mean we sacrifice ourselves and our reputations. If we have truth that people would benefit from hearing, we should not be silent. Athanasius was a great defender of the faith of Christianity in a world of controversy. He said, "If the world is against the truth, then I am against the world."

Personal truth is also costly. Do you say one thing but do another? Are you a truthful person, or are you living a lie? Some people put their wedding vows up for sale because they think they have found someone who will better meet their needs. Others put their career up for sale; they sacrifice their integrity to get a promotion in the world. Others put their soul up for sale in exchange for money. In these and in other ways, people, in effect, put up a sign that says, "Truth for sale."

Years ago, my wife and I visited the city of Ephesus in Turkey, and we saw a store with a sign that read, "Genuine Fake Watches."

The watches kept time perfectly; to the untrained eye they looked genuine. The coins in the store could be passed off as valuable currency, but again, they were fakes. But they were said to be *genuine* fakes.

Are you a fake Christian? Like a counterfeit coin that makes the rounds and even buys some groceries, when the divine coin collector examines your life, will He reveal that you are a fake? A *genuine* fake, but a fake nonetheless? God knows who you are better than you know yourself.

You want God to answer your prayers? "The LORD is near to all who call on him, to all *who call on him in truth*" (Psalm 145:18). We can't expect God to hear us if we come to him with a pack of lies safely hidden in our souls.

God expects us to *speak* the truth and to *do* the truth. And who can come before the Lord and be received? The answer: "He who… speaks truth in his heart" (Psalm 15:2).

Pay whatever you must to buy the truth, and when you have it, don't sell it!

There is a story that when Lloyd C. Douglas, the author of *The Robe* and other novels, was a university student, he lived in a boarding house. On the first floor was an elderly, retired, infirm music teacher. Douglas said that every morning they had a ritual they would go through together. He would come down the stairs, open the old man's door, and ask, "Well, what is the good news?" The old man would pick up his tuning fork, tap it on the side of his wheelchair, and say, "That is middle C. It was middle C yesterday; it will be middle C tomorrow; it will be middle C a thousand years from now. The tenor upstairs sings flat. The piano across the hall is out of tune, but, my friend, that is middle C!"[26]

The noise of the world interrupts us through our smartphones, tablets, and television screens; everyone is shouting, trying to get us to dance to their music. But in the midst of trying to figure out what to believe or not believe, we can be thankful we have a tuning fork. We have a "middle C."

Jesus Christ, our Middle C!

OUR DECLARATION OF DEPENDENCE

We should weep for this directionless generation, "always learning and never able to arrive at a knowledge of the truth" (2 Timothy 3:7). And we can do more: We can give this world a message of hope, light, and yes, *truth*.

But as we end this chapter on truth and truthiness, let us take time to reflect on how we use words to speak about one another as Christians. Truth is powerful, but it is most powerful when it is combined with love. Paul admonished us, "Speaking the truth in love, we are to grow up in every way into him who is the head, into Christ" (Ephesians 4:15). This is a rebuke to those among us who claim to speak the truth but do so out of anger, revenge, jealousy, and a spirit of self-righteousness. Unwise speech has brought hurtful divisions among members of the body of Christ. While criticism of each other has always been a part of church life, social media has exacerbated the problem tenfold. Many Christians who are on X (formally Twitter) are busy sniping with each other, often lacking charity, fairness, and mutual respect. And, sadly, failures that at one time were handled within the church are now amplified and used as fodder for sensational headlines. Yes, transparency is important, but today, transparency is sometimes interpreted to mean that every accusation (whether fully understood or not) can be broadcast around the world.

Why am I concerned? I have spoken to pastors and Christian leaders whose reputations have been tarnished or even ruined because of one-sided reports of events in which a part of the story is presented as the whole story. And once a leader is targeted, he or she cannot defend themselves; if they did, they would be vilified in a public "he said, she said" tug of verbal war. Social media has made redemption of an individual practically impossible because the story is permanently accessible. And many are eager to believe the worst about someone else.

We don't need the culture to destroy us; we are destroying ourselves.

Yes, there is a place for exposing wrongdoing, especially in instances where the church or organization has not been open to correction and its failure impacts believers beyond their own circle. So, if there is a need to expose a leader or ministry, let us do it with a heavy heart, with respect, and with fervent prayer that the situation be remedied. Let us treat others the way we would want to be treated, and as much as possible, let's keep our differences in the realm of ideas rather than personal attacks.

My plea: Let's disagree respectfully, fairly, and above all, with a spirit of helpfulness. "You who are spiritual should restore him in a spirit of gentleness. Keep watch on yourself, lest you too be tempted. Bear one another's burdens, and so fulfill the law of Christ" (Galatians 6:1-2). I always remind myself that God loves the believers I disagree with as much as He loves me!

ACTION STEP

Let us ask God for wisdom as to when we should speak the truth and when we should remain silent. And before we criticize another believer, we should ask: Will this help the body of Christ, or do damage to the body? Are we doing this because we want to compare them unfavorably to ourselves? James gives us this assurance: "If anyone does not stumble in what he says, he is a perfect man, able also to bridle his whole body" (James 3:2). Let us confess our stumbling and ask God to guard our mouths so that all we say would be for His glory. Truth is powerful; let's handle it well.

CHAPTER 8

Returning to the God of Creation, Not Blind Chance

The Devolution of Man and the Way Back

n creation, God went public: "The heavens declare the glory of God" (Psalm 19:1).

But some people want to steal this glory from God and take it for themselves. Read these astounding words from Jeremy Rifkin:

> We no longer feel ourselves to be guests in someone else's home and therefore are obligated to make our behavior conform with a set of preexisting cosmic rules. It is our creation now. We make the rules. We establish the parameters of reality. We create the world, and because we do, we no longer have to justify our behavior, for we are now the architects of the universe. We are responsible for nothing outside ourselves, for we are the kingdom, the power, and the glory for ever and ever.[1]

The final triumph of man over God!

"We are the kingdom, the power, and the glory for ever and ever."

Atheist Richard Dawkins writes, "Even if there were no actual evidence in favour of the Darwinian theory…we should still be justified in preferring it over all rival theories."[2]

Another evolution biologist, Richard Lewontin, writes,

> Our willingness to accept scientific claims that are against common sense is the key to an understanding of the real struggle between science and the supernatural. We take the side of science in spite of the patently absurdity of some of its constructs…because we have a prior commitment, a commitment to materialism…no matter how counter-intuitive, no matter how mystifying to the uninitiated. Moreover that materialism is absolute, for we cannot allow a Divine Foot in the door.[3]

No divine foot allowed in the door!

SO WHO CREATED GOD?

"The cosmos is all that is or ever was or ever will be."[4]

So began the television series *Cosmos*, written by the famous scientist Carl Sagan. In his view, the universe was created by the big bang; he believed we could trace the universe back to the nanosecond of an explosion and we won what one scientist called "the cosmic jackpot." And with unprecedented luck, the universe, and life as we know it, came to be. As one scientist put it: The universe was not created out of nothing, but "next to nothing."

But from where did the "next to nothing" come from?

When I was in Bible college, I was taught that God created the world. But I would look at the stars and wonder, *Who created God?* I was told that God was not created; He existed from all eternity. I've often pondered that throughout the years, but I find myself on the edge of a great mystery.

So let's discuss this: Who created God?

Some people use this question as an argument for atheism. Here's the argument: Creationists say the cosmos is so complex it must have been created by God. But if that's true, it must mean that God, the Creator, is even more complex than the cosmos. So if the cosmos needed a Creator, surely this higher-class being called *God* needed a creator! To put it differently, if it is improbable that the cosmos exists without a beginning, it is even more improbable that God exists without a beginning. So why believe in this highly improbable God?

Let's break down this argument and see if we can get some clarity on the subject.

Nothing from Nothing

Skeptics and Christians alike agree with this basic proposition: Out of nothing, nothing comes. Quite obviously, if nothing had ever existed, there would be nothing now and nothing forever. Atheists and theists (those who believe in God) therefore agree that because something exists, something had to exist from all of eternity. Atheists say the cosmos existed from all of eternity; theists say God existed from all of eternity.

Follow me carefully here—you have probably heard this argument:

- Every event has a cause.
- The universe is an event.
- Therefore, the universe has a cause. (And, of course, Christians are told this cause was God.)

But atheists, looking at this argument, respond by saying that if we believe every event has a cause, it follows therefore that God must have a cause.

Distinguishing the Physical from the Spiritual

So how do theists respond? We clarify the first premise by saying the idea that every event has a cause is true only in the observable empirical world. There is no reason to believe it applies to the invisible spiritual world.

In other words, in the empirical observable world, every event has a cause, but we should be hesitant to impose such laws on the unseen spiritual world. Physical laws are for the physical world and do not apply beyond it. So God does not need a cause.

Edgar Andrews, of the University of London, England, an international expert on the science of large molecules, writes this in defense of God's existence:

> Because cause and effect is only proven for the physical
> world, we can no longer insist that cause and effect are
> relevant when it comes to the origin of a spiritual entity
> like God. Therefore God doesn't have to have a cause—
> he can be the ultimate uncaused cause, a being whom
> no one has made.[5]

So we are faced with a choice. Because we've already established that something has existed from all eternity, is it more reasonable to believe the cosmos has existed from all of eternity, or that God has existed from all of eternity? Theists insist that the answer is *God* simply because there is no evidence that the cosmos has within itself the energy and wisdom to be the cause of its own existence. Nature, the cosmos, left to itself, always drifts toward randomness and deterioration, not complexity. Everything we know about the cosmos demonstrates that it had a beginning and could not have been self-created.

. . . .

When faced with the choice of the cosmos existing from all of eternity, or the Divine Spirit (God) existing from all eternity, the Christian answer is *God*.

. . . .

Who created God? That's like asking, Who created the uncreated one? Back in Bible college, I memorized this definition: "God is the infinite and perfect spirit in whom all things have their source, support, and end." Theists affirm that God is the uncaused cause of all things.

Certainly God is mysterious, but it's not a contradiction to say God existed from all eternity. When faced with the choice of the cosmos existing from all of eternity, or the Divine Spirit (God) existing from all eternity, the Christian answer is *God*.

Evolutionists have the unenviable task of trying to account for life as we know it. But first they must ask, Where did the first bit of material come from? Or equally important, Where did the massive force come from to create the big bang? And, interestingly, there is a correspondence between our brains and the structure of the universe: Without an intelligent creator we would not have a *cosmos*; we would have *chaos*.

So which is it more rational to believe: The universe created itself, or God existed from all eternity and created all that is? I submit that believing in a personal, eternal, and omnipotent God is more satisfying to the mind. And satisfying to the human heart. As one person put it, "Where is atheism when it hurts?"

The twelfth-century book *The Book of the Twenty-Four Philosophers* makes this interesting statement: "God is an intelligible sphere whose center is everywhere and circumference nowhere." In the Psalms, we read these comforting words: "Lord, you have been our dwelling place in all generations. Before the mountains were brought forth, or ever you had formed the earth and the world, from everlasting to everlasting you are God" (90:1-2). God is in an eternal dimension, and yet He dwells with us.

THE GREAT EVANGELICAL COMPROMISE

For many years, evangelicals have had disputes when trying to harmonize the Bible with science. Some argue that the days in Genesis 1 should be interpreted as a 24-hour period. This certainly seems to be the straightforward reading of the text. However, others argue, with great erudition, that given paleontological and archaeological research, Earth is billions of years old, and thus the word *day* encompasses a longer period of time, perhaps even millions of years.

But once we let paleontology and archaeology dictate how we interpret Scripture, that might lead to an even more serious departure from the biblical doctrine of creation—namely, that there was no literal Adam and Eve. Having lived as long as I have, I should not be surprised at this doctrinal concession to the culture, but I confess I was initially unprepared for this great surrender of Christianity to the *zeitgeist*.

Be warned: As the evangelical church capitulates to the culture, we will find many instances when the Bible is interpreted through the lens of culture rather than critiquing the culture through the lens of Scripture. When there is conflict, expect much of the evangelical community to abandon the Scriptures. Even now, the biblical story about Adam and Eve is being canceled in light of supposed contemporary scholarship.

Briefly, here are some troubling quotations from scholars who insist they are in the evangelical camp. Dennis Venema, a biologist at Trinity Western University in Vancouver, Canada, when asked how likely it was that all humans descended from Adam and Eve, said, "That would be against all the genomic evidence that we've assembled over the last 20 years, so not likely at all."[6] John Schneider, who taught at Calvin College, wrote that it is time we face the facts: "There was no historical Adam and Eve, no serpent, no apple, no fall that toppled man from a state of innocence…there never was any such paradise to be lost."[7]

I was most surprised by the book *In Quest of the Historical Adam* by William Lane Craig, otherwise an influential apologist for the Christian faith. He says that he does believe in the existence of a historical Adam, but he distinguishes this Adam from the biblical "literary Adam" as described in Scripture. Craig must then reinterpret all the New Testament passages that refer to Adam as if they are purely a reference to the "literary Adam"—that is, not the actual historical Adam who Craig believes existed much earlier.

Craig had this to say about Jesus' reference to the creation account of Adam and Eve and their original mandate: "Jesus is interpreting the story of Adam and Eve to discern its implications for marriage and divorce, not asserting its historicity. Similarly, many of Paul's references to Adam may be understood not to go beyond the literary Adam."[8]

In a lengthy article in *First Things*, Craig concludes, "But for now, that name [Adam] serves as a placeholder for the large-brained human species that was ancestral to *Homo sapiens* and the various sister species of the human family. We can live with uncertainty. For though we now see through a glass darkly, we shall one day see face to face."[9]

So what do we make of this? Numerous books, of course, have been written to defend the literal biblical account. For my purposes,

I simply list what we would lose if Adam and Eve as described in the creation account were not historical figures: (1) There would be no fall of man into sin; (2) we would have to admit that Paul misled the Athenians when he said God "made from *one man* every nation" a reference to the biblical Adam (Acts 17:26); (3) we would lose the parallelism Paul makes between Adam and Christ: "Therefore, just as sin came into the world through one man" (Romans 5:12) and then follows a contrast between the one man Adam and the one man Christ (verses 12-21). And finally, (4) we would have to deal with the fact that Adam is presented in Scripture as being an actual person. For example, his genealogy is given, and he was 130 years old when he fathered Seth (see Genesis 5:3).

Evangelicals who deny the historicity of the Adam and Eve account as described in Scripture generally concede that at some point along the evolutionary journey, God did choose two developing *Homo sapiens* and did invest in them the divine image. But we are told there was no paradise to be lost. What this means is that human nature should not be seen as fallen, but rather, the evils people commit were our original state. We are left with Darwin's explanation for the existence of evil as the remnants of our animal nature coming though the line of baboons.[10]

So without the fall of man into sin, without the biblical Adam standing in contrast with Christ, and with the misleading references in the New Testament to "one man" (Adam) in contrast to Christ— what is left?

Shattered before us are the foundational pieces that make up what we call the gospel. No tree of good and evil, no warning to Adam and Eve, no shame that came as a result of their rebellion, and perhaps no literal promise of enmity between the seed of the serpent and the seed of the woman.

I agree with Richard Gaffin: "The truth of the Gospel stands or falls with the historicity of Adam as the first human being from whom all other human beings descend. What Scripture affirms about creation, especially the origin of humanity, is central to its teaching about salvation."[11]

Interestingly, it has been pointed out that those who deny the existence of a literal, biblical account of Adam and Eve take the word of current scientific assumptions literally, and therefore feel forced to interpret the Bible according to these "findings." Clearly, they have more faith in secular science than they do in God's Word. Meanwhile, there are archaeologists and paleontologists who refute the current scientific assumptions and believe the literal account of Adam and Eve need not be abandoned to be consistent with the evidence.[12]

I encourage you to check out your Christian school and find out what it teaches about the biblical account of creation. The denial of the literal Adam and Eve as presented in Genesis is cropping up everywhere. When the questionable assumptions of science and archaeology clash with the Bible, tragically, science and present archaeological assumptions often win.

What biblical domino will be the next to fall?

WHEN PEOPLE RE-CREATE THEMSELVES

The apostle Paul gives a summary of man's spiritual journey that has led us to where we are today. In contrast to Darwin's book *The Ascent of Man*, in Romans 1, we read about the *descent of man* into anarchy and disgrace. A key phrase explains, "They exchanged the truth about God for a lie and worshiped and served the creature rather than the Creator, who is blessed forever! Amen" (verse 25).

* * * * * * * * * * * *

The eclipse of God gives the human race
permission to define itself, choose its
lifestyles, and behave without restraint.

* * * * * * * * * * * *

When humanity exchanges places with the Creator—worshipping itself rather than God—depravity is the inevitable result. The eclipse of God gives the human race permission to define itself, choose its lifestyles, and behave without restraint. This means mankind can now live with abandon, without having to fear submission to or judgment by an omniscient God.

Mankind, Animal Rights, and the Environment

In a fascinating twist, when man exalts himself above God, he must immediately devalue himself. Because man differs from animals only in degree but not in kind, it follows that we as human beings are brought low to identify with our "ancestors." If we are merely animals, we have no special significance in the world.

If we differ from animals just in matters of degree and we are not unique in kind, then animal rights advocates can insist that we give animals the dignity they deserve as our ancestors and relatives. They can tell us we should be giving long-overdue attention to our great-grandfathers, grandmothers, and their cousins. But when moderns insist that animals be raised up toward mankind, mankind is brought low toward the animal kingdom.

We should not be surprised that a February 2023 article appeared in *The New York Times* titled "The War on Rats: Is it Ethical?" It speaks about reasons to control the rat population but wrestles with this: "But rats are also cognitively advanced social animals and questions about how to effectively control them can raise tricky ethical questions."[13]

Now, of course, all of us agree that animals should not be tortured, and their extermination should be done as humanely as possible. But my point is that if we are distantly related to the rat population, as evolution would teach, then the question we must answer is this: Do we even have a right to exterminate them? *The New York Times* article admits that there are good reasons to exterminate rats, but wrestles with their relative value over against humans. One person summed up the dilemma by saying, "For me, rats are not the enemy, people are the enemy."

At last, it is clearly stated: Man is the problem; nature might be better served without us. We as humans should not have unilateral authority over rats; we should acknowledge their dignity. Humans are biologically chained to their own past, interrelated with the animal kingdom.

In an evolutionary world, killing a preborn infant should not be considered unethical or immoral because often, deformed animals are "put to sleep." So even after the human infant is born, should he or she have a disability, the parents and their caregivers should not have any qualms about putting the infant to death. Or as Ralph Northam, a former governor of Virginia, put it, "If a mother is in labor…the infant would be delivered. The infant would be kept comfortable. The infant would be resuscitated if that's what the mother and the family desired, and then a discussion would ensue between the physicians & mother."[14]

To see an animal suffer is painful because our attachment to our pets can truly be meaningful and loving. But reality sets in when, because of old age or a terminal disease, we want to deliver our pet out of its misery. In the same way, why should we not support euthanasia rather than filling our retirement centers with people who will never regain the strength or cognitive abilities of their youth?

Following this logic even further, we should be able to choose the time of our own death. After all, only we know how much we are suffering and whether our life is still worth living. And if, in our estimation, our usefulness is past, why should our relatives not make such a decision for us? In Canada, 10,000 people are euthanized each year.[15] And "the right to die" soon becomes "the duty to die."

I heard one politician say, "Abortion is a God-given right." Anyone who agrees with that could just as easily say, "Choosing our time to die is a God-given right." How could it be otherwise if God is whatever we want Him to be, and the baboon was our grandfather, and rats our distant cousins?

The result? We are left living by the law of the jungle—living with cruelty, self-indulgence, and the destruction of others. In a world in which God is eclipsed, darkness is normalized. Nietzsche's nihilism quickly arrives.

Choosing Our Gender

Recently, the American Medical Association concluded that there are more than two genders.[16] Since secularists teach there is no created order, sexuality can be separated from gender, and promoted and experienced in any number of ways. We are told there are a variety of genders, and one can choose where he, she, or they wish to stop on the gender spectrum.

When Jill Biden awarded a transgender woman with the International Woman of Courage award—Alba Rueda of Argentina—the First Lady was essentially signaling that the women's movement no longer existed.[17] Today, men with cosmetic and irreversible anatomical surgery are now "women," thus erasing the entire category that was once labeled *women*.

No wonder spokespersons for the women's movement have become largely silent. Now that men have invaded their space, only a few women have the courage to still fight for women's rights.

Biological women are leaving sports such as swimming and cycling because they know they cannot compete against males who masquerade as women. In other words, women are vacating the very space they fought for that gave them a sense of belonging and identity.

Just to make sure that no one was excluded, Alba, the trans woman who received the International Women of Courage award, had campaigned to change the name of the National Women's Conference to the "Plurinational Conference of Women and Lesbian, Cross-Dresser, Transgender, Bisexual, Intersex and Non-Binary Persons." This was done in order "to include diverse, dissident and racialized identities."[18]

Consider Hollins College, founded in 1842, a historically women's college. Today, in order to keep up with the "changing world and evolving understanding of gender identity," the college's "guiding principle on admissions is that it will consider applications from those who 'consistently live and identify as women.'"[19] In other words, they must accept trans women (men who identify as women); but they cannot accept trans men, that is (women who identify as men) at this women's college.

Gender ID laws that have been passed in several countries say a person can self-identify as whatever sex they want to be without any medical requirements or certification by the medical community.[20] The transgender rights movement promotes such laws to make it easier for trans people to identify as their preferred gender without having to bear the onerous burden of surgery or the humiliation of seeing a medical professional. And recently I read the headline, "Post-World Truth: Man Wins Miss Netherlands"—and this trans woman competed in the Miss Universe contest in El Salvador in 2023.[21] Why not?

Cleary, some people are not plagued with the task of facing reality.

This is the final example of the deification of men, women, boys, and girls by an act of the will; by a fluctuating feeling, it is possible for anyone to defy biology and recreate oneself and become any gender of choice. This is a radical rejection of reality. Thus humans have moved from creature to creator, from clay to potter. Finally, humans have ascended the throne and displaced God.

And the confusion continues.

The Sin of Deadnaming

Not until recently was I acquainted with the word *deadnaming*. To deadname someone is to call them by a name they asked you not to use. To wit,

> A transgender person may decide to no longer use their birth or legal name. Instead, they'll choose a name that better aligns with their identity. When someone uses their old name after being asked not to, that is what we call "deadnaming." The person who they once were is dead, but the new person is alive, so their current name should be used.[22]

Please note the language here: "The person who they once were is dead, but the new person is alive, so their current name should be used." So, who do we blame for a crime? The person who is now dead, and not the person who is alive?

The moral insanity this creates was highlighted when, in California, a *Los Angeles Times* headline read, "Prosecutor Suspended for Misgendering Hannah Tubbs." Tubbs is a transgender woman who was convicted of a crime when he was a previous gender—namely, a male. Now that he is a female, is he really the same person? The prosecutor was accused of deadnaming Tubbs, referring to him by his legal name and the pronoun *he*, found in legal documents. But the point is, even though Tubbs now identifies as a woman, there is no doubt that the crime he committed was done by a male body.[23]

Of course the court case can still move forward even as prosecutors wrestle with the perplexing question, Did "he" do it, or did "she" do it? After all, "the old has passed away; behold, the new has come."

The IRS is facing this question: How do they deal with someone who paid into their social security with one name and gender, but now assumes a new name and gender? Do they pay the "dead" person, or the "new" person? Are they really the same person?

I find it interesting that Caitlyn Jenner (aka Bruce Jenner) says that he appreciates it when his biological children send him flowers on Father's Day! He says, "I'm always going to be your father. That's never going to change."[24] An interesting admission. To call him Bruce would be to deadname him, but apparently now "she" was the "he" who fathered "her" children. So a "she" impregnated his wife, who had the children.

Really?

The Challenge of Pronouns

Perhaps you are a parent or a grandparent of a child who claims that he or she is transgender, and you have been asked to respect his/her pronouns. My advice is to proceed with love, caution, and truth; don't give a hurried response, but a thoughtful one. Children deserve to be heard. There are a small number of people who actually struggle with gender dysphoria, but today, it is spreading like a contagion given our culture, the media, and the educational system. I heard someone say, with a touch of sarcasm, "If you give your teenager a cell phone, don't be too surprised if they believe they are trans."

We must remember: Many who claim they are trans may actually be grasping for hope and seeking internal peace. That's why we must always treat them with respect, love, and a sense of acceptance; to condemn them often cuts off communication and widens the gap between them and us. We are called to speak the truth, but with thoughtfulness, humility, and compassion.

If your daughter was born Betty but now wants to be called Bert, in my judgment, you can honor her request because names are not necessarily gendered. In fact, many couples today give what used to be thought of as a boy's name to their daughter, or vice versa.

But honoring pronouns is a different story.

Think through the implications. If a girl says her new pronouns are *he* and *him* and you affirm her, what argument would you have if she now wants her breasts removed? You have already agreed to pretend that she is not a girl, but a boy. And boys don't have the breasts of a girl.

We must help people understand that our self-perception is not always a reliable guide as to who we are. There are men in psych wards who actually believe they are Napoleon. Young women who suffer from anorexia see themselves as overweight when, in point of fact, they are starving to death. We must lovingly help those who are confused about their identity know that biology matters, and who they are was determined by their creator, not their feelings. We must help those who expect us to switch their pronouns to realize that they do not have a body problem, but a mind problem.

Our discussions with those who struggle with their identity should always be characterized by sensitivity and politeness. But we can answer, "You are asking me to deny my authenticity and be a hypocrite. I cannot call you what I am convinced you are not."

We must especially sound a warning to teenagers who want to change their biological gender to overcome their depression, self-hatred, and sexual confusion. If they follow through with hormone blockers and eventual surgery, they are doing irreversible damage to themselves. You cannot be a more productive person as a man who pretends to be a woman or vice versa. The outer cosmetic changes do not change your biological gender. We must tell people that they may believe they can choose their gender, but what they cannot do is avoid the consequences of their decision.

To mutilate the body is a forgivable sin, but the consequences are irreversible. And with these changes, a person will never be able to become a biological parent. Also, would a woman be attracted to a trans man? Would a man be attracted to a trans woman? The future implications of body-altering surgery are huge. These topics have been adequately covered by others. But the issues are not going away.

Transgenderism is as old as the gods of the pagan world. Siproites[25] was the name of a male hunter who was transformed into a woman when he observed a woman bathing. Hermaphroditus[26] was the two-sex child of Aphrodite and Hermes, and was a symbol of androgyny (the union of characteristics of both genders in one person). We've all heard of Ishtar, who had various names, but "she was known as the Queen of Heaven," and "was also believed to have the ability to change a person's gender. This power of Inanna's [another name for Ishtar], the ability to change a man into a woman and vice versa… The gender-blurring members of her cult have often been included in poems and dedications written for her."[27]

Because the Bible is clear that those who worship pagan deities worship demons (Deuteronomy 32:16-17; Psalm 106:34-38; 1 Corinthians 10:20), we can be sure that Satan is at work in a culture given to the gender dysphoria cult of today. Online, I discovered various clothes for sale with the slogan "Satan Respects Pronouns." This is true, of course.

I am not suggesting that all who believe they are nonbinary or gender fluid are knowingly worshipping demons. But given how transgenderism is destroying the lives of people—especially young ones—the slogan "Satan Respects Pronouns" is certainly true.

Let us remember that those who struggle with these issues cannot simply walk away free; *they must be set free* (John 8:32-33).

BLAME THE CHRISTIANS

I have a friend who is an attorney and has been litigating on behalf of Christian organizations for nearly 50 years, and he fears that the same hatred we have witnessed against the Jews since the October 7, 2023 attack in Israel may soon be directed toward Christians. That sounds extreme, but what is extreme in one era often is normalized in the next.

When Audrey Hale, a woman who became a trans male, smashed "his" way into a Christian school in Nashville and killed three adults and three children (each child approximately nine years old), immediately the trans community went into defense mode, not blaming Hale, but blaming Christians who would not get on board with the trans community.

In their eyes, the violent rampage was not "his" fault; it was the fault of those who failed to affirm trans people. Blame fell on the allegedly stubborn Christians who refuse to bow before all spectrums of the rainbow. At all costs, exonerate the perpetrator who is a victim of an unsupportive public.[28]

To the church, I offer this warning: When a trans woman (a man dressed as a woman) enters a public woman's bathroom or dressing room, those who object will be vilified. Biological women will not be asked what they think or feel about sharing bathrooms and locker rooms with biological men. The rights of trans people will almost certainly reign supreme. Those who honor God will be targeted as needing therapy and sensitivity training. The man who identifies as a woman, with his fetishes and pathologies, will be affirmed as having more rights than the women he is offending.

Let us never forget we represent Christ to a confused world. We must return to the teaching of Paul: "When reviled, we bless; when persecuted, we endure; when slandered, we entreat. We have become, and are still, like the scum of the world, the refuse of all things" (1 Corinthians 4:12-13).

> We must stand up for truth even as we are compassionate toward those who have been caught up by lies.

Our model is Christ: "When he was reviled, he did not revile in return; when he suffered, he did not threaten, but continued entrusting himself to him who judges justly" (1 Peter 2:23). Let us not react with anger but with compassion, brokenness, and humility. It is tragic when people are swept up with obvious delusions, but for them, it can appear as truth.

And as we learned in the previous chapter, we must stand up for truth even as we are compassionate toward those who have been caught up by lies.

THE ROAD BACK TO MORAL SANITY

The creation story of Genesis gives us the only basis for human dignity that is available. We must respect every person; to disrespect others is unchristian. Though we may disagree with another's opinion, we must deal with them with kindness; love and truth are not enemies.

We have a better story to tell:

> God said, "Let us make man in our image, after our like-
> ness. And let them have dominion over the fish of the
> sea and over the birds of the heavens and over the live-
> stock and over all the earth and over every creeping thing
> that creeps on the earth." So God created man in his own
> image, in the image of God he created him; male and
> female he created them (Genesis 1:26-27).

Let us be grateful that the baboon is not our grandfather.

We are not on a continuum with animals; each individual person is created in God's image, is capable of connecting with God, is
held responsible for their choices, and is a person of value as the pin-
nacle of God's creative activity. And as the story progresses, Adam
and Eve were created uniquely for each other, and to serve God in
unity and worship.

Let me summarize what God teaches us in the creation story.

First, both men and women are created equally in the image of
God. Men and women are different in some respects, but they are
similar in others. Genesis 1:26-27 focuses on what they have in common. The terms *male* and *female* are not cultural constructs. "They
are not social roles foisted upon mankind by the accretion of culture and tradition."[29] Gender is what is given to us at conception;
it is not for us to choose. God gave us this dignity to serve and glorify Him. "God crowns no other creature with image-bearing status.
Human beings alone wield this honor, and man and woman share
equally in the image of God."[30]

The equality of men and women as unique creations of God
gave impetus to Christians to abolish slavery and lift the dignity of
women. Yes, of course progress has often been slow with painful

disagreements as to what roles various groups and genders should play, but the ideal of equality of value has guided Christian history. Just compare Christian influence historically over against pagan societies, and the difference is remarkable.[31]

And children who die in infancy, created as they are in the image of God, are precious to God, for "their angels always see the face of my Father who is in heaven" (Matthew 18:10). And Jesus, holding a child in His arms, reminded us that "to such belongs the kingdom of heaven" (Matthew 19:14). By virtue of creation, each child is precious. Each human life should be treated with dignity, recognized as uniquely valuable.

Contrary to those who believe that there was no fall into sin, no paradise that was lost, a Dutch theologian, Herman Bavinck (1854–1921), perceptively wrote, "Sin ruined the entire creation, converting its righteousness into guilt, its holiness into impurity, its glory into shame, its blessedness into misery, its harmony into disorder, and its light into darkness."[32]

We all are more sinful, more evil than we are willing to admit.

. . . .

Left to ourselves, not one person is better
than another; the difference between any of
us is entirely dependent on God's grace.

. . . .

The Puritan writer Thomas Brooks rightly said, "There is the seed of all sins; of the vilest and worst of sins, in the best of men… there is not a worse nature in hell, than that that is in [you]; and it would discover itself accordingly, if the Lord did not restrain it."[33] The seeds of every conceivable evil lies coiled like a serpent in every human heart. Left to ourselves, not one person is better than another; the difference between any of us is entirely dependent on God's grace.

But in every reasonable way at our disposal, we must oppose our culture's obsession with the array of LGBTQ+ agendas that confuse, destroy, and ultimately lead to damnation all who give themselves over to aberrant sexuality. We must, at the same time, also address the other sinful practices listed in passages such as 1 Corinthians 6:9-11.

We come with a message of hope that is true only because of the God who is the Creator: "If anyone is in Christ, he is a new creation. The old has passed away; behold, the new has come" (2 Corinthians 5:17). God, who created the worlds, can and does create within us a new nature. This is the gift of His grace, given to all who repent and believe the good news of Christ and the forgiveness He offers us.

For all eternity, we will worship the God of creation: "Worthy are you, our Lord and God, to receive glory and honor and power, for you created all things, and by your will they existed and were created" (Revelation 4:11).

Before our Creator and Redeemer, we humbly bow.

OUR DECLARATION OF DEPENDENCE

Let us worship our Creator, giving thanks that He has crowned each human being with dignity. As we read this psalm to God, we must include in our prayers the children of this nation both born and unborn, thrust into a world of confusion, a world in which their value is diminished.

> O Lord, our Lord,
>   how majestic is your name in all the earth!

You have set your glory above the heavens.
    Out of the mouth of babies and infants,
you have established strength because of your foes,
    to still the enemy and the avenger.

When I look at your heavens, the work
        of your fingers,
    the moon and the stars, which you have set
        in place,
what is man that you are mindful of him,
    and the son of man that you care for him?

Yet you have made him a little lower than
    the heavenly beings
    and crowned him with glory and honor.
You have given him dominion over the works
    of your hands;
    you have put all things under his feet,
all sheep and oxen,
    and also the beasts of the field,
the birds of the heavens, and the fish of the sea,
    whatever passes along the paths of the seas.

O Lord, our Lord,
    how majestic is your name in all the earth!
(Psalm 8).

ACTION STEP

Let us become a safety net for those who have made destructive decisions about their sexuality regardless of the path they have chosen. We should be known as "go-to people" who offer hope, acceptance, and love to the broken, to those who feel abandoned and are struggling with guilt and self-hatred. As much as possible, become conversant about gender ideology. Research terms such as *heteronormativity*, *cisgender*, and *nonbinary*. Be ready to politely defend your convictions if you are accused of transphobia. Above all, pray earnestly for those who are caught in the tight grip of demonically inspired guilt and confusion. Let's be here for a needy world.

CHAPTER 9

Returning to the God of Moral Absolutes, Not Our Personal Preferences

Without God, Everything Is Permissible

H ow difficult is it to distinguish right from wrong or good from evil? What about premarital sex, same-sex relationships, killing in self-defense or in war? Should mothers have the right to kill their preborn infant? Is crime always evil, or should we evaluate criminals (without using the word *criminal*) as "people who have issues with the law"? Of course this list of questions could continue indefinitely.

No matter how we or others answer such questions, if we answer them at all, we are appealing to some objective standard by which conduct should be judged. In order to believe there is such an objective standard, you must believe in some kind of a transcendent (objective) morality, and in doing so, whether you know it or not, you are actually assuming the existence of God.

C.S. Lewis, an Oxford scholar and a one-time atheist, eventually became a Christian and is considered one of the most influential

Christian writers of the twentieth century. In part, the change began when he realized, "My argument against God was that the universe seemed so cruel and unjust. But how had I got this idea of *just* and *unjust*? A man does not call a line crooked unless he has some idea of a straight line."[1] His point is that a moral standard or law implies there is a moral lawgiver. This is what Paul meant when he said, "The truth about God is known to them instinctively" (Romans 1:19 TLB).

This chapter addresses this question: Can we find the answers to questions about morality by appealing to human reason alone? I intend to show that moral sanity cannot exist without an appeal to an objective standard that is ultimately a reflection of God. When God is eclipsed and darkness is normalized, Fyodor Dostoevsky is proven right: "Without God and the future life...It means everything is permitted now, one can do anything."[2] Only if God exists can we have a rational basis for moral decisions.

Atheism cannot establish the existence of any moral standards whatsoever. Yes, of course some atheists believe in basic decency and morality. But the reason they believe is because they, too, are created in the image of God. Atheists might not realize it, but they also assume God exists even as they lecture us about their dedication to morality and their own inherent goodness. But of course they also acknowledge the existence of evil, and as Frank Turek likes to say, "The existence of evil actually establishes the existence of God!"[3]

In the pages that follow, I hope to explain why Turek is right.

Someone objects, "You can stamp out religion from our schools and government and still have morality because morality can exist independently of religion." Admittedly, nonreligious people have morality, but as we will see, they do so at the price of living inconsistently with what they profess to believe. Though they deny God, they nevertheless live *as if* they were created by Him.

Let me say with clarity: From the standpoint of reason, *God is absolutely necessary for moral values.* No moral theory can arise out of atheism. Those who wish to create a secular state where religion has no influence will, of logical necessity, eventually bring about meaninglessness, lawlessness, and despair. Such conditions often spawn a totalitarian state, instituted to restore order by brute force. When a nation loses its moral roots, a dictator often arises who takes away personal freedoms to restore order. Just ask the citizens of China and Russia.

To think we can have morality without
God is like believing we can have trees
without roots, or fish without water.

Morality is a child of religion. If, like the prodigal son, it leaves home without its parents, it will end up in the swamp of moral bankruptcy. To think we can have morality without God is like believing we can have trees without roots, or fish without water. All atheists can hope for is that they have the smile without the Cheshire cat.

Humanists [read atheists] themselves admit they are attempting a difficult task in trying to erect morality without religion. Decades ago, in the February 1977 issue of *Humanist* magazine, Will Durant said, "Moreover, we shall find it no easy task to mold a natural ethic strong enough to maintain moral restraint and social order without the support of supernatural consolations, hopes, and fears."[4] He continued, "There is no significant example in history, before our time, of a society successfully maintaining moral life without the aid of religion."[5] Durant underestimated the problem. It is not merely *difficult* to have morality without religion, it is *impossible*.

Stay with me as we discuss this.

REASONS THE ECLIPSE OF GOD
SPELLS MORAL DARKNESS

Can human wisdom be the basis for moral values?

The Limits of Human Wisdom

One of the most startling statements in the Bible is Paul's remark, "Has not God made foolish the wisdom of the world?" (1 Corinthians 1:20). This statement seems to contradict the great advances in science we have witnessed in the past and present. Man is able to go to the moon and return safely; he can build computers that perform complex mathematical problems in split seconds; he has developed artificial intelligence that enables surgeons to perform delicate operations on the human body, correcting everything from a person's vision to a blocked artery or even replacing the entire heart. And yet, God says the wisdom of man is foolishness. Don't the results of science appear to conflict with God's dismal evaluation of human wisdom?

The discrepancy can be easily resolved. As long as man explores the physical creation, he is able to discover laws that can creatively be used in scientific experiments. God has given this world almost unlimited resources and predictable laws, and mankind is learning how to use them. The discovery of electricity resulted in lighting up our world; millions of tons of steel can be manufactured from the earth's resources for cars and airplanes and much more.

Why the difficulty of deriving values from our vast reservoir of knowledge? The reason is because knowledge of the physical world is of no help when it comes to metaphysical ideas (such as found in matters of religion and morality). Science can teach us how to make a bomb, but it cannot give guidance as to when the bomb should be detonated—or whether it should. Therefore, the truly important matters—the difference between right and wrong, ultimate

questions about the purpose of man's existence, and finding last-
ing meaning—cannot be discovered by human reasoning. Science
is silent regarding values.

The skeptic David Hume was among the first to articulate this
dilemma. He argued that even murder is not a vice but is simply an
act that excites passions within us.[6] Stealing and other crimes simply elicit negative feelings; the murderer who kills a family in a fit of
anger did not do wrong, but what he did makes us feel bad.

Jacques Monod, a French molecular biologist, in an interview in
The New York Times, agreed that it is impossible to derive what *ought*
to be from what *is*. He said that if there was no intention in the universe (no creator), and if we are pure accidents of evolution, then we
cannot discover what *ought* to be. He concluded that values must be
chosen arbitrarily, without any standard by which to judge them.[7]

Artificial Intelligence (AI), which is repeatedly in the news, can
simulate intelligence, and the details of various cultures can be analyzed, but such research cannot take the next step and say what
ought to be done. The old dilemma still stands: "My conscience tells
me to burn a widow with her dead husband," shouts the devoted
pagan. "My conscience tells me I should hang you if you do," replies
a British officer. Cultures have different values, laws, and punishments. How do we decide between them?

To explain further: All we have at our disposal are bits and pieces
of experience. We are like a mole who encounters a clump of dirt
and a blade of grass but is unable to see the whole landscape. William James once remarked, "We may be in the Universe as dogs
and cats are in our libraries, seeing the books and hearing the conversation, but having no inkling of the meaning of it all"[8]—an apt
description of man's dilemma if he is alone in the universe.

Albert Camus, staring the implications of atheism in the face, in
the first sentence of *The Myth of Sisyphus*, wrote, "There is but one

truly serious philosophical problem, and that is suicide."[9] He understood that if his atheism is to be consistently applied, man cannot find values in the world. In fact, when Camus spoke of values, even saying that there were values, he was unknowingly assuming an objective standard, though he did not know what it could be, nor did he realize such an objective standard had to be rooted in God.

Atheistic morality collapses like a house of cards held together by ropes of mist. It is a house without a foundation, suspended in mid-air. Morality becomes but a matter of personal preference. Good cannot be distinguished from evil; right from wrong is whatever anyone wants it to be.

And there is more.

The Existence of Your Thought Life

What are you thinking right now? Perhaps you are thinking this chapter is boring, or difficult to follow, or even irrelevant. Or maybe your mind has wandered from this page, and you are daydreaming about an exciting future, or a dismal one. Either way, because you are awake, you are conscious of existing as a human being. From where did your consciousness arise? When did the neurons in your brain become aware that "you" existed? Are your thoughts just calcium and phosphate and electrons forming in interesting patterns, then suddenly—behold!—these become conscious and aware so that you exist and have a mind?

Think of it this way: The evolutionary view of man says that life began somewhere in Darwin's "warm little pond." The atoms randomly assembled themselves into a complex pattern, and suddenly, a living cell appeared. This cell began to reproduce itself, and then at some point, these cells became self-conscious and began to give you thoughts. But, if this is true, if evolution is right, we are forced to conclude that *matter can actually think.*

Consider this unwelcome conclusion—French philosopher Julien Offray de LaMettrie put it this way: "Let us then conclude boldly that man is a machine and that there is in the whole universe only one diversely modified substance."[10] He accepted the implications of a mechanistic theory of origin and stated that all human actions were predetermined by chemistry and physics. Freedom, in any sense of the word, is an illusion.

Let me repeat: If matter can think, we have a difficulty. Because we don't control the physical and chemical laws pertaining to matter, we have no control over our thoughts. In a purely naturalist world, what arises in our thoughts depends on the chemical reactions of the neurons of calcium and phosphate in our brain. Because we can't say that one combination of chemical reactions is more ethical or moral than another, we have to conclude that all thoughts are morally neutral. Whatever *is, is*. Morality, as we generally think of it, does not exist.

Reread the last paragraph if you have to. Evolutionists are caught in a dilemma. If ideas are reduced to special combinations of atoms (as is necessary in an evolutionary worldview), and because those atoms are out of our control, our thoughts are predetermined by natural law. Obviously, we are not moral beings.

Another atheist said it more clearly. Pierre Cabanis wrote, "The brain secretes thought as the liver secretes bile."[11] We don't control the quality of our bile; therefore, we can't control our thoughts either—they are determined for us by the laws of physics and chemistry. Neurons do whatever neurons do without asking our permission.

If you have followed the argument this far, you can see that if we are the result of the haphazard forces of nature, we cannot even trust our ability to reason. In other words, if Darwinism is true, there is no way of establishing its plausibility. In a chance universe, logic and reason must be ruled out.

But, to return to what we said at the beginning of this chapter, someone may object, "Can't the humanist argue for morality simply on the basis that we should do whatever is best for humanity?" We have already shown that if our thoughts are merely combinations of atoms, the words *best* and *value* simply do not apply. It's like saying there are ten hours in a mile, or a tree has a phlegmatic personality, or the choir music was orange. Remember, the conclusion of humanism must be that whatever *is*, just *is*. Nothing more can be said.

Occasionally, one finds atheists who are willing to admit the inescapable conclusion of their presuppositions. Jean-Paul Sartre understood clearly where atheism led. "All activities are equivalent... thus it amounts to the same thing whether one gets drunk alone or is a leader of nations."[12] It is not just a matter of having an inadequate morality or a wrong morality; rather, it is a matter of morality not existing at all.

Oliver Wendell Holmes, a US Supreme Court justice from 1902 to 1932, would agree. He said:

> I see no reason for attributing to man a significant difference in kind from that which belongs to a baboon or a grain of sand. I believe that our personality is a cosmic ganglion, just as when certain rays meet and cross there is white light at the meeting point.[13]

Bertrand Russell, the famous British atheist, stated that

> man is the product of causes which had no prevision of the end they were achieving; that his origin, his growth, his hopes and fears, his loves and his beliefs, are but the outcome of accidental collocations of atoms...blind to

good and evil, reckless of destruction, omnipotent matter rolls on its relentless ways.[14]

This, of course, is precisely where the atheistic-evolutionary view
leads. Man may be more complex, but he has no more significance
than a baboon or a grain of sand. As we have already argued, abortion, infanticide, and euthanasia all become reasonable in a world
where human life is seen as the product of random evolutionary
forces.

When humanists attempt to destroy belief in God, they cannot
do so without destroying themselves. They may champion human
rights and speak of the need for morality, but their philosophy has
no metaphysical basis to sustain such values. They are planting their
feet on a free-floating illusion. They are assuming the existence of a
moral standard that could not have arisen out of atheism. They are
like a fish swimming in an ocean, arguing that water does not exist.

Allan Bloom, author of *The Closing of the American Mind*, wrote,
"Reason cannot establish values, and its belief that it can is the stu-
pidest and most pernicious illusion."[15]

To further clarify: Do atheists live in accordance with their atheistic presuppositions? Of course not. An atheist's reason tells him
that he is of no more value than a speck of dust, yet his life contra-
dicts such a conclusion. He may provide for his spouse and family,
and if you were to steal his car, he would want you punished—all
because he is created in the image of God. An atheist may appeal for
justice without knowing that even the concept of justice assumes
there is a God. Atheists live off the perfume of a theistic worldview.

Is there a way out of this moral uncertainty and the resulting
arbitrary laws?

The answer is *yes*. But first, let me introduce you to a humanistic philosopher by the name of Ludwig Wittgenstein (with a name

like that, he must be German, don't you think?). He admitted that if we really want to know right from wrong, we need this information to come from outside the universe. He wrote, "If a man could write a book on Ethics which really was a book on Ethics, this book would, with an explosion destroy all the other books in the world." Then he added, "Ethics, if it is anything, is supernatural…"[16]

It's too bad that Wittgenstein did not believe that such a supernatural book existed. But at least he knew that only such a book could give us the perspective we need. There is ample evidence that the Bible is the supernatural book he was looking for—a book that tells us the truth about ourselves, our world, and what we need to do to experience divine redemption.

THE BIBLE'S LIFE-GIVING ANSWER TO QUESTIONS OF MEANING AND MORALITY

The Bible opens by telling us about our origin and inherent value. Mankind was created "in the image of God" (the imago Dei, Genesis 1:27)—that is, with a conscience and an internal, rudimentary knowledge of God. This means that although we are physical beings with a body, we are also a soul or a spirit. Exactly how the spirit (or we could use the word *mind*) influences the brain is not known; the two connect in ways beyond our ability to understand. But this must be said: We can be held accountable for our actions because our minds or spirits are not subject to the inflexible scientific laws of impersonal neurons and chemical reactions.

Bob Perry writes in *Salvo*,

> We learn from biology that the cells that make up our bodies constantly die off and get replaced…Physically,

you become a completely different individual over and over again throughout your lifetime. Yet we all recognize that though we may grow older and slower, we are the same person we've always been...And that means that the persistent "self" is made of a different substance than the body.[17]

To repeat: your mind could not have evolved out of a physical substance like your body.

For those who would like to study this further, I recommend a fascinating article in *The Philosophical Review*, published by Thomas Nagel back in 1974, titled, "What Is It Like to Be a Bat?"[18]

The Bible teaches that at death, our mind or spirit will separate from the body and go on in existence either into the presence of Christ or to a place too horrid to describe here. To the scientist who says he has analyzed the brain, dissected all of its parts, and not found a "spirit" or "mind," we say it is possible to take a piano apart, lay out all of its individual pieces, and not find music. The astronomer who looks into the heavens does not see God; but sober-minded astronomers know He exists—not just in the heavens, but everywhere. As Solomon put it, "Behold, heaven and the highest heaven cannot contain you, how much less this house that I have built!" (2 Chronicles 6:18). We don't have to see the mind or soul, nor do we have to see God to know that both exist.

As C.S. Lewis put it,

> The dullest and most uninteresting person you can talk
> to may one day be a creature which, if you saw it now,
> you would be strongly tempted to worship, or else a hor-
> ror and a corruption such as you now meet, if at all, only
> in a nightmare...There are no ordinary people...But it is

immortals whom we joke with, work with, marry, snub, and exploit—immortal horrors or everlasting splendours.[19]

THE GOD WHO SPEAKS AND WARNS

We are called by God to proclaim the Scriptures as an authoritative revelation from a sovereign God who pronounces judgment on those who regard evil as good and good as evil (see Isaiah 5:20). The biblical doctrines of sin, judgment, and salvation must once again be heard with clarity and power.

On September 7, 1864, Abraham Lincoln was presented with a Holy Bible given to him by a delegation of Black Americans. In response, he said these words: "In regard to this Great Book, I have but to say, it is the best gift God has given to man. All the good the Savior gave to the world was communicated through this book. But for it we could not know right from wrong."[20]

Have you ever heard of the McGuffey Readers (also known as the Eclectic Readers)? William Holmes McGuffey was a Presbyterian clergyman and educator who wrote the McGuffey Readers and taught in many schools during the mid-nineteenth to early twentieth centuries. They gave great impetus to America's religious heritage and are still used today by homeschoolers and some private schools. McGuffey wrote,

> Erase all thought and fear of God from a community, and selfishness and sensuality would absorb the whole man. Appetite, knowing no restraint, and suffering, having no solace or hope, would trample in scorn on the restraints of human laws. Virtue, duty, principle, would be mocked and spurned as unmeaning sounds. A sordid self-interest would supplant every other feeling; and

man would become, in fact, what the theory of atheism declares him to be—a companion for brutes.[21]

Without God, we have appetites without restraint!

MY PLEA TO YOU AND ME

Do we who claim to be followers of Christ conduct ourselves in ways that reflect our biblical convictions? We are quick to defend biblical morality, but are we living what we profess? Years ago, I heard this challenging question: "If you were accused of being a Christian, would there be enough evidence to convict you?"

If you are a politician or in business, your temptations to compromise your convictions are exponentially greater. When I was in a country that had been under the brutal heel of Communism, Christian businessmen and politicians were living by the theory, "You have to join hands with the devil until you get across the bridge." But many discovered that after they had "crossed the bridge," they could not relinquish the devil's grip.

There is a story I have not been able to confirm about Gustav Dore, a famous French artist (1832–1883). When he was crossing a border in Europe, he had no passport or identifying papers. The border crossing officials were not sure whether he was who he claimed to be, so they challenged him: "If you are Gustav Dore, take this piece of paper and sketch the landscape around you." Within minutes, they saw extraordinary ability in his sketch. They immediately knew he was who he claimed to be.

Are we the person we claim to be?

> O Lord, who shall sojourn in your tent?
> Who shall dwell on your holy hill?

He who walks blamelessly and does what is right
   and speaks truth in his heart;
who does not slander with his tongue
   and does no evil to his neighbor…
   and does not take a bribe against the innocent
(Psalm 15:1-3, 5).

If we believe in our Redeemer, let us live as those who are redeemed!*

OUR DECLARATION OF DEPENDENCE

We are glad that the Bible is a revelation from God that helps us discern right from wrong. But thankfully, it also has a message of redemption. When we see people seek to manage their own sin by self-directed destructive paths, we must call out to the Lord on their behalf.

Even when the prophet Daniel was told that anyone who prayed to the God of heaven would be thrown into the lions' den, he kept praying to the God of heaven. We read, "He went to his house where he had windows in his upper chamber open toward Jerusalem. He got down on his knees three times a day and prayed and gave thanks before his God, as he had done previously" (6:10).

After being spared from the lions' den, Daniel learned that earnest prayer attracts the opposition of the spirit world. His answer was delayed because "the prince of the kingdom of Persia" withstood the messenger God had sent until the angel Michael came to his rescue (10:13). Evidently an evil spirit, perhaps Satan himself, was

---

* Portions of this chapter were excerpted from Erwin W. Lutzer, *Exploding the Myths That Could Destroy America* (Chicago, IL: Moody Publishers, 1986), 45-59. Used by permission of Moody Publishers.

trying to direct the policies of the kingdom of Persia and attempted to block the revelation Daniel was about to receive. But Daniel persisted, and the answer came. Daniel's primary concern was for the people who were called by God's name. *The world can't be made right until the people of God are made right.*

Recently, I read Daniel's prayer each day for a week, substituting the church and America in the references to the nation Israel (Daniel's entire prayer is found in Daniel 9:3-19).

My own heart was challenged and the burden I have for our country increased. "For we do not present our pleas before you because of our righteousness, but because of your great mercy" (Daniel 9:18).

Join me as we set aside the distractions of Babylon to focus on what is most important. Yes, the survival of our nation is at stake, but more importantly, the souls of many people are spiritually confused. Jesus is the Savior they need to meet.

Corrie ten Boom said, "The wonderful thing about praying is that you leave a world of not being able to do something, and enter God's realm where everything is possible."[22]

ACTION STEP

Pray to restore someone who has fallen into the error of sin, and do so with a spirit of gentleness. "Keep watch on yourself, lest you too be tempted" (Galatians 6:1).

Who is Christ for you today? An unwed mother? A grieving widower? A woman in an abusive marriage? An addicted teenager? Or an unwanted child? We might not always be able to prevent someone from making a destructive moral decision, but we can be there to pick them up when they stumble. Look around you; Christ's hands and heart is needed everywhere in an amoral world.

CHAPTER 10

Returning to God as Lawgiver, Not as Vacillating Ruler

That Which Men Might Rule as Legal *Might Actually Be* Evil

Thankfully, America is not Nazi Germany.

I return to Nazi Germany because it is perhaps the best example of how Christianity, under intense pressure, both political and legal, adjusted its teaching and influence to fit in with the *zeitgeist*—that is, the spirit of the times. The hard edges of Christianity were softened; the message and goals of the church were reshaped, and "positive Christianity" was adopted. The values of heaven were replaced with the values of Earth. And the swastika took the place of the cross.

This chapter is intended to help us answer several questions: What happens when justice becomes whatever a dictatorial regime wants it to be? What should be the basis of law in a just society? Are there transcendent principles that should undergird our understanding of justice? And how does this apply to our present situation in the West?

THE PROMISE OF HOPE IN
EXCHANGE FOR LIBERTY

When a country lurches toward becoming an oppressive regime and the citizens experience the loss of individual freedoms, the changes generally follow a somewhat predictable path. It begins with a state of rampant chaos, which means that the beleaguered populace is willing to accept a leader who promises to restore order. This leader must be heralded as a liberator, as someone who secures his position of power by identifying an enemy and convincingly arguing that he is able to bring stability out of anarchy. Desperate times necessitate desperate measures.

Seeking a Crisis

Those who would be dictators need a reason to clamp down on their citizens. Historically, they have sought a crisis to suspend civil liberties and increase their power. Any crisis will do—it could be an economic crisis, a pandemic, anarchy, or war. Desperate citizens seek stability in the midst of chaos.

Adolf Hitler had an opportunity and took it. On February 27, 1933, just a month after he had been installed as Chancellor, the Reichstag—the massive German parliament building in Berlin—was set ablaze, apparently by a Dutchman, Marinus van der Lubbe, though many believe Hitler's henchmen were the instigators. Be that as it may, Hitler blamed the Communists. Now he had a crisis that would give him the right to dispense with the present laws of Germany and institute new laws that would "protect" the Germans from three enemies: Communism, the present economic crisis, and the Jews, who were blamed for Germany's defeat in World War I. This began the journey of Hitler taking the role of lawgiver and bringing Germany under his control. Historians would agree that the burning of the Reichstag was, as reportedly said in the words of one writer, a "gift from the gods"!

A month after the Reichstag fire, the opening of the new session of parliament was moved into the Garrison Church in Potsdam. There, Hitler passed the Enabling Act (a law "to Remedy the Distress of the People and the Reich"[1]), which would give him control of legislation, including the authority to violate the Weimar Constitution (ratified in the city of Weimar to cope with Germany's crisis after World War I). Thus, Hitler could deal with emergencies quickly and decisively.

To restore order, civil liberties were curtailed: no freedom of assembly, no freedom of the press, no freedom to form opposition parties. Dissidents were summarily isolated, publicly identified, then executed. Hitler did not seek to hide these atrocities; in fact, he proudly said they were necessary for the "protection" of the German people.

With anarchy on the streets and soup lines in the cities, the people were understandably desperate to trust a strong leader who could bypass parliamentary procedures and restore order. Gerald Suster wrote,

> Many welcomed the abolition of individual responsibility for one's actions; for some it is easier to obey than to accept the dangers of freedom. Workers now had job security, a health service, cheap holiday schemes; *if freedom meant starvation, then slavery was preferable.*[2]

Satan was quite right when he said of Job, "All that a man has he will give for his life" (Job 2:4). For the Germans, as it would likely be for us, food on the table was more important than the freedom of speech or assembly.

Steps to Appease the Church

Hitler knew any moral opposition he received would come from the church. To my knowledge, he never once suggested to the

Germans that they should stop attending church. In fact, he even encouraged church attendance, as long as those churches accommodated themselves to the new German Era. It was a new day in Germany, and the churches had to adapt to the times.

Despite Christianity's concessions to liberal theology, the influence of the churches was still too powerful for Hitler to ignore. He needed the support of the churches, and for the most part, he got what he wanted. After he was sworn in as Chancellor, he paid tribute to Christianity as "an essential element for safeguarding the soul of the German people" and promised to respect the rights of the churches. He declared his ambition was to have a "peaceful accord between Church and State."[3] Article 24 of the Nazi Party Platform said, "We demand freedom for all religious denominations in the State, provided they do not threaten its existence nor offend the moral feelings of the German race."[4]

Churches were given freedom with limits, *as long as they didn't offend the German race's sense of decency or morality*. Pastors were to preach positive sermons about the glitter of a revived economy and harmonize the teachings of the Bible with the blessings of a new prosperity. Many pastors preached messages that neither offended anyone, nor, most likely, did not save anyone from their sins.

Of course, it would be Hitler who determined what would pose a danger to the "moral feelings" of the Germans or what would be considered a "threat" to the state. In his early speeches, Hitler frequently spoke about the need for "religious freedom" and the "independence" of the church. Those two words, *freedom* and *independence*, were the words he used to plot tyranny.

Hitler called his views "Positive Christianity."

What was this Positive Christianity? It emphasized that which was hopeful and refrained from exposing the erosion of law and freedom. Rather than hearing messages about the cruelty of Hitler's policies, the persecution of the Jews, and the need for redemption from sin, the people were to be affirmed as Germans, as decent citizens. They needed to be encouraged by the positive transformation of culture that was happening before their eyes. It was much akin to what, in our day, we call progressive Christianity.

Nazism was presented as the light that would dispel the economic and cultural darkness and usher in a new day of optimism and the dawning of hope brought on by self-confidence and innovation. To continue Hitler's words from Article 24 mentioned above: "The party as such stands for a positive Christianity, without binding itself denominationally to a particular confession."[5]

Positive Christianity was exactly as it sounded: The German people should not be offended but affirmed. Of course many evangelicals in our day also fit this description and water down the messages of sin and grace so as to affirm everyone—no matter their lifestyle. A.W. Tozer said it best: "In many churches Christianity has been watered down until the solution is so weak that if it were poison it would not hurt anyone, and if it were medicine it would not cure anyone!"[6]

Thankfully, in Hitler's day, as in ours, there was pushback.

Hermann Sasse, who had previously edited the 1932 *Church Year Book,* saw the issues clearly and defied the Nazi Party decree that Germans should not be offended in church. He wrote regarding Article 24, "No discussion at all is possible...For the Protestant church would have to begin such a discussion with a frank admission that its doctrine constitutes a deliberate, permanent insult to the 'German race's sense of decency and morality.'"[7] He was saying that the gospel itself was offensive to Germans and non-Germans alike.

Then Sasse followed with this rebuke: "According to the Protestant doctrine of original sin," the supposed superiority of the German race meant nothing:

the newborn infant of the noblest Germanic descent, endowed in body and mind with the optimal racial characteristics, is as much subject to eternal damnation as the genetically gravely compromised half-caste from two decadent races...We are not much interested in whether the Party gives its support to Christianity, but we would like to know whether the church is to be permitted to preach the Gospel in the Third Reich without hindrance, whether, that is, we will be able to continue undisturbed with our insults to the Germanic or Germanistic moral sense, as with God's help as we intend to do...[8]

Sasse understood that a baby from any race—even the German race—is born a sinner, and a preacher cannot be true to the gospel without insulting those who insist otherwise. If we preach a gospel that does not offend people, if we are afraid that our affirmation of human sinfulness might insult our listeners, we can no longer claim we are true to the core of the gospel.

Even Swiss theologian Karl Barth, with his penchant for universal salvation, stood up to Hitler's decree. He gave a withering critique and said that it is not enough to say, "Jesus Christ: even if she [the church] says it a thousand times...[the church] is talking into the wind, blind to the real distress of real men, just as she is deaf to the Word of God...It is high time to stop taking this path, high time to retrace our steps."[9]

Churches were free to say "Jesus Christ" as often as they liked, but Barth said what was really needed was a full-throated commitment to all that the gospel entails—therefore, to be quiet about Nazism is a betrayal of the gospel. Of course we are reminded of Jesus' warning that many who say "Lord, Lord" and even do miracles will not enter the kingdom of God (see Matthew 7:21-22).

Only if we say "Jesus Christ is Lord!" with personal conviction do the words count.

When a Catholic bishop said he would oppose the Nazi interference in the church, Hitler responded by saying the rights of the churches (both Protestant and Catholic) "would not be infringed." He sought only their cooperation in agreeing to fight against "a materialistic view of the world" and establishing a "genuine national community." After this speech, the Catholic church said it saw no reason to continue to oppose Hitler's policies.[10]

But Christianity would have to be remade if it were to survive in the German Third Reich; the churches had to be persuaded they could support Hitler without betraying their religious convictions. Eventually, most of them would place a swastika on their altar or on the front door so if there were a purging of churches, they would be seen as being on the right side of Germany's rise to greatness. The death of historic Christianity was presented as liberation and a step toward a new spirit of democracy.

The great temptation of the church has always been to trim its sails to float along with the world. And as Karl Barth said, people think that as long as they say "Jesus Christ" enough times, they must be on solid theological ground. But the gospel includes teaching about sin, righteousness, and judgment. And what we do about Jesus Christ is most critical.

. . . .

A cross bedecked with flowers cannot save; only a blood-stained cross can redeem needy sinners.

. . . .

Churches can dance around the gospel and make it appear as if they are preaching the gospel without preaching the gospel. When

England transitioned from a predominantly Christian nation to the secularism of today, one observer wrote these words: "I believe that the cross was there, but it was so heaped up with flowers I could not see it."[11] But a cross bedecked with flowers cannot save; only a blood-stained cross can redeem needy sinners. Interestingly, the pastors who objected to the compromises of the church in England were called out as being divisive and causing factions.

Whether in England, Germany, or America, contending for the faith is not easy. Love is often assumed to supersede truth, and heresy is tolerated in the interest of unity. And, as already emphasized, churches often drift from the gospel because of the weakness of otherwise good men.

HITLER, THE LAWGIVER

Hitler's commitment to transform Germany had teeth because he created new laws. The Nazis proclaimed, "Hitler is the law!" Or, as Hermann Göring put it, "The law and the will of the Fuehrer are one."[12] Right and wrong were determined by Hitler and his cronies.

Hitler would put an end to the equality of all people under the law; the law would not be "blind," but would target political enemies. Today we call it the weaponization of our justice system.

The Need for a Scapegoat

Any nation drifting toward totalitarianism needs a scapegoat, some entity to blame for all the nation's woes. The Germans blamed the Jews for the loss of World War I and the world's economic crisis. So Hitler generated hatred against them, and laws were put in place to destroy their influence.

The Nuremberg Laws of September 15, 1935 deprived the Jews of German citizenship, confining them to the status of "subjects."

These laws forbade marriage between Jews and Aryans (Germanic peoples), as well as sexual relationships between them. This was the basis for 13 administrative regulations against the Jews that would later outlaw them completely. Many of them were deprived of their livelihood and faced starvation. In many towns, Jews were forbidden to purchase food or do business.

As early as May 1923, Hitler, during a speech in Munich, said, "The Jews are undoubtedly a race, but not human. They cannot be human in the sense of being an image of God, the Eternal. The Jews are the image of the devil. Jewry means the racial tuberculosis of the nations."[13] He would change the law to ensure that extinguishing this race was not a crime.

With Hitler's declaration that Jews were beneath animals came the assertion that non-Aryans were *Untermensch*—that is, subhuman. Heinrich Himmler had the green light to use his SS troops to exterminate them. The SS were now free to kill without breaking laws; they were free to eliminate Jews without being charged for committing murder. There would be no trials for poisoning such vermin; the land must be cleansed of alleged filth so that it might be peopled with those who have Aryan blood flowing through their veins. If evil is called good, then it becomes good.

Adolf Hitler said so.

Police power became independent of judicial review; the police could arrest anyone they deemed to be acting or speaking contrary to the goals of the German Reich, and the accused had no judicial recourse. By 1934, the People's Court was established to try acts of treason. Treason was defined as anything contrary to the will and the purposes of the Reich. Criticism was treason; freedom of the press was treason; a failure to further the agenda of the Reich was treason. Treason was whatever Hitler said it was.

The proceedings were secret, the punishments were severe. Crimson red posters announced the names of those who died under the axe of the executioner. Threats and intimidation kept the people in line.

A Dangerous Path

Clearly, historic Christianity had to be cleansed from the fabric of society; its foundational principles were destroyed to make room for a more optimistic, humanistic, and equitable future. Science would replace religion; the collective human consciousness would replace God. And the new optimism of a revived Germany fit in well with the spirit of Positive Christianity.

Many churches were so enamored by Hitler's successes that they did not pause to ask in whose name these benefits came to them. Their buildings remained open, Christ was still honored, but repentance from personal sin was not needed and scarcely mentioned.

Nazi propaganda propelled the nation along a dangerous path.

THE POWER OF LAWS

One powerful reason Nazism flourished is because the laws of Germany no longer honored the equal application of the law and a basic respect for equality. When laws are based on the desire for power and not the principle of equality, brutality reigns. R.J. Rushdoony observed that behind every system of law there is a god. "If the source of law is the individual, then the individual is the god of that system…if our source of law is a court, then the court is our god. If there is no higher law beyond man, then man is his own god… When you choose your authority, you choose your god, and when you look for your law, there is your god."[14] *Look behind the law and there is your god!*

With Hitler's power to make laws, he could mock his power-less opposition. Without a law in their favor, opponents had no defense against the accusations made against them. Pastors, for example, could be tried for hate crimes such as "abuse of pulpit" or treason. And if accused, they had no recourse but to accept their fate. They were frequently confronted with false evidence accusing them of theft or sexual malpractices. Lurid details of the accusations hurled against them, often sexual in nature, were published in the newspapers.

Then, as now, public exposure and ridicule caused the best of people to remain quiet. Parents who refused to have their children join the Hitler Youth were blackmailed. History has shown the truth of the words of Scripture: "The fear of man lays a snare" (Proverbs 29:25). We can only imagine what Hitler and his cronies would have done with today's social media!

Once a ruler has the power to censor alternative opinions, he can do whatever he likes. The restraints are gone. That's why Hitler could belittle the pastors and say with contempt, "You can do anything you want with them…They will submit…they are insignificant little people, submissive as dogs, and they sweat with embarrassment when you talk to them."[15] He knew he could crush their resistance because the law was on his side!

What else? When laws are not rooted in some transcendent (absolute) morality, the perpetrators of evil can be exonerated, and their victims can be blamed for their fate. Repeatedly, Heinrich Himmler spoke of his SS troops as the ones who were making a sacrifice even as they tortured men, women, and children and put them in ovens. It was as though the torturers suffered more than the people they tortured. "To have stuck it out," he said to his officers, "and at the same time…to have remained decent fellows, that is what has made us hard. This is a page of glory in our history which has never been written and shall never be written."[16] According to Himmler, torturing and killing Jews was a real sacrifice made by the SS troops, who were "decent fellows."

This leads to a question: If laws should not be created arbitrarily, on what should they be based? What objective values should they reflect?

THE BASIS OF LAW

After Hitler was defeated, war crimes trials were held in Nuremberg to judge the guilt of Hitler's henchmen. But a dispute arose as to what laws should be used to try the accused. After all, Hitler's cronies argued, they had not broken any laws; their actions were carried out with the protection of their own legal system. They could not be accused of murder because "personhood" had been redefined to exclude Jews and other undesirables. These men were simply following the laws handed down by the courts of their day. As Adolf Eichmann protested before his execution, "I am guilty of having been obedient, having subordinated myself to my official duties and the obligations of war service and my oath of allegiance and my oath of office."[17] He was simply faithful to the laws of his country.

Moral relativists who believe laws are nothing more than the result of social conditioning and are subject to the whims of various cultures and nations would have to agree with Göring, Hitler's designated successor, who is quoted by some as saying, "This court has no jurisdiction over me; I am a German!" Should Germans be judged by British law? By American law? What laws should have jurisdiction over them?

Let's not hurry over this. If laws are simply what a culture or state says they are, then as the culture and laws change, atrocities can become legal. And just as water cannot rise above its source, so transcendent laws cannot rise above the shifting sands of diverse relativistic cultures. So the questions at the famous trials at Nuremberg were, What gives us the right to judge Germans who were obeying the laws of their country? Would we want some other country's laws to be imposed on us?

Robert H. Jackson, Chief of Counsel of the United States, broke the impasse and argued that there was a law above the law that stood in judgment of all men in all countries and societies. There is a universal law that is above all cultures, all forms of government, and all peoples; there is a superior law that puts a price tag on human life. I might add that only an appeal to God and His revelation can give us the laws by which individuals and countries can be uniformly judged. Either God, who created man in His own image, is supreme, or the vacillating rulers of the world are supreme.

In our fallen world, we must distinguish between legal justice and moral justice; often they are not the same. In 1973, the US Supreme Court, reminiscent of Hitler, changed the law to exclude a whole class of people from constitutional protection. Under the court's ruling and its progeny, the courts held that as long as a baby was in the womb, it was not human and thus could be killed. Our Supreme Court made *abortion legal, but please note that it could not make it moral.*

Several years ago, a group of pro-life protesters who picketed an abortion clinic were sued for slander for calling abortionists murderers. The abortionists argued, just as Hitler's emissaries had done, that they could not be murderers because they were not breaking any laws![18] The experience of Nuremberg and the silent holocaust in our abortion clinics bear eloquent witness to the fact that when a state is accountable to no one except itself, it simply assumes that whatever is legal is moral. (Thankfully, a more recent Supreme Court affirmed the unconstitutionality of the 1973 decision and returned the issue to be resolved by the individual states.)

Show me your laws, and I will show you your God!

LAW IN AMERICA

I was born and raised in Canada but became a naturalized US citizen. As I have become acquainted with the Declaration of Independence, the Constitution, and the Bill of Rights, I am amazed at the wisdom of our Founding Fathers. Fearing the possibility of tyranny, they wrote documents that insisted our government have checks and balances and would ultimately be accountable to the people.

The Founders knew that giving people freedom had risks, and only a people with basic moral values could sustain the republic. A so-called deist, Benjamin Franklin, gave what is now a famous acknowledgement of God's sovereignty in the affairs of men:

> I have lived, Sir, a long time, and the longer I live, the more convincing proofs I see of this truth—*that God governs in the affairs of men.* And if a sparrow cannot fall to the ground without his notice, is it probable that an empire can rise without his aid? We have been assured, Sir, in the sacred writings, that "except the Lord build the House they labour in vain that build it." I firmly believe this; and I also believe that without His concurring aid we shall succeed in this political building no better than the Builders of Babel.[19]

There is a debate today as to how Christian the Founding Fathers were, but whether they were individually Christian or not, there was a general consensus of theism, the belief that God existed, and this meant that "all men were created equal" and from our Creator we receive "unalienable Rights, that among these are Life, Liberty and the pursuit of Happiness."[20] This, of course, differs from the Marxist teachings that rights are granted by the state; the state can give them and the state can take them. Our Founding Fathers believed that because man was responsible to his Creator, there were absolute rights and standards by which moral judgments could be measured.

A theistic view of law was passed on to the American colonies through Samuel Rutherford's book *Lex, Rex*, or *The Law and the Prince*, written in 1644. This book spoke against the "divine right" of kings, insisting that even kings and princes should be subject to the law.

Rutherford reasoned that because all men are sinners, no man is superior to any other. This meant even the king had to be subject to the law—there were no exceptions. All were equal, all had certain unalienable rights (i.e., absolute rights). All live under the law of God. This was another incredible blow against "the divine right of kings" who had been deemed above the law.

The eighteenth-century jurist William Blackstone also influenced the early American understanding of the Bible and nature. Because God is the personal, omnipotent Creator, He works and governs the affairs of men. Law should be consistent with His revelation in the Bible and nature (such as the relationship between parents and their children). No law should be passed that would be contrary to the law of God.

This Christian view of the world greatly influenced the founding of the United States. In the words of C. Gregg Singer, it "so permeated the colonial mind that it continued to guide even those who had come to regard the Gospel with indifference or even hostility. The currents of this orthodoxy were too strong to be easily set aside by those who in their own thinking had come to a different conception of religion and hence of government also."[21]

To our shame, our nation did not live up to the promises of "equality under the law" as specified in the Constitution. During slavery, there was not equality under the law, and even during what is called the Jim Crow era, we lived with a two-tiered justice system. Thankfully, much progress has been made since those days, yet unfortunately, human justice will never be perfectly administered. But the goal of equality for various religions (or no religion) and various ethnicities remains before us. Human courts seldom do justice perfectly, but strive toward this goal we must.

But no document(s) can save us from unequal justice.

Politicians and judges can place their hands on a Bible and swear to uphold the Constitution, but that means nothing if they lack the integrity to follow through with their promise. Both Russia and China have constitutions that guarantee freedoms, but words on a page are meaningless to those who substitute power in the place of justice.

WHITHER AMERICA?

What jumps out at you as you read these verses of Scripture?

> A single witness shall not suffice against a person for any crime or for any wrong in connection with any offense that he has committed. Only on the evidence of two witnesses or of three witnesses shall a charge be established (Deuteronomy 19:15).

> You shall not pervert justice. You shall not show partiality, and you shall not accept a bribe, for a bribe blinds the eyes of the wise and subverts the cause of the righteous.

Justice, and only justice, you shall follow (Deuteronomy 16:19-20).

It is not good to be partial to the wicked or to deprive the righteous of justice (Proverbs 18:5).

Evil men do not understand justice, but those who seek the LORD understand it completely (Proverbs 28:5).

The LORD is our judge; the LORD is our lawgiver; the LORD is our king; he will save us (Isaiah 33:22).

Justice is turned back, and righteousness stands far away; for truth has stumbled in the public squares, and uprightness cannot enter. Truth is lacking (Isaiah 59:14-15).

This last verse is especially significant: Without truth, justice and righteousness cannot enter the public square. Please notice how repeatedly Scripture warns about favoritism or the unequal application of the law, as well as a form of justice that is not based on truth.

Without a respect for justice that is based on truth, there is tyranny.

Justice for Thee, but Not for Me

Unless confronted by light, the darkness of secularism will always expand its reach and cast its shadow over matters of justice and fairness. In recent years, we have seen the weaponization of our justice system. Some politicians have been prosecuted, while others with compelling evidence of greater crimes have been either neglected or the evidence buried.

Justice should be blind in an unbiased manner, but unfortunately, it is sometimes blind to those whose crimes certain people seek to hide.

The more that we here in America see the law unequally applied, the more we can expect our downward spiral to continue. In other words, crimes will be overlooked if done by the "right" people. The result will be a de facto one-party system with totalitarianism not far behind.

· · · · · · · · · · · ·

Unless confronted by light, the darkness of secularism will always expand its reach and cast its shadow over matters of justice and fairness.

· · · · · · · · · · · ·

Let us remember the ominous words attributed to Lavrentiy Beria, the police chief for Joseph Stalin: "Give me the man, and I will give you the case against him!"[22] Other dictators have said similar statements based on the presumption of guilt. If a presumed enemy of the state is to be neutralized, any crime will do. Thankfully, we are not there yet here in the West, but given the weaponization of our justice system, this is the direction we are headed.

Protesting is allowed under the Constitution, but not blocking major highways, vandalizing property or looting. But if the mob doing these acts represents an aggrieved party, there are few consequences. Sometimes "smash and grab" robberies are, in effect, romanticized with turnstile justice. As one police officer here in Chicago told me, "We arrest a person but often before we have the paperwork filled out, he or she is back out on the street."

What can we expect in the future? Ominously, perhaps there will be harsh penalties for "lawbreakers" who refuse to comply with the woke agenda, but leniency toward those who break the law as they promote wokeness: transgenderism, socialism, critical race theory, and minorities who view America as racist and in need of a socialist revolution. When power is substituted for justice, our safeguards are gone.

Going forward, let us pray that our laws will be equally applied.

The Battle for Free Speech

We never believed it could come to this.

At the time of this writing, House Bill 4474 has been passed by the Michigan House of Representatives (it presently is stalled in the Senate). The bill criminalizes hate speech, and as attorney David A. Kallman writes, it "will be used to attack anyone opposing the progressive ideology sweeping the nation. If you speak against transgender issues, illegal immigration, BLM protestors, or simply refuse someone's preferred pronouns, you can be charged with a felony and face 5 years in prison and a $10,000.00 fine."[23] Kallman goes on to explain the bill line by line and points out that the phrase "regardless of the existence of any other motivating factors" means that if you speak, even peacefully, about these matters because of your faith or conscience, the law will not protect you. Even if this bill doesn't become law, it signals the loss of our freedoms and the use of law to impose Leftist moral standards on our society.

Sadly, so many people favor censorship for those who disagree with them. They applaud when those with conservative values are deplatformed and cancelled; they are in favor of intolerance if it is directed against people with whom they disagree. Apparently they don't realize that the very purpose of the First Amendment (freedom of speech) was to protect the right of unpopular ideas to be spoken. But of course these same radical Leftists would quickly appeal to the First Amendment if they were to suffer the same fate.

SOGI laws (Sexual Orientation and Gender Identity) are not just intended to protect certain groups; these laws will most probably be used to *compel agreement*, often enforced either by the courts or in businesses. Sadly, our neighbor to the north, Canada, passed a so-called conversion law that could be so broadly interpreted that parents who try to talk their teenagers out of transgender surgery could be tried as lawbreakers.[24]

Christians in the marketplace have some difficult decisions to make. We must all ask: "At what point does my love for Christ outweigh my need to feed my family? At what point am I willing to accept vilification for refusing to bow to the legalities that violate my convictions?" If we choose to violate our conscience because of fear or the possibility we might lose our livelihood, then let's not be critical of the church in Germany, when bread on the table was more important than standing up for freedom and accepting costly consequences.

It is not farfetched to predict that we're on our way to the creation of a "digital prison" that surveils and controls all people. At the time I am writing this, there is a great deal of discussion about the development of a digital dollar. Let us not think that we will always be able to spend these dollars according to our discretion; they possibly will be programmed according to government restrictions in connection with "financial inclusion and equity" and "reduc[ing] climate change and pollution."[25] This could eventually mean that dollars cannot be sent to churches or Christian ministries that continue to teach biblical sexuality and therefore are not seen as inclusive. Furthermore, people's accounts will possibly be frozen if compliance with certain directives is resisted.

Let me say it again: When the rule of law is replaced by the quest for power, freedom ends.

Are we ready?

WHEN DISOBEDIENCE
TO LAWS HONORS GOD

Should we always obey the laws of the land? In Nazi Germany, even Christians believed that obedience to the state should be absolute. When Martin Bormann requested that the pastors of Germany swear personal allegiance to Hitler, many pastors complied, citing Romans 13:1-7. Read this controversial passage carefully:

> Let every person be subject to the governing authorities. For there is no authority except from God, and those that exist have been instituted by God. Therefore whoever resists the authorities resists what God has appointed, and those who resist will incur judgment. For rulers are not a terror to good conduct, but to bad. Would you have no fear of the one who is in authority? Then do what is good, and you will receive his approval, for he is God's servant for your good. But if you do wrong, be afraid, for he does not bear the sword in vain. For he is the servant of God, an avenger who carries out God's wrath on the wrongdoer. Therefore one must be in subjection, not only to avoid God's wrath but also for the sake of conscience. For because of this you also pay taxes, for the authorities are ministers of God, attending to this very thing. Pay to all what is owed to them: taxes to whom taxes are owed, revenue to whom revenue is owed, respect to whom respect is owed, honor to whom honor is owed.

Without taking a deep dive here, let us ask: Could Paul really be advocating for unquestioning obedience to the powers that be? Commentators have pointed out that he wrote this at a time when the evil Emperor Nero was on the throne. Yet Paul himself disobeyed laws when they conflicted with his own conscience—after all, he did end up in a Roman prison chained to guards. And there is evidence that he was executed under Nero.

In Romans 13:1-7, I believe Paul is describing the ideal government, a government as envisioned by God. As Paul says, God's intention is that a government reward the good and punish the guilty. Obviously, the passage isn't calling for blind obedience to a nation's laws. At the most basic level, *if we say we should always obey the government, we put the government in the place of God.* The Bible and church history are replete with examples of when believers disobeyed governing authorities in order to obey God.

Consider the words of the Reformer John Knox, who refused to obey the laws of Scotland when they forbade him to practice his Protestant faith:

> True it is, God has commanded kings to be obeyed; but likewise true it is, that in things which they commit against his glory—or when cruelly without cause they rage against their brethren, the members of Christ's body—he has commanded no obedience, but rather he has approved, yea, and greatly rewarded, such as have opposed themselves to their ungodly commandments and blind rage.[26]

Amid many examples of government overreach here in America, I refer to the COVID-19 mandates, which included many employers requiring their employees to receive the vaccine. Also, in my home city of Chicago, businesses such as abortion clinics and marijuana stores were deemed "necessary" to keep open, but churches were told to suspend their worship services (or limit attendance to 50 people) because they apparently were deemed "unnecessary." Without getting into the pros and cons of the vaccine, to compel compliance with the unconstitutional mandates of any politician or business is a frightening overreach.

I spoke to a pastor in Canada who spent 37 days in jail for keeping his church open during the COVID-19 lockdown. He had the personal conviction that being faithful to the Scriptures meant that for the church to assemble was necessary, but this was contrary to the arbitrary laws made by Canadian politicians. Thankfully, eventually, Canada's Charter of Rights was on his side. Meanwhile his experience is a warning to others: obey, or else!

Should we have another pandemic, we might be wise to keep in mind the words often spoken in the world of mathematicians and statisticians: "If you torture the data long enough, it will confess to anything."

Secularism is never neutral. It will always move in slow yet relentless fashion, smashing any opposition it may encounter. Unless reversed, even here in America, some form of totalitarianism with its disregard for human freedoms can be expected to emerge. And groups like the ACLU know the average church or ministry cannot bear the legal costs to fight the legislation that will shrink personal liberties. Businesses and churches will be expected to either go along with the changes or face the consequences.

Remember this: When Shadrach, Meshach, and Abednego were faced with the decision of whether to bow before the image or be thrown into the fiery furnace, they chose the furnace. They feared God more than the fire. Yes, God delivered them, but thousands of Christians have been burned at the stake for their faith and there was no visible fourth man to deliver them. Those who have gone before us teach us *there is something more important than life itself—namely, pleasing the Lord.*

We must always remember that all that
really matters is what matters forever.

We must be grateful for organizations such as the Alliance Defending Freedom, committed to fighting for our constitutional freedoms. The most basic principle of biblical justice is equality under the law, but this must be balanced with the freedom for us to practice religion. We must always remember that all that really matters is what matters forever.

THE COMING OF THE TWO LAWGIVERS

This world still has two coming lawgivers who will insist that their word be followed, and for those who disobey, there will be consequences.

Both will take it upon themselves to enact laws.

The first is the Antichrist, who, for a brief while, will rule the world.

> Let no one deceive you in any way. For that day will not come, unless the rebellion comes first, and the man of lawlessness is revealed, the son of destruction, who opposes and exalts himself against every so-called god or object of worship, so that he takes his seat in the temple of God, proclaiming himself to be God (2 Thessalonians 2:3-4).

By calling him "the man of lawlessness," Paul meant that the Antichrist would not be subject to any laws, but will invent many new laws for others to follow. "He shall speak words against the Most High, and shall wear out the saints of the Most High, and shall think to *change the times and the law*" (Daniel 7:25, emphasis added). Antichrist's weapon will be laws that force compliance at the pain of death.

Worldwide government, religion, and economics will finally be united in one person. There will be laws about worship (all must worship him or be killed). There will be laws about buying and selling (all must take his mark or starve to death), and objectors will be killed with the sword. And there will be laws about political agreement (no rivals allowed).

But there is another lawgiver who will return to Earth. "Out of Zion shall go forth the law, and the word of the LORD from Jerusalem. He shall judge between the nations, and shall decide disputes for many peoples" (Isaiah 2:3-4). And later we read, "Of the increase of his government and of peace there will be no end, on the throne of David and over his kingdom, to establish it and to *uphold it with justice and with righteousness* from this time forth and forevermore. The zeal of the LORD of hosts will do this" (Isaiah 9:7, emphasis added).

This Divine Lawgiver will rule with impeccable justice, and He will rule forever.*

OUR DECLARATION OF DEPENDENCE

Herrmann Göring, Hitler's designated successor, is widely quoted as having said that people can be easily controlled—"If you find something to scare them, you can make them do anything you want."[27]

Fear is used today to compel us to bow to devious cultural norms. But the early church experienced vicious legal persecution in all the territories ruled by Rome. Countless Christians, unwilling

---

* Portions of this chapter were excerpted from Erwin W. Lutzer, *Exploding the Myths That Could Destroy America* (Chicago, IL: Moody Publishers, 1986), 61-78. Used by permission of Moody Publishers.

to yield to Caesar, were put to death. Peter, who himself would die as a martyr, wrote to these scattered, beleaguered Christians and encouraged them to not yield to threats but to hold fast to promises from God:

> Beloved, do not be surprised at the fiery trial when it comes upon you to test you, as though something strange were happening to you. But rejoice insofar as you share Christ's sufferings, that you may also rejoice and be glad when his glory is revealed. If you are insulted for the name of Christ, you are blessed, because the Spirit of glory and of God rests upon you...Yet if anyone suffers as a Christian, let him not be ashamed, but let him glorify God in that name...Therefore let those who suffer according to God's will entrust their souls to a faithful Creator while doing good" (1 Peter 4:12-14, 16, 19).

Earth's viewpoint counts for little; heaven's viewpoint counts for much. Let us ask the Lord for grace to do what is right and gladly accept the consequences.

ACTION STEP

Churches, Christian schools, and even Christian charitable ministries are under attack by those who hope to use laws to stifle our witness. It is our duty and privilege to search out ministries and identify attorneys who are worthy of our financial contributions and our prayers as they fight to maintain our constitutional freedoms. And let all of us defend parental rights by whatever reasonable means we have at our disposal. Above all, we must cry up to God for the courage to do and support what is right, no matter the laws of the land.

"Show me your laws, and I will show you your God!"

CHAPTER 11

Returning to the God of Wrath and Grace, Not Unconditional Love

Sinners in the Hands of an Angry God,
or God in the Hands of Angry Sinners?

Ask any Christian if they would like to see a genuine revival in America—a time of national repentance and a return to God—and they would almost certainly say, "Yes!" Indeed, many of us are praying for just that.

But what they might not know is that revival is difficult. Repentance—a deep travail of soul—is difficult because it exacts a price. Issues of reconciliation and restitution are often humiliating and costly. Cheaters have to confess their cheating and betrayers have to confess their betrayal. Brokenness and humility before God are the fruit of deep and true repentance.

Johnathan Edwards believed that for revival to take place—an outpouring of God's blessing—we need to have a right view of God. God's undeserved grace must be seen against the background of His holiness and hatred for sin.

Let me ask a question.

How many times have you heard that God loves everyone unconditionally? That is not found anywhere in Scripture. Yes, God loved the world and sent His Son to redeem us, but this love was, by no means, unconditional, which, in the minds of moderns, means "Since He loves me unconditionally, He accepts me and my behavior unconditionally."

Let's not overlook other passages of Scripture: "God is a righteous judge, and a God who feels indignation ['anger with the wicked,' KJV] every day" (Psalm 7:11). And again, "If a man does not repent, God will whet his sword; he has bent and readied his bow; he has prepared for him his deadly weapons, making his arrows fiery shafts" (verses 12-13).

Read the following verses, and even if you think the words are only symbolic, ask yourself: Does this sound like unconditional love? "Behold, the name of the LORD comes from afar, burning with his anger, and in thick rising smoke; his lips are full of fury, and his tongue is like a devouring fire; his breath is like an overflowing stream that reaches up to the neck; to sift the nations with the sieve of destruction, and to place on the jaws of the peoples a bridle that leads astray" (Isaiah 30:27-28).

And, if you are still not convinced, "The LORD tests the righteous, but his soul hates the wicked and the one who loves violence" (Psalm 11:5). The idea that God loves everyone unconditionally is simply a concession to the culture that has opted for a more tolerant, inclusive, and socialized deity who treats everyone the same.

The purpose of this chapter? To get us to deeply appreciate the radical blessing of God's grace. But we cannot do so unless we see it against the background of God's wrath and eternal hell. It is the wrath of God that causes us to worship the "God of all grace" with a deeper sincerity and devotion.

Without Christ, we are far worse off than
we can possibly realize; with Him we are
more blessed than we can imagine.

To begin: Our understanding of human nature will determine our understanding of the gospel of grace. If we don't know how far humanity has fallen into sin, we will not know the pit from which God redeems us—and we will not be as astounded that He invites us to rule with Him eternally on His throne. Without Christ, we are far worse off than we can possibly realize; with Him we are more blessed than we can imagine.

WHEN HUMAN NATURE IS UNRESTRAINED

"If God is dead, then everything is permissible."[1]

I have quoted that paraphrase of Fyodor Dostoevsky a few times in this book, and it can be proven true. Without God, there is no reason to set boundaries, to be rational, or to cultivate civility. To quote Dostoevsky again, "Indeed, people speak sometimes about the 'animal' cruelty of man, but that is terribly unjust and offensive to animals, no animal could ever be so cruel as a man, so artfully, so artistically cruel."[2]

What an indictment of humanity! Think of the deliberate torture of millions in the gulag; think of the genocide of the Armenians; think of the tortures the Nazis inflicted on the Jews. No animal, no matter how vicious, has such an appetite for wanton cruelty. And given humanity's superior intellect, combined with the ability to create weapons and modern technology, the evils multiply.

The reprobate mind is a mind out of control—it defies reason, logic, and common sense.

So, let me ask: Is it inhuman to drug children and sell them into sexual slavery? Is it inhuman to force parents to watch as their children are tortured to death? Is it inhuman to commit rape, incest, and mass killings? If you think doing such is inhuman, you might have to revise your opinion of human nature because these evils and others like them are being committed by human beings even as you read this. Clay Jones, a visiting scholar for the Christian apologetics MA program at a major seminary, has studied the atrocities people have committed around the world. He wrote, "I realized that horrendous evils weren't the doings of a few deranged individuals or even hundreds of thousands but were done by humankind *en masse*."[3]

Eva Braun, Hitler's mistress, enjoyed making home movies. When the films were discovered, some people wanted them destroyed because they portrayed Hitler as a human being, playing with children, petting his dog, and entertaining his friends. They wanted people to think of der Führer as a man with horns, a man in a category of evil all by himself. But alas, he was a part of the human race, with a nature just like ours.

Aleksandr Solzhenitsyn, who suffered eight years in a Soviet gulag, asks: "Where did this wolf-tribe [officials who torture and kill] appear from among our people? Does it really stem from our own roots? Our own blood? It is our own. And just so we don't go around flaunting too proudly the white mantle of the just, let everyone ask himself: 'If my life had turned out differently, might I myself not have become just such an executioner?' "[4] It is a dreadful question if one answers it honestly.

To quote Solzhenitsyn, once more, he said that every evil committed in the twentieth century could be committed in any century. Why? Men have forgotten God.[5] We should be deeply grieved because of the evil in the human heart, but we should not be surprised. The biblical diagnosis is correct: "The heart is deceitful above all things, and desperately wicked: who can know it?" (Jeremiah 17:9).

In Cologne, Germany, there is a Documentation Center that has won many awards for exposing the evils of Nazism with numerous exhibits, a research library, and even displays of torture chambers. Mirrors are strategically placed in various rooms and hallways so that when you look up, you see yourself. It forces you to ask: Could I have done this?

The answer is *yes*, we most likely could have done this. Given a different time, the hypnotic effect of a national ideology, the deadening of emotions by the power of herd instinct, and the widespread notion that we have no accountability to God for our actions, we all could have done this. Thankfully, God often restrains evil by what theologians call *common grace*, that is there is a common shared humanity blessed by God (Matthew 5:45; Luke 6:35). But when God-given institutions such as the family, the church, and human government break down, anarchy reigns. And people will do in a mob what they almost certainly would not do individually.

To be clear, we have the capacity to do evil, but as humans created in the image of God, we also have the capacity to do good. We are grateful that not all human beings are as evil as they could be; in fact, human beings sometimes astound us with their goodness, their generosity, and their sacrifice for others. For example, in my community in the Chicago area, most people are decent, reliable, and we are surrounded by good neighbors. But because we are also deeply fallen, we also have the capacity to commit unthinkable evils.

. . . .

Great sin can be met with great grace.

. . . .

But without a belief in God and the subsequent breakdown of cultural deterrents, all that we are left with is insatiable appetites gone wild. Whatever an evil mind can envision, it can do. And yet—and yet—for the greatest of sinners, there is hope.

Great sin can be met with great grace.

CONTINUING WITH A DEEP DIVE INTO THE HUMAN HEART

For the most part, our therapeutic culture believes that no one is bad; it is just that they have bad thoughts about themselves. So, with proper counseling and by enhancing one's self-esteem, the individual is able to remake themselves, wash away their own guilt, and begin anew. In varying degrees, this is the default position of the human heart. Just try to find someone who confesses to being bad; everyone sees themselves as basically good, with just some lapses of bad judgment.

The Bible begs to differ with our optimistic view of human nature. You have probably read this passage before, but read it again with a pencil in hand. You might want to underline some of its phrases, such as "God gave them up," or "they exchanged." We are going to take some time to unpack this text and find out its implications for all of us. It begins by explaining that the wrath of God is directed toward the whole human race. The bad news comes before the good news:

> For the wrath of God is revealed from heaven against all ungodliness and unrighteousness of men, who by their unrighteousness suppress the truth. For what can be known about God is plain to them, because God has shown it to them. For his invisible attributes, namely,

his eternal power and divine nature, have been clearly perceived, ever since the creation of the world, in the things that have been made. So they are without excuse. For although they knew God, they did not honor him as God or give thanks to him, but they became futile in their thinking, and their foolish hearts were darkened. Claiming to be wise, they became fools, and exchanged the glory of the immortal God for images resembling mortal man and birds and animals and creeping things.

Therefore *God gave them up* in the lusts of their hearts to impurity, to the dishonoring of their bodies among themselves, because they exchanged the truth about God for a lie and worshiped and served the creature rather than the Creator, who is blessed forever! Amen.

For this reason *God gave them up* to dishonorable passions. For their women exchanged natural relations for those that are contrary to nature; and the men likewise gave up natural relations with women and were consumed with passion for one another, men committing shameless acts with men and receiving in themselves the due penalty for their error.

And since they did not see fit to acknowledge God, *God gave them up* to a debased mind to do what ought not to be done. They were filled with all manner of unrighteousness, evil, covetousness, malice. They are full of envy, murder, strife, deceit, maliciousness. They are gossips, slanderers, haters of God, insolent, haughty, boastful, inventors of evil, disobedient to parents, foolish, faithless, heartless, ruthless. Though they know God's righteous decree that those who practice such things deserve to die, they not only do them but give approval to those who practice them (Romans 1:18-32, emphasis added).

In a sermon, Dr. S. Lewis Johnson made reference to a minister, Walter Luthi, preaching to his Sunday congregation in Bern, Switzerland, in the Reformed cathedral. He said, "In the words that we have just read [Romans 1:18-32] we are told the whole truth about our condition. There may well be people among us who cannot bear to hear the truth and would like to creep quietly away out of this church. Let them do so if they wish."[6]

So, if you wish, you can put this book down because as we delve into Romans 1, the truth about ourselves might be just a tad much for you to accept. On the other hand, you might want to keep reading and enhance your understanding of our present condition and emerge with praise for the wonder of the grace of the gospel.

S. Lewis Johnson, goes on to describe the depravity of mankind with these words:

> [Romans 1 is] Paul's canvas upon which he has painted his picture—dark, foreboding, threatening, flashing with lightning and crashing with thunder—is crammed with forms and figures, fights and shadows, of sin, wrath, and judgment. And the revelation of wrath is total and complete, encompassing all and rendering all without excuse and under condemnation, both individually and collectively.[7]

Like a patient who doesn't want to hear the doctor tell him he has cancer, the truth we learn about ourselves will not be pleasant. But for many, it will lead to forgiveness and a new sense of freedom and a proper sense of self-worth. Grace will finally be understood to be truly amazing.

So the diagnosis must precede the cure.

Paul begins this passage, "For the wrath of God is revealed from heaven against all ungodliness." You often hear it said—and I'm sure I've said it myself—that we as a nation are going to be judged for our sins. And that is true, of course, but what we often fail to say is that the entire human race is already under judgment. This judgment began as far back as the garden of Eden. God's wrath is continuously being revealed throughout human history. Thankfully, those whose faith is in Christ are no longer under that condemnation. But when a nation is judged, God's people suffer in this life along with others.

Is the human race blameless? Paul answers that God's wrath is revealed against "men, who by their unrighteousness suppress the truth." That is readily seen through nature (the wonder of the heavens above) and our consciences. Like a metal detector at an airport, sometimes the conscience is more finely tuned than at other times, but every person has a conscience that says, "You have done wrong." Every one of us has known this indictment; we've all experienced shame, guilt, and regret. In other words, not one of us lives up to what we know to be right. And we all know intuitively that we are accountable to God. Therefore, we are "without excuse."

Yet despite this rudimentary knowledge of God, many harden their conscience and feel no guilt for their sin. Paul says, "They suppress the truth." Thomas Watson, a Puritan writer (1620–1686), spoke of those who have their conscience so impervious to their sins and crimes, "They are like the blacksmith's dog that can lie and sleep near the anvil when all the sparks fly about."[8]

And now, instead of *progress*, we have *regress*; instead of upward advancement, we have a downward slide. Imagine a stairway leading downward to a basement called perversity. Step number one, they did not honor God or give Him glory; rather, they showed their disdain for Him through ingratitude (verse 21a). Step number two, they chose darkness over light (verse 21b). Step number three, they chose foolishness over wisdom. And finally, on the last step, they worshipped the creature, not the creator (verse 25).

Paul said, "They…worshiped and served the creature rather than the Creator." Thus, we return to the issues of radical individualism, self-identity, and rebellion discussed earlier in this book. This self-worship has given this generation the sexual freedom to be and to do whatever they desire. Thus, much of our generation is comfortable with perversity. Sexual anarchy is rampant because self-worship is the most widespread of all the religions of the world. Yet God is not neutral about these developments. He responds.

RETRIBUTIVE JUSTICE: GOD "HANDED THEM OVER"

God takes His holiness and sovereignty seriously.

Three times in Romans 1:18-32, God "gave them up." The Greek phrase here is *paredōken autous*. This is an active verb and means more than God simply withdrawing His hand and letting humanity go its own way. A faithful translation is that "He handed them over." Someone has said the imagery is that "God withdrew His hand and handed them over to be dragged away by a raging river."

God handed these people over to intensified lusts and every kind of sexual perversion. Paul wrote about women having sex with women; he did this because usually we associate same-sex relationships with men, but he wrote *"even their women"* (verse 26 NIV, emphasis added). In other words, lesbianism would not necessarily be expected, but there it is.

> [Pitirim] Sorokin in his *The American Sex Revolution* pointed out that sex anarchy leads to mental breakdowns, rather than the other way around, as the Freudian psychologists have taught…he pointed out that increasing sexual license leads to decreasing creativity and productivity in the intellectual, artistic, and economic spheres of life.[9]

Now comes the bombshell.

I've read this passage many times, but only recently did I note the sequence that appears within. It is not just that the sinfulness of the human race caused God to "give them up," but rather, that *the sexual debauchery is the result of God "handing them over."* Or to put it more clearly: Sexual debauchery is not the reason God handed them over, it is *proof* that He handed them over. People are not merely in danger of judgment; they are already being judged.

Paul ended this "handing them over" by saying that the end result is a "debased mind" (verse 28)—a mind that is not given to rationality, decency, or even the common grace of human reason. Finally, we understand why the culture says men can have babies and women can become fathers. Teenage girls are having their breasts removed and boys are undergoing the horrors of transgender surgery in order to have their genitalia surgically changed so they can resemble a woman.

The reprobate or debased mind has no limits. The mutilation of the human body—even young bodies—is done under the guise of "affirming healthcare." When you see darkness celebrated as light and light condemned as darkness, you can be sure that Satan is hiding behind the curtain calling the plays. When God withdraws Himself, darkness follows.

Despite Paul's strong language, let us never be harsh, angry, nor condemning toward those who struggle with various forms of gender dysphoria. Let us love them even as we warn them, and let us be filled with compassion for them even as we seek to understand them. My limited experience has taught me that those who wrestle with this confusion already feel condemned. Perhaps they were introduced to this lifestyle by predatory individuals, even within their own circle of friends and relatives. Whatever the cause (which, in some instances, cannot be known), we must love with patience and care. In her book *The Secret Thoughts of an Unlikely Convert,* author Rosaria Butterfield shares about how she came out of lesbianism, and says it was the hospitality she experienced from Christians that won her over to the gospel.[10]

Let us repent of the slightest hint of self-righteousness that might arise within us; whether or not we participate in the sins listed so far, every one of us is born under the wrath of God. Only God, in Christ, can rescue us. A finger-pointing self-righteousness has driven many a person deeper into their own struggles and pathologies.

And now, a diagnosis for the so-called "better people" in the human race.

THE INDICTMENT OF THE
WHOLE HUMAN RACE

Yes, all of us are included in the experience of God's wrath and condemnation. Every sin imaginable is now listed. Read this and ask, *How many of these sins have I committed?*

> They were filled with all manner of unrighteousness, evil, covetousness, malice. They are full of envy, murder, strife, deceit, maliciousness. They are gossips, slanderers, haters of God, insolent, haughty, boastful, inventors of

evil, disobedient to parents, foolish, faithless, heartless, ruthless. Though they know God's righteous decree that those who practice such things deserve to die, they not only do them but give approval to those who practice them (Romans 1:29-32).

Paul ended by saying that all sinners want allies; they want people to join them as they confidently march toward destruction. They do evil and "give approval to those who practice them [the sins]." Having been carried along with their sinful desires, they want to recruit as many people as they can to participate in their sin. Children are recruited and groomed for sexual exploitation; young people are recruited to join the sexual revolution. People don't want to march toward hell alone.

In Romans 3, Paul gave an even more chilling description of the human heart. Read it for yourself (verses 9-18). He ended with ominous words that state we are all declared guilty before God, "that every mouth may be stopped, and the whole world may be held accountable to God" (verse 19). Before God, we all stand under the condemnation of His wrath; we are all indicted, guilty as charged.

Standing before God, every mouth is stopped and every person confesses guilt. The radical nature of our sin demands a radical cure. It is not enough that we tell people to "do better" or make promises to change the direction of their lives. They cannot do that on their own; human nature is not able to bring about genuine change except with God's help.

And in case you think you can escape God's judgment because you are better than others, Paul put an end to such a delusion when he said, "All have sinned and fall short of the glory of God" (verse 23). And without Christ, there is no escape from God's wrath. None of us is more deserving of God's grace than another.

God hates sin with a vengeance.

But let us remember, that although we hate the lies of our culture, we should still be compassionate toward those who are deceived by those lies. Love compels us to tell the truth, though we must do so with humility, sensitivity, and care. And thankfully, we have the privilege of pointing everyone to Jesus Christ for forgiveness and hope.

Keep reading.

Centuries ago, there was a theologian who wanted to correct the casual understanding of God that prevailed in his community. He warned a careless generation that an eternal hell existed and would forever be the abode of all who did not come under the protection Christ provided for sinners. What he said was frightening, but judge for yourself whether it was biblical.

This theologian feared the acceptance of two doctrines that destroy the mission of the church: As I mentioned in a previous chapter, those two doctrines are belief in the essential goodness of mankind, and the endless tolerance of God. Today, as in the past, these errors are the default position of the human heart.

This theologian wanted us to see ourselves as God sees us.

SINNERS IN THE HANDS
OF AN ANGRY GOD

I can't say this often enough: By nature we want a tolerant, inclusive, and endlessly gracious God who would never severely judge anyone—a God who is responsive to our needs and will commend us for our effort. We want a God whose holiness is not an offense to our unholiness. A God who grades on the curve and makes allowances for our imperfect performance. We'd love to have a God whom we can approach on our own without a mediator, Christ, and without His sacrifice. We'd love to have a God who gives us an *A* for making an effort to do better.

> Until we see hell as it is, we cannot
> appreciate grace as it is.

As for hell? Hell has been cooled; the flames have been doused, and the very concept is treated like a relic in a musty museum. Universalism—the belief that in the end, everyone will make it to that "blissful shore"—is widely assumed even in evangelical circles. But if we take the subject at face value, as described multiple times in Scripture, we cannot and should not avoid it. *Until we see hell as it is, we cannot appreciate grace as it is.*

The most famous sermon ever preached in America was preached by a theologian named Jonathan Edwards back in 1741: "Sinners in the Hands of an Angry God." A few years ago, my wife, Rebecca, and I visited his church in Northampton, Massachusetts, and discovered that it gives full support to the LGBTQ+ agenda. But to its credit, near the outside entrance, it does have a small plaque referencing this sermon—no doubt an embarrassment to the church leadership but also a cause for celebration that the church has moved beyond such vitriol. The God of Jonathan Edwards, in the minds of many, no longer exists. Today, we could say that God *is in the hands of angry sinners.*

Edwards loved his congregation and felt it was his duty to warn them about what would happen if they did not come to Christ in repentance and faith to receive pardon and protection from the arrows of God's wrath. Love seeks to warn; love seeks the truth; love helps us deal with reality as it is, not as we wish it to be.

Edwards's message is so offensive to modern ears that some seminary professors require their students to read it as an example of how *not* to preach. It is seen as an embarrassing relic of a previous era obsessed with God's holiness and anger toward sinners. This view, we are told, stands in conflict with the unconditional love of God for all people of good will.

Caution: There are some people who do not need this sermon, and that is those who already feel condemned by God. I was speaking to a person who works with Muslims who told me that it is neither necessary nor wise to speak to Muslims about the wrath of God because they were brought up with belief in Allah, who is seen as a vengeful deity who is filled with unpredictable wrath and anger. For them, we can immediately transition to the underserved grace of God.

But Westerners, schooled on notions of an endlessly tolerant God, need to hear Edwards's message. Here is my challenge: I want you to read at least a few paragraphs of his sermon (of course, it would be better to read it in its entirety) and ask yourself: *What did Edwards get wrong? What did he say that is inconsistent with Scripture?* Read these excerpts and ask: *If he is correct, does our view of God need to be changed?*

Read carefully these next few paragraphs:

> There is nothing that keeps wicked men, at any one
> moment, out of hell, but the mere pleasure of God…
> They deserve to be cast into hell; so that divine justice
> never stands in the way, it makes no objection against
> God's using his power at any moment to destroy them…
> Unconverted men walk over the pit of hell on a rotten
> covering, and there are innumerable places in this cover-
> ing so weak that they won't bear their weight, and these
> places are not seen.[11]

...So that thus it is, that natural men are held in the hand of God over the pit of hell; they have deserved the fiery pit, and are already sentenced to it; and God is dreadfully provoked, his anger is as great towards them as to those who are actually [already] suffering the executions of the fierceness of his wrath in hell, and they [those who have not yet fallen into hell] have done nothing in the least to appease or abate that anger, neither is God in the least bound by any promises to hold 'em up one moment...the flames gather and flash about them, and would fain lay hold on them, and swallow them up; the fire pent up in their own hearts is struggling to break out; and they have no interest in any mediator, there are no means within reach that can be any security to them. In short, they have no refuge, nothing to take hold of, all that preserves them every moment is the mere arbitrary will, and uncovenanted unobliged forbearance of an incensed God.[12]

Then near the end of his sermon comes this plea:

And now you have an extraordinary opportunity, a day wherein Christ has flung the door of mercy wide open, and stands in the door calling and crying with a loud voice to poor sinners; a day wherein many are flocking to him, and pressing into the kingdom of God; many are daily coming from the east, west, north and south; many that were very lately in the same miserable condition that you are in, are in now a happy state, with their hearts filled with love to him that has loved them and washed them from their sins in his own blood, and rejoicing in hope of the glory of God.[13]

Time for a deep breath.

Somewhere I saw a sign that read, "If the living knew what the dead now know, the whole world would follow Jesus." Let me tweak that a bit: "If the living knew what the dead now know, the living would rush to Jesus and accept His mercy and grace; they would repent in dust and ashes."

Horace was a Roman poet and playwright who objected to plays that brought a god in to untangle the plot too quickly. He said, "Do not bring a god onto the stage unless the problem is one that deserves a god to solve it."[14] The Bible teaches that our sin runs so deep, our self-deception is so well protected, and our minds are so quick to rationalize our sin that only God has an answer to our predicament.

Thankfully, the God whom we have offended has a cure for the vilest human being, which means He has a cure for us all. The God who demands righteousness also supplies what He demands. His holiness is His standard—a standard we cannot meet—so He meets that standard on behalf of all who repent and believe.

AMAZING GRACE THAT SAVED A WRETCH LIKE ME

Only when sin is bitter does grace become truly sweet.

The same book of the New Testament that spends so much time exposing our sin now urges us to receive God's grace. "We are justified by his grace as a gift through the redemption that is in Christ Jesus, whom God put forward as a propitiation by his blood to be received by faith" (Romans 3:25). That word "propitiation" means that Christ's death turns away God's wrath for all who believe on Christ.

Who is qualified to turn God's wrath away? Only He Himself can do so, through the work of Christ. So Christ became the propitiation for sin—that is, He diverted the wrath of God to Himself so that we could be forgiven. God demanded a sufficient sacrifice, and God Himself, through Christ, supplied what He demanded. Yes, some other religions also require a blood sacrifice, but only in Christianity does God become the sacrifice. "God was in Christ, reconciling the world unto himself" (2 Corinthians 5:19).

Undeserved Grace

To rescue us, God didn't just throw us a life preserver; Jesus got into the murky water of this world to scoop us to safety. Only He could rescue us from the dark rebellion of our own hearts. Let us never move from "I appreciate grace" to "I deserve grace."

If we deserved grace, it would not be grace.

How far does God's grace extend? To the vilest of sinners, to criminals of every stripe. To evil Nazis? Yes, to evil Nazis. That's what I learned from the book *Mission at Nuremberg* by Tim Townsend. It is the story of a devout Christian chaplain, Henry Gerecke, who was sent to Nuremberg to represent the Allies as a spiritual advisor to the 21 war criminals held at Nuremberg, Germany, in 1945 (15 were Protestant, 6 were Catholic). Gerecke invited them to religious services and most came; some did not. He spent time with them, sharing the gospel, and refused to give them communion unless they repented and believed the gospel. He thinks that five did so, perhaps as many as seven.

I give but one example:

Joachim von Ribbentrop was Hitler's foreign affairs minister, found guilty of war crimes and the first to be hung at Nuremberg in 1946. Thanks to Gerecke's witness, God overcame this criminal's hard heart. Before his death, he affirmed, "I put all my trust in the blood of the Lamb, that taketh away the sins of the world." He asked that God would have mercy on his soul. Then, taken to the trap door to be hung, his last words to the chaplain were, "I'll see you again."[15]

Of course, we don't know the real state of Ribbentrop's heart because words can be cheap; God alone is judge. But do you recoil at the idea that someone who had done such evils would be in heaven? God says, in effect, "What Jesus did in His death and resurrection is so complete, so sufficient that I can forgive a Nazi if he repents and believes on My Son, but I cannot forgive an upstanding, decent, and kind person who does not believe on My Son!"

. . . .

There is more grace in God's heart
than sin in your past.

. . . .

Hell can be avoided and heaven gained; the wrath of God need not terrify us if we understand His provision and come under the protection of Christ, for "where sin increased, grace abounded all the more" (Romans 5:20). There is more grace in God's heart than sin in your past.

Jesus "delivers us from the wrath to come" (1 Thessalonians 1:10).

Unconditional Love

And finally, yes, we are introduced to unconditional love! Those who belong to Christ are loved by God even as Jesus Himself is loved by God, completely and eternally. Jesus prayed, "The glory that you have given me I have given to them, that they may be one even as we are one, I in them and you in me, that they may become perfectly one, so the world may know that you sent me and loved them even as you have loved me…because you loved me from before the foundation of the world" (carefully read all of John 17:22-28).

For those who belong to Christ, nothing they do will cause God to love them less, or to love them more. They are loved because of Christ—*in* Christ, I repeat, they are loved unconditionally and loved eternally!

The following words were written by a pastor who was blind, who went through a period of doubt about God's goodness but returned to fellowship with God:

> O Love that will not let me go,
> I rest my weary soul in thee.
> I give thee back the life I owe,
> that in thine ocean depths its flow
> May richer, fuller be.[16]

Love beyond all measure, given to all who believe on Christ.

WHAT ABOUT THOSE WHO HAVE NOT HEARD THE GOSPEL?

The subject of the justice of God in condemning sinners who did not have the privilege of hearing the gospel deserves a much longer discussion than I can give here. But briefly, there is scriptural evidence that all children of all religious or nonreligious backgrounds who die will be in heaven. Second, we must realize that responsibility is based on knowledge (Luke 12:47-48; Romans 2:12, 14-15). Everyone will be judged by the light that was available to them, not the light that was unavailable. Third, those who seek the true God will find Him (Jeremiah 29:13). Finally, the general revelation that all people receive through the light of nature and conscience will be the basis of judgment, even though there is no evidence in Scripture that it will be a basis for salvation.

Be assured that God's punishments will be proportionately administered. As I mentioned in chapter 5, only once did God punish an innocent human being—He punished Christ on our behalf and "laid on him the iniquity of us all" (Isaiah 53:6).

As we consider similar mysteries that are beyond our understanding, we are driven back to the New Testament, where Paul said,

> Is there injustice on God's part? By no means…But who are you O man, to answer back to God? Will that which is molded say to its molder, "Why have you made me like this?" Has the potter no right over the clay to make out of the same lump one vessel for honorable use and another for dishonorable use? (read all of Romans 9:14-25).

The bottom line: We do not need to understand the details of how God judges sinners in order to know that for all of eternity the redeemed will sing, "Great and amazing are your deeds, O Lord God the Almighty! *Just and true are your ways, O King of the nations!*" (Revelation 15:3, emphasis added).

The God of the universe will deal justly.

OUR DECLARATION OF DEPENDENCE

I conclude this chapter with a plea to you, the reader, because apart from Christ, you will definitely be without excuse. I ask: Do you have the assurance that your faith is in Christ alone? Jesus spoke with utmost clarity: "Whoever believes in the Son has eternal life; whoever does not obey the Son shall not see life, *but the wrath of God remains on him*" (John 3:36, emphasis added).

The words of this prayer alone will not save you; *Christ* saves you. But if this prayer expresses the desire of your heart, it will be the means God will use to transfer your trust to Christ, and you will be saved.

Pray:

> O God, I know that I am a sinner under judgment, but at this moment I turn from my sin to Christ, receiving His acceptance, mercy, and grace. Take from me my burden of sin and give me the assurance that You have received me. Thank You for Your assurance that "to all who did receive him, who believed in his name, he gave the right to become children of God" (John 1:12).

I end this chapter with two stanzas and the chorus of one of my favorite hymns:

> Marvelous grace of our loving Lord,
> Grace that exceeds our sin and our guilt!
> Yonder on Calvary's mount out-poured—
> There where the blood of the Lamb was spilt.

> Dark is the stain that we cannot hide;
> What can we do to wash it away?
> Look! There is flowing a crimson tide,
> Brighter than snow you may be today.

> Grace, grace, God's grace
> Grace that will pardon and cleanse within;
> Grace, grace, God's grace,
> Grace that is greater than all our sin!

> Oh, the depth of the riches and wisdom and knowledge of God! How unsearchable are his judgments and how inscrutable his ways!

"For who has known the mind of the Lord,
or who has been his counselor?"
"Or who has given a gift to him
that he might be repaid?"

For from him and through him and to him are all things.
To him be glory forever. Amen (Romans 11:33-36).

Let us walk in the light and not let darkness overtake us.

ACTION STEP

Let us remember that the unrepentant have no idea of the danger they are in. Let us all be a witness to others of the grace of God, and the danger that awaits those who "neglect so great salvation" (Hebrews 2:3 KJV). Invite neighbors for lunch or dinner to personally share your testimony and why you believe it is urgent for them to transfer their trust to Christ alone both for now and their eternal future.

Shine the light without rancor, without judgmentalism and without manipulation. Let us be as approachable as Christ in a world that is terribly dark and terribly lost.

Determine that, as much as possible, your words and actions will shine as light to all who are around you, and help people to see God for who He really is, and not what the world has made Him to be.

A Glorious Darkness

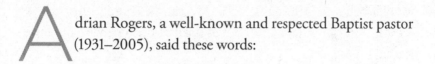drian Rogers, a well-known and respected Baptist pastor (1931–2005), said these words:

> We're living in strange days, are we not? When I see what's happening to this world, if I didn't know the Lord Jesus Christ, I'm not sure what I would do. Yet, knowing the Bible and Bible prophecy, when I see all these things coming to pass, they do not shake me. Sometimes they grieve me, sometimes they sadden me, but they do not shake me. That's because I know God's Word. I know they're a fulfillment of prophecy. I can say with all the saints, "Praise God, it's getting gloriously dark."[1]

It's getting *gloriously dark*!

Moral and spiritual darkness have bedeviled this world since the fall of man in Eden. And amid the darkness, God has always raised up a remnant—that is, a group of people who are distinctly His, shining light into the darkness. Those who can see God despite the darkness will understand what it means to say it is gloriously dark.

If we can stay focused on Christ in the darkness, we will gladly redouble our efforts to shine the light of the gospel as far and wide as possible. We know that darkness never retreats on its own; only light can push back the darkness. We will serve the Lord with joy, despite the cultural headwinds, and we will not see ourselves as *victims*, but *victors*.

Someone has said that we are like a tourist arriving in a strange country in which people speak a language we do not understand and the culture is being destroyed. But we stand at the curb, offering hope to all who pass by even as we wait, knowing that someone has promised to pick us up. "Now is our salvation nearer than when we first believed" (Romans 13:11). We can be courageous because our hope is in another world. But as the darkness deepens, our faith is tested.

One man who was baffled by God's lack of attention to the darkness of his world was the prophet Habakkuk, who lived back in the seventh century BC. He complained to God because He was silent in the face of growing violence, cruelty, and injustice. As if living in our day, Habakkuk wrote, "The law is paralyzed, and justice never goes forth. For the wicked surround the righteous; so justice goes forth perverted" (1:4).

God surprised the prophet by telling him that *yes*, He was actually doing something about it: He was raising up the Babylonian Empire to come and crush the small Israelite nation. This enemy would swoop down from the north, whose armies were "guilty men, whose own might is their god" (verse 11). The prophet thought things were bad, and God warned him that when this evil army arrived, things would get a lot worse.

Habakkuk complained about this, just like we might do. But then as God reminded the prophet of His faithfulness to His people, the prophet changed his point of view: He admitted his fear, but also chose to rejoice despite the horror that awaited the nation. Of his fears, he said,

> I hear, and my body trembles;
> my lips quiver at the sound;
> rottenness enters into my bones;
> my legs tremble beneath me.
> Yet I will quietly wait for the day of trouble
> to come upon people who invade us
> (Habakkuk 3:16).

Then upon remembering the faithfulness of God, Habakkuk burst out in a song of praise and gratitude. Read carefully, keeping in mind that he lived in an agrarian culture. He said what he would do if his livelihood was destroyed:

> Though the fig tree should not blossom,
> nor fruit be on the vines,
> the produce of the olive fail
> and the fields yield no food,
> the flock be cut off from the fold
> and there be no herd in the stalls,
> yet I will rejoice in the LORD;
> I will take joy in the God of my salvation.
> God, the LORD, is my strength;
> he makes my feet like the deer's;
> he makes me tread on my high places (verses 17-19).

Habakkuk was a lone voice, but a voice testifying to both coming judgment and the joy awaiting those whose hope was entirely in God. He proved you don't need to be part of a majority to be faithful. He taught us that we can live with imminent danger and still rejoice in God.

Let's jump over to the New Testament and remind ourselves that there is not so much as a single prayer offered by Paul that asked God for a change of circumstances. Rather, Paul's prayers asked for grace and strength to be a faithful witness *within* his circumstances. Many centuries later, Martin Luther, in the darkness of his world, would write:

> And though this world, with devils filled,
>   should threaten to undo us,
> we will not fear, for God has willed
>   his truth to triumph through us.
> The prince of darkness grim,
>   we tremble not for him;
> his rage we can endure,
>   for lo! his doom is sure;
>   one little word shall fell him.[2]

That one little word has six letters: C-H-R-I-S-T.

Jesus said to His small army of disciples, "You are the light of the world. A city set on a hill cannot be hidden" (Matthew 5:14). Christ's call that we "let [our] light shine" (verse 16) even amid hostile cultural winds means we will have the opportunity to guide many who are seeking hope to find shelter in Him alone. The darker the night, the more necessary every single light becomes.

        · · · · · · · · · · ·

The darker the night, the more necessary
every single light becomes.

        · · · · · · · · · · ·

As I have said repeatedly in this book, we are called to expose the lies of today's culture even as we have compassion on those who are deceived by these lies. In this book, we have exposed much of the darkness. Now let us gaze on the Light. With Him on our side, we can face the future with confidence and joy.

On the other side of the eclipse, the sun shines just as brightly. Glorious darkness!

Soli Deo gloria!

ACTION STEP

What is the overarching lesson God has taught you as you have rethought your view of Him and the collapsing culture around us? Ask God to imprint those lessons on your soul, and seek wisdom to act on them.

Notes

INTRODUCTION: FROM MY HEART TO YOURS

1. The expression "three dollars worth of God" comes from the title of a book by Wilbur Rees—*$3.00 Worth of God* (King of Prussia, PA: Judson Press, 1971).

CHAPTER 1—LIFE IN THE SHADOWS: THE ECLIPSE OF GOD

1. C.S. Lewis, *The Weight of Glory: And Other Addresses* (San Francisco, CA: HarperOne, 2001), 140.

2. TimCast News (@TimcastNews), "NYC Drag Marchers chant 'we're here, we're queer, we're coming for your children,'" Twitter, June 23, 2023, https://twitter.com/TimcastNews/status/1672410287251529735.

3. Matt Walsh, "Activists & Celebrities Openly Admit They're Coming For Our Kids," *The Matt Walsh Report*, archived email from May 13, 2023, https://rec.arts.tv.narkive.com/mwP9XPXy/activists-celebrities-openly-admit-they-re-coming-for-our-kids.

4. Mirjam Heine, "Why Our Perception of Pedophilia Has To Change" TEDx Event, University of Würzburg, 2018, https://archive.org/details/TEDxMirjamHeineWhyOurPerceptionOfPedophiliaHasToChange.

5. Os Guinness, *A Free People's Suicide* (Downers Grove, IL: InterVarsity, 2012), 99.

6. Theodore Beza, as quoted in Stephen Abel Laval, *A Compendious History of the Reformation in France: And of the Reformed Churches in that Kingdom, Vol. 2* (London: H. Woodfall, 1738), 33-34.

7. A.W. Tozer, *The Attributes of God, Vol. 2* (Camp Hill, PA: WingSpread Publishers, 2007), 59.

8. Dennis Peacocke, as quoted by David Lane, "We've boarded the wrong train...," *American Renewal Project*, November 21, 2023, https://myemail.constantcontact.com/We-ve-boarded-the-wrong-train—.html?soid=1106253726374&aid=I4BYFyW6S-s.

9. Apollon Maykov, a nineteenth-century Russian poet, from an untitled poem dated 1878.

10. William Booth, as quoted in "William Booth's army of blood and fire," *New Life Publishing*, https://www.newlifepublishing.co.uk/articles/william-booths-army-of-blood-and-fire/.

11. John Piper, "What Does It Mean to Seek the Lord?," *desiringGod*, August 19, 2009, https://www.desiringgod.org/articles/what-does-it-mean-to-seek-the-lord.

CHAPTER 2—THREE GRAVEDIGGERS
WHO PREPARED A COFFIN FOR GOD

1. Stephen R.C. Hicks, *Nietzsche and the Nazis: A Personal View* (Loves Park, IL: Ockham's Razor Publishing, 2010), 51.

2. Friedrich Nietzsche, "The Madman," a section of *Gay Science* in Walter Kaufmann, ed., *The Portable Nietzsche* (New York: Viking, 1954), 125.

3. As quoted by David McLellan, *Karl Marx: His Life and Thought* (London: The Macmillan Press LTD, 1973), 22.

4. Leslie Houlden, gen. ed., *Jesus in History, Legend, Scripture, and Tradition: A World Encyclopedia, Vol. 1* (Santa Barbara, CA: ABC-CLIO, 2015), 357.

5. Karl Marx, *The Communist Manifesto,* Gateway Edition (Chicago, IL: Henry Regnery, 1954), 56-57.

6. Marx, *The Communist Manifesto*, 81-82.

7. Dave Breese, *Seven Men Who Rule the World from the Grave* (Chicago, IL: Moody Press, 1990), 60.

8. Breese, *Seven Men Who Rule the World from the Grave*, 71.

9. Aleksandr Solzhenitsyn, "Men Have Forgotten God: Remembering Solzhenitsyn's profound speech on the centenary of his birth," *National Review*, December 11, 2018, https://www.nationalreview.com/2018/12/aleksandr-solzhenitsyn-men-have-forgotten-god-speech/.

10. Karl Marx, "On the Jewish Question," 1844, https://www.marxists.org/archive/marx/works/download/pdf/On%20The%20Jewish%20Question.pdf.

11. Ida Auken, "Welcome to 2030. I own nothing, have no privacy, and life has never been better," *World Economic Forum*, November 12, 2016, https://medium.com/world-economic-forum/welcome-to-2030-i-own-nothing-have-no-privacy-and-life-has-never-been-better-ee2eed62f710.

12. Klaus Schwab and Thierry Malleret, *COVID-19: The Great Reset* (Geneva: Forum Publishing, 2020); Klaus Schwab, *The Fourth Industrial Revolution* (New York: Currency, 2016); Klaus Schwab and Thierry Malleret, *The Great Narrative* (Geneva: Forum Publishing, 2021).

13. To see the many articles World Economic Forum has written on DEI, go to *World Economic Forum*, and do a search for "Diversity, Equity, Inclusion," https://www.weforum.org/search?query=Diversity,+Equity,%20INclusion. To see a biblical response to DEI written by a Christian apologist, see Neil Shenvi, "DEI Done Right: Disentangling Christian Community from Critical Theory," *Neil Shenvi—Apologetics*, https://shenviapologetics.com/dei-done-right-disentangling-christian-community-from-critical-theory/.

14. Christopher Marty, "Darwin on a Godless Creation: 'It's like confessing to a murder,'" *Scientific American,* February 12, 2009, https://www.scientificamerican.com/article/charles-darwin-confessions/.

15. Charles Darwin, letter to Frederick McDermott, November 24, 1880, "Darwin Correspondence Project," *University of Cambridge*, https://www.darwinproject.ac.uk/letter/?docId=letters/DCP-LETT-12851.xml.

16. Charles Darwin, letter to Nicolai Mengden, June 5, 1879, "Darwin Correspondence Project," *University of Cambridge*, https://www.darwinproject.ac.uk/letter/?docId=letters/DCP-LETT-12088.xml.

17. Nora Barlow, *The Autobiography of Charles Darwin 1809–1882* (London: Collins, 1958), 87.

18. Charles Darwin, *Notebook M,* eds. Paul Barrett and John van Wyhe, 123, http://darwin-online.org.uk/content/frameset?pageseq=2&itemID=CUL-DAR125.-&viewtype=side.

19. Francis Galton, *Inquiries into Human Faculty and Its Development* (London: Macmillan, 1883), 25.

20. Charles Darwin, *The Descent of Man: Selection in Relation to Sex* (New York: D. Appleton, 1878), 2.

21. Darwin, *The Descent of Man: Selection in Relation to Sex*, 5.

22. John Jackson Jr. and Nadine M. Weidman, *Race, Racism, and Science: Social Impact and Interaction* (Santa Barbara, CA: ABC-CLIO, 2004), 71.

23. As quoted in Jerry Bergman, *Hitler and the Nazi Darwinian Worldview* (Kitchener, Ontario: Joshua Press, 2012), 11.

24. Daniel C. Dennett, *Darwin's Dangerous Idea: Evolution and the Meaning of Life* (New York: Simon & Schuster, 1995), 61ff.

25. Carl R. Trueman, *The Rise and Triumph of the Modern Self* (Wheaton, IL: Crossway, 2020), 203.

26. Sigmund Freud, *Civilization and Its Discontents,* trans. James Strachey (New York: W.W. Norton, 1989), 56.

27. Matt Walsh, *What Is a Woman?* (Nashville, TN: DW Books, 2022), 33-35.

28. Quoted in David F. Wells, *God in the Wasteland* (Grand Rapids, MI: Eerdmans, 1994), 88.

29. Howard Hendricks, as cited by Maina Mwaura in *The Influential Mentor* (Chicago, IL: Moody Publishers, 2023), 111.

CHAPTER 3—GOD IS GIVEN A RESPECTFUL BURIAL, BUT HE IS IN ATTENDANCE

1. Friedrich Nietzsche, "Thus Spoke Zarathustra," in *The Portable Nietzsche,* trans. Walter Kaufmann (New York: Penguin, 1976), 124.

2. Friedrich Nietzsche, "The Madman," a section of *Gay Science* in Walter Kaufmann, ed., *The Portable Nietzsche* (New York: Viking, 1954), 125.

3. Stephen R.C. Hicks, *Nietzsche and the Nazis: A Personal View* (Loves Park, IL: Ockham's Razor Publishing, 2010), 53.

4. Hicks, *Nietzsche and the Nazis*, 55.

5. Friedrich Nietzsche, *Basic Writings of Nietzsche*, trans. and ed. Walter Kaufmann (New York: The Modern Library, 2000), 23.

6. Oscar Levy, "Nietzsche to Mussolini," *The New York Times*, August 22, 1943, Section E, Page 8, https://www.nytimes.com/1943/08/22/archives/nietzsche-to-mussolini.html.

7. "Adolf Hitler looks at a bust of Friedrich Nietzsche during a visit at Villa Silberblick in Weimar," *Hitler Archive*, https://www.hitler-archive.com/photo.php?p=mlop7789.

8. See "Adolf Hitler on Cruelty," *Jewish Virtual Library*, https://www.jewishvirtuallibrary.org/adolf-hitler-on-cruelty-1942.

9. Friedrich Schleiermacher, *The Christian Faith* (Edinburgh: T&T Clark, 1928), 17.

10. Roland H. Bainton, *Here I Stand: A Life of Martin Luther* (Nashville, TN: Abingdon Press, 1978), 182.

11. David Schley Schaff, *John Huss: His Life, Teachings and Death After Five Hundred Years* (New York: Charles Scribner's Sons, 1915), 257-258.

12. H. Richard Niebuhr, *The Kingdom of God in America* (Middleton, CT: Wesleyan University Press, 1937), 193.

13. Friedrich Nietzsche, "The Madman," 125.

14. Douglas Murray, *The Strange Death of Europe: Immigration, Identity, Islam* (New York: Bloomsbury, 2027), i.

15. Albert Mohler, "Now They Are Taking Names: The Oxford Safe Churches Project Releases Report Rating Churches on LGBTQ Acceptance, Parts 1 and 2, *The Briefing*, September 27, 2023, https://albertmohler.com/2023/09/27/briefing-9-27-23.

16. K.V. Turley, "G.K. Chesterton Was Right: The Church Will Rise Anew," *The National Catholic Register*, August 29, 2018, https://www.ncregister.com/blog/g-k-chesterton-was-right-the-church-will-rise-anew.

17. Turley, "G.K. Chesteron Was Right."

18. Dietrich Bonhoeffer, *The Cost of Discipleship* (London: SCM Press, 2015), 44.

CHAPTER 4—"NEARER MY GOD TO ME"

1. Catherine Nixey, "The Church of England's God is becoming more liberal," *The Economist*, November 8, 2021, https://www.economist.com/the-world-ahead/2021/11/08/the-church-of-englands-god-is-becoming-more-liberal.

2. Nicola Heath, "If God is neither male nor female, should we change God's pronouns?," *ABC News (Australia)*, May 7, 2022, https://www.abc.net.au/news/2022-05-08/should-we-change-gods-pronouns-in-the-bible-liturgy/101024214. See also Albert Mohler, "'Feminism Cannot Be Done from the Existing Base of the Christian Bible': The Background to Feminist Reconsiderations of Terms Used for God," *The Briefing*, February 20, 2023, https://albertmohler.com/2023/02/20/briefing-2-20-23.

3. Bill Chappell, "Gender-neutral terms for God are up for discussion, the Church of England says," *NPR*, February 10, 2023, https://www.npr.org/2023/02/10/1155792333/god-gender-pronouns-church-of-england.

4. Amanda Holpuch, "Church of England Considers Gender-Neutral Language for God," *The New York Times*, February 2, 2023, https://www.nytimes.com/2023/02/09/world/europe/england-church-gender-neutral-god.html.

5. Jon Brown, "Cambridge dean defends sermon about Jesus' 'trans body,' 'vaginal' side wound blasted as 'heresy,'" *Fox News*, November 27, 2022, https://www.foxnews.com/world/cambridge-dean-defends-sermon-jesus-trans-body-vaginal-side-wound-new-heresy-age.

6. Albert Mohler, "God Gets to Name Himself: Why We Must Never Tamper with God's Self-Revelation," *The Briefing*, February 20, 2023, https://albertmohler.com/2023/02/20/briefing-2-20-23.

7. C.S. Lewis, *The Screwtape Letters* (New York: Macmillan, 1943), 39.

8. Thomas Paine, *The Age of Reason* (New York: D.M. Bennett: Liberal and Scientific Publishing House, 1877), 6.

9. Neale Donald Walsch, *The Complete Conversations with God* (New York: G.P. Putman's Sons, 2005), 21.

10. Walsch, *The Complete Conversations with God*, 17.

11. Walsch, *The Complete Conversations with God*, 142.

12. Neale Donald Walsch, *Conversations with God for Teens* (Charlottesville, VA: Hampton Roads, 2012).

13. Sigmund Freud, *Civilization and Its Discontents*, trans. James Strachey (New York: W.W. Norton, 1989), 56.

14. Carl R. Trueman, *The Rise and Triumph of the Modern Self* (Wheaton, IL: Crossway, 2020), 206.

15. Nadia Bolz-Weber, *Shameless: A Sexual Reformation* (New York: Convergent Books, 2019), 60.

16. Donald W. McCullough, *The Trivialization of God* (Colorado Springs, CO: NavPress, 1995), 13-14.

17. C.S. Lewis, *Miracles* (New York: Macmillan, 1960), 93.

18. John Stott, *The Cross of Christ* (Downers Grove, IL: InterVarsity Press, 1986), 335-336.

CHAPTER 5—SHOULD WE STILL BE WORSHIPPING THE "SMITEY ALMIGHTY" OF THE OLD TESTAMENT?

1. Catherine Nixey, "The Church of England's God is becoming more liberal," *The Economist*, November 8, 2021, https://www.economist.com/the-world-ahead/2021/11/08/the-church-of-englands-god-is-becoming-more-liberal.

2. Richard Dawkins, *The God Delusion* (Boston, MA: Houghton Mifflin, 2006), 51.

3. Gregory Boyd, *Crucifixion of the Warrior God, Vols. 1 and 2* (Minneapolis, MN: Fortress, 2017), 493.

4. Paul Copan, *Is God a Vindictive Bully?* (Grand Rapids, MI: Baker Academic, 2022), 4.

5. Boyd, *Crucifixion of the Warrior God, Vol. 2*, 926.

6. For further reading on this topic, I recommend Jeremiah J. Johnston's 2017 book *Unimaginable: What Our World Would Be Like Without Christianity*. This scholarly book details how Christianity elevated culture, including what the world was like before and after Christ's influence.

7. Gregory Boyd, *Crucifixion of the Warrior God, Vols. 1 and 2* (Minneapolis, MN: Fortress, 2017), 589.

8. Boyd, *Crucifixion of the Warrior God, Vols. 1 and 2*, 590.

9. Andy Stanley, *Irresistible: Reclaiming the New that Jesus Unleashed for the World* (Grand Rapids, MI: Zondervan, 2018), 158.

10. Fleming Rutledge, *And God Spoke to Abraham: Preaching from the Old Testament* (Grand Rapids, MI: Eerdmans, 2011), 6.

11. Alexander Pope, "An Essay on Man," *Poetry Foundation*, https://www.poetryfoundation.org/poems/44899/an-essay-on-man-epistle-i.

12. Bill Moyers, "Apocalypse: Genesis: A Living Conversation," *BillMoyers.com*, November 3, 1996, https://billmoyers.com/content/genesis-apocalypse/.

13. L. Daniel Hawk, *Violence of the Biblical God: Canonical Narrative and Christian Faith* (Grand Rapids, MI: Eerdmans, 2019), 31.

14. See Walter Brueggemann, *Genesis* (Louisville, KY: Westminster John Knox Press, 1982), 77.

15. Copan, *Is God a Vindictive Bully?*, 106.

16. Clay Jones, *Philosophia Christi*, Vol. 11, No. 1, 2009, 53, https://www.clayjones.net/wp-content/uploads/2011/06/We-Dont-Hate-Sin-PC-article.pdf.

17. Quoted by Andy Patton in "God-Ordained Genocide? Making Sense of the Invasion of Canaan," *The Crossing*, October 13, 2021, https://info.thecrossingchurch.com/blog/god-ordained-genocide-making-sense-of-the-invasion-of-canaan. From John H. Walton and J. Harvey Walton, *The Lost World of the Israelite Conquest* (Downers Grove, IL: InterVarsity Press, 2017).

18. James Emery White, "How Do We Explain the Slaughter of the Canaanites?," *Outreach*, November 4, 2020, https://outreachmagazine.com/features/evangelism/61070-how-do-we-explain-the-slaughter-of-the-canaanites.html.

19. R.C. Sproul, *The Holiness of God* (Carol Stream, IL: Tyndale, 2013), 128.

20. Nadia Bolz-Weber, *Shameless: A Sexual Reformation* (New York: Convergent Books, 2019), 70-71.

21. Walter C. Kaiser, *Toward Old Testament Ethics* (Grand Rapids, MI: Zondervan, 1983), 91-92.

22. R.C. Sproul, *The Holiness of God* (Carol Stream, IL: Tyndale, 2013), 117.

CHAPTER 6—IS GOD MORE TOLERANT
THAN HE USED TO BE?

1. Voddie Baucham, "This is WHY we pick and choose from the Old Testament," *Grace Bible Church*, https://www.youtube.com/watch?v=-pmlol_4rSc.

2. E.J. Dionne Jr., "A question to conservative Christians on gay marriage: Why draw the line here?," *The Washington Post,* December 11, 2022, https://www.washingtonpost.com/opinions/2022/12/11/gay-marriage-conservative-christians-lgbtq-plea/.

3. Albert Mohler, "Answering E.J. Dionne: Explaining Why Conservative Christians Cannot Just Accept Same-Sex Marriage and Move On," *The Briefing,* December 13, 2022, https://albertmohler.com/2022/12/13/briefing-12-13-22.

4. See Matthew Vines's book *God and the Gay Christian* (New York: Convergent Books, 2014). This book seeks to justify same-sex marriage by interpreting Scripture through the lens of contemporary understandings of homosexuality as an orientation.

5. R.C. Sproul, *The Holiness of God* (Carol Stream, IL: Tyndale, 2013), 43.

6. C.S. Lewis, *The Lion, the Witch and the Wardrobe* (New York: Macmillan, 1950), 75-76.

7. Donald W. McCullough, *The Trivialization of God* (Colorado Springs, CO: NavPress, 1995), 20.

8. Taken from "O Christ, what burdens bow'd Thy head," lyrics by Anne Ross Cousin, music by Ira David Sankey, *Hymnal.net*, https://www.hymnal.net/en/hymn/h/94.

CHAPTER 7—RETURNING TO THE GOD
OF TRUTH, NOT "TRUTHINESS"

1. "Road Trip to Truth," Season One, *Wretched Radio*, https://shop.wretched.org/product/road-trip-to-truth/.

2. *Merriam-Webster.com*, s.v. "truthiness," accessed July 31, 2023, https://www.merriam-webster.com/dictionary/truthiness. See also Merriam-Webster, "'Truthiness': Can Something 'Seem,' Without Being True?" *Merriam-Webster.com*, https://www.merriam-webster.com/grammar/truthiness-meaning-word-origin.

3. *Merriam-Webster.com*, s.v. "gaslighting," accessed July 31, 2023, https://www.merriam-webster.com/dictionary/gaslighting.

4. George Orwell, *Nineteen Eighty-Four* (New York: Signet Classics, 1977), 298.

5. G.K. Chestertson, *The Collected Works of G.K. Chesterton, Vol. 34* (San Francisco, CA: Ignatius Press, 1991), 145.

6. Jim Leffel, "Our New Challenge: Postmodernism," *The Death of Truth,* gen. ed. Dennis McCallum (Minneapolis, MN: Bethany House, 1996), 33.

7. This quote is attributed to Omar Bradley. Original source unknown.

8. Jim Leffel, "Postmodern Impact: Literature," *The Death of Truth,* gen. ed. Dennis McCallum (Minneapolis, MN: Bethany House, 1996), 91.

9. Leffel, "Postmodern Impact: Literature," 92.

10. Carl R. Truman, *The Rise and Triumph of the Modern Self* (Wheaton, IL: Crossway, 2020), 49.

11. Dennis McCallum, gen. ed., *The Death of Truth* (Minneapolis, MN: Bethany House, 1996), 17.

12. Gary DeLashmutt and Roger Braund, "Postmodern Impact: Education," *The Death of Truth,* gen. ed. Dennis McCallum (Minneapolis, MN: Bethany House, 1996), 119.

13. DeLashmutt and Braund, "Postmodern Impact: Education," 103.

14. George Orwell, "Politics and the English Language," *The Orwell Foundation,* https://www .orwellfoundation.com/the-orwell-foundation/orwell/essays-and-other-works/politics-and-the -english-language/.

15. Alexander Hall, "Michigan State's language guide chides against using words like 'America,' 'Christmas tree' or 'bunny,'" *Fox News,* March 30, 2023, https://www.foxnews.com/media/ michigan-states-language-guide-chides-against-using-words-like-america-christmas-tree-bunny.

16. Giulia Heyward, "A USC office removes 'field' from its curriculum, citing possible racist connotations," *NPR,* January 14, 2023, https://www.npr.org/2023/01/14/1148470571/usc-office-removes -field-from-curriculum-racist.

17. See: Erwin W. Lutzer, *No Reason to Hide* (Eugene, OR: Harvest House, 2022).

18. Joseph A. Wulfsohn, "James Carville: 'Christian nationalists' like Speaker Mike Johnson are a 'bigger threat than al-Qaeda,'" *Fox News,* December 2, 2023, https://www.foxnews.com/media/ james-carville-christian-nationalists-speaker-mike-johnson-bigger-threat-than-al-qaeda.

19. Chuck Colson and Timothy George, "Flaming Truth: Recalling Francis Schaeffer's Challenge," *Christianity Today,* February 15, 2012, https://www.christianitytoday.com/ct/2012/february/ remembering-francis-schaeffer.html. See also Francis A. Schaeffer, *Escape from Reason* (Westmont, IL: InterVarsity Press, 2014).

20. Melanie Phillips, *The World Turned Upside Down: The Global Battle Over God, Truth, and Power* (New York: Encounter Books, 2010), 265.

21. Frank Turek, *Stealing from God: Why Atheists Need God to Make Their Case* (Colorado Springs, CO: NavPress, 2014), 32.

22. Turek, *Stealing from God,* 35.

23. Selwyn Duke, "George Orwell is stealing my work," *American Thinker,* November 14, 2016, https://www.americanthinker.com/blog/2016/11/george_orwell_is_stealing_my_work.html.

24. Henry M. Morris, *Men of Science, Men of God* (Green Forest, AR: New Leaf, 2020), 19.

25. Lee Weeks, "Playbook for Life by Tony Dungy and James Brown," *Decision,* June 1, 2023, 16.

26. The original source of this account is unknown, but it can be found on multiple sites online.

CHAPTER 8—RETURNING TO THE GOD
OF CREATION, NOT BLIND CHANCE

1. Jeremy Rifkin, *Algeny: A New Word—A New World* (New York: Viking Press, 1983), 244.

2. Richard Dawkins, *The Blind Watchmaker: Why the Evidence of Evolution Reveals a Universe Without Design* (New York: W.W. Norton, 1996), 287.

3. Richard Lewontin, "Billions and Billons of Demons," *New York Times Book Review* 44, No. 1 (January 9, 1997), https://www.nybooks.com/articles/1997/01/09/billions-and-billions-of-demons/.

4. Carl Sagan, "The Shores of the Cosmic Ocean," *Cosmos* 1980 S01E01, *Internet Archive*, https://archive.org/details/Cosmos-1980-S01E01-The-Shores-Of-The-Cosmic-Ocean-720p-by-Vaibhav-khade.

5. Edgar Andrews, *Who Made God?—searching for a theory of everything* (Carlisle, PA: Evangelical Press, 2009), 25.

6. Dennis Venema, as cited by Barbara Bradley Hagerty, "Evangelicals Question The Existence Of Adam And Eve," *NPR Morning Edition*, August 9, 2011, https://www.npr.org/2011/08/09/138957812/evangelicals-question-the-existence-of-adam-and-eve.

7. John Schneider, as cited by Barbara Bradley Hagerty, "Evangelicals Question The Existence Of Adam And Eve."

8. William Lane Craig, "The Historical Adam," *First Things*, October 2021, https://www.firstthings.com/article/2021/10/the-historical-adam.

9. Craig, "The Historical Adam."

10. Charles Darwin, *Notebook M*, eds. Paul Barrett and John van Wyhe, 123, http://darwin-online.org.uk/content/frameset?pageseq=2&itemID=CUL-DAR125.-&viewtype=side.

11. Subby Szterszky, "Adam and Eve really existed, and why that matters," *Focus on the Family Canada*, https://www.focusonthefamily.ca/content/adam-and-eve-really-existed-and-why-that-matters.

12. See "The Case for Adam and Eve" by Christopher Eames, *Armstrong Institute of Biblical Archaeology*, November 21. 2018, https://armstronginstitute.org/126-the-case-for-adam-and-eve. Also, "In Light of Genetics...Adam, Eve, and the Creation/Fall" by Dr. John C. Sanford and Dr. Robert Carter, *Christian Apologetics Journal*, 2014, Southern Evangelical Seminary, https://docs.wixstatic.com/ugd/a704d4_f5f5f851384f4767889ad115b1e52f65.pdf. And "Is Genesis History?," by Kurt Wise, PhD, transcript from *Genesis History Movie*, 2017, https://isgenesishistory.com/wp-content/uploads/The-Interviews-Kurt-Wise-at-Old-Archway.pdf.

13. Albert Mohler, "Now Hiring, Rat Czar: New York City Has a Rat Problem—and a Bigger Ethical Dilemma of How to Terminate Them 'Humanely,'" *The Briefing*, March 2, 2023, https://albertmohler.com/2023/03/02/briefing-3-2-23.

14. Dr. Susan Berry, "Gov. Ralph Northam: Aborted 'Infant' Saved if 'Mother and Family Desired,'" *Breitbart*, January 30, 2019, https://www.breitbart.com/politics/2019/01/30/gov-ralph-northam-aborted-infant-saved-if-mother-and-family-desired/. See also video posted by @CalebJHull on Twitter, January 30, 2019, https://www.breitbart.com/politics/2019/01/30/gov-ralph-northam-aborted-infant-saved-if-mother-and-family-desired/.

15. "Third annual report on Medical Assistance in Dying in Canada 2021," *Government of Canada,* https://www.canada.ca/en/health-canada/services/publications/health-system-services/annual -report-medical-assistance-dying-2021.html. See also Alex Schadenberg, "Canada Releases 2021 Euthanasia Report. More than 10,000 Deaths Representing 3.3% of All Deaths," *Canada Health Alliance,* December 10, 2022, https://canadahealthalliance.org/canada-releases-2021-euthanasia -report-more-than-10000-deaths-representing-3-3-of-all-deaths/.

16. "Medical Spectrum of Gender," *American Medical Association,* https://policysearch.ama-assn .org/policyfinder/detail/gender?uri=%2FAMADoc%2Fdirectives.xml-D-295.312.xml. See also "Affirming the Medical Spectrum of Gender," *American Medical Association,* https://policysearch .ama-assn.org/policyfinder/detail/gender%20spectrum?uri=%2FAMADoc%2FHOD.xml-H -65.962.xml.

17. Jesse O'Neill, "White House dragged for honoring trans woman on International Women's Day," *New York Post,* March 9, 2023, https://nypost.com/2023/03/09/alba-rueda-trans-woman -honored-by-white-house-on-international-womans-day/.

18. "2023 International Women of Courage Award," *U.S. Department of State,* https://www.state .gov/2023-international-women-of-courage-award/.

19. Albert Mohler, "'My Femininity Does Not Define Me': Historic Women's College Faces Reckoning of the LGBTQ+ Revolution as Non-Binary Students Demand Recognition," *The Briefing,* December 16, 2021, https://albertmohler.com/2021/12/16/briefing-12-16-21.

20. Azadeh Ansari, "Transgender rights: These countries are ahead of the US," *CNN,* February 23, 2017, https://www.cnn.com/2017/02/23/health/transgender-laws-around-the-world/index.html. See also *U.S. Department of State,* November 7, 2022, https://travel.state.gov/content/travel/en/ passports/need-passport/selecting-your-gender-marker.html.

21. Ben Whitehead, "'Post-Truth World': Man Wins Miss Netherlands, Sparking Outrage On Twitter," *DailyWire.com,* July 9, 2023, https://www.dailywire.com/news/post-truth-world-man-wins-miss -netherlands-sparking-outrage-on-twitter.

22. "Why Deadnaming Is Harmful," *Cleveland Clinic,* November 18, 2021, https://health.cleveland clinic.org/deadnaming/.

23. James Queally, "Prosecutor in controversial Hannah Tubbs case suspended for 'misgendering' defendant," *Los Angeles Times,* March 1, 2023, https://www.latimes.com/california/story/2023 -03-01/l-a-county-prosecutor-hannah-tubbs-case-suspended-misgendering-defendant.

24. Michael Rothman and Joi-Marie McKenzie, "Caitlyn Jenner Shares a Photo from Her Father's Day Celebration," *ABC News,* June 22, 2015, https://abcnews.go.com/Entertainment/ caitlyn-jenner-shares-photo-fathers-day-celebration/story?id=31939242.

25. See Wikipedia: https://en.wikipedia.org/wiki/Siproites.

26. See Wikipedia: https://en.wikipedia.org/wiki/Hermaphroditus.

27. Morg Daniels, "Ancient Mesopotamian Transgender and Non-Binary Identities," *Academus Education,* June 30, 2021, https://www.academuseducation.co.uk/post/ancient-mesopotamian -transgender-and-non-binary-identities.

28. Kate Anderson, "Trans Activists Criticize Right-Wingers, Christians In Aftermath Of Nashville School Shooting," *Daily Caller*, March 28, 2023, https://dailycaller.com/2023/03/28/trans-activists-nashville-school-shooter-real-victim-massacre/. See also Ariel Zilber, "NBC freelance reporter ripped for linking Nashville shooting to Ben Shapiro, Daily Wire," *New York Post*, March 28, 2023, https://nypost.com/2023/03/28/nbc-reporter-ripped-for-linking-nashville-shooting-to-ben-shapiro-daily-wire/.

29. Denny Burk, *What Is the Meaning of Sex?* (Wheaton, IL: Crossway, 2013), 160.

30. Burk, *What Is the Meaning of Sex?*, 161.

31. I recommend Jeremiah J. Johnston's 2017 book *Unimaginable: What Our World Would Be Like Without Christianity* for further reading on this topic. This scholarly treatise examines a wide range of social, moral, and cultural changes made possible by Christianity. Those who read it will be amazed at the positive impact Christianity has had in the midst of our fallen, unjust, and chaotic world.

32. Herman Bavinck, *Reformed Dogmatics: Vol. 3: Sin and Salvation in Christ* (Grand Rapids, MI: Baker Academic, 2006), 28.

33. Thomas Brooks, *The Selected Works of... Thomas Brooks, Vol. 1* (London: L.B. Seeley and Son, 1824), 41.

CHAPTER 9—RETURNING TO THE GOD OF MORAL ABSOLUTES, NOT OUR PERSONAL PREFERENCES

1. C.S. Lewis, *Mere Christianity*, The Complete C.S. Lewis Signature Classics (San Francisco, CA: HarperOne, 2007), 41.

2. Fyodor Dostoevsky, *The Brothers Karamazov*, trans. and annotated by Richard Pevear and Larissa Volokhonsky (New York: Farrar, Straus and Giroux, 2007), 589.

3. Frank Turek, *Stealing from God: Why Atheists Need God to Make Their Case* (Colorado Springs, CO: NavPress, 2014), 116.

4. Will Durant, *The Humanist*, February 1977, 26.

5. Will and Ariel Durant, *The Lessons of History* (New York: Simon & Schuster, 2012), 38.

6. See David Hume, *A Treatise of Human Nature* (London: John Noon, 1888), 677.

7. John C. Hess, "French Nobel Biologist Says World Based on Chance Leaves Man Free to Choose His Own Ethical Values," *The New York Times*, March 15, 1971, https://www.nytimes.com/1971/03/15/archives/french-nobel-biologist-says-world-based-on-chance-leaves-man-free.html.

8. William James, *A Pluralistic Universe: Hibbert Lectures at Manchester College on the Present Situation in Philosophy* (New York: Longmans, Green, 1909), 309.

9. Albert Camus, *The Myth of Sisyphus and Other Essays* (New York: Knopf Doubleday, 2012), 3.

10. Julien Offray de La Mettrie, *La Mettrie: Machine Man and Other Writings* (Cambridge: Cambridge University Press, 1996), 39.

11. Pierre Jean Georges Cabanis, *Rapports du Physique et du Moral de l'homme* (Paris: Chez Crapart, Caille et Ravier, 1805).

12. Jean-Paul Satre, *Being and Nothingness,* trans. Hazel E. Barnes (New York: Washington Square, 1965), 627.

13. Quoted in John Whitehead, *The Second American Revolution* (Elgin, IL: David C. Cook, 1982), 52.

14. Bertrand Russell, *Mysticism and Logic, and Other Essays* (New York: Longmans, Green, 1918), 47, 56.

15. Allan Bloom, *Closing of the American Mind* (New York: Simon & Schuster, 2008), 194.

16. Ludwig Wittgenstein, *Lecture on Ethics*, eds. Edoardo Zamuner, Ermelinda Valentina Di Lascio, D. K. Levy (New York: John Wiley & Sons, 2014), 32.

17. Bob Perry, "Four Lines of Evidence for the Existence of a Nonmaterial Soul," *Salvo*, No. 63, https://salvomag.com/article/salvo63/souls-searched-out.

18. Whomas Nagel, "What Is It Like To Be A Bat?," *The Philosophical Review*, Vol. 83, No. 4 (Durham, NC: Duke University Press, 1974), 435-450, https://www.sas.upenn.edu/~cavitch/pdf-library/Nagel_Bat.pdf.

19. C.S. Lewis, *The Weight of Glory and Other Addresses* (San Francisco, CA: HarperOne, 2000), 45-46.

20. Abraham Lincoln, "Reply to Loyal Colored People of Baltimore Upon Presentation of a Bible, September 7, 1864," *The Collected Works of Abraham Lincoln, Vol. 7*, The Abraham Lincoln Association, https://quod.lib.umich.edu/l/lincoln/lincoln7/1:1184?rgn=div1;view=fulltext.

21. William H. McGuffey, *The Eclectic Fourth Reader: Containing Elegant Extracts in Prose and Poetry from the Best American and English Writers* (Cincinnati, OH: Truman and Smith, 1838), 143-144, reproduced in John H. Westerhoff III, *McGuffey and His Readers: Piety, Morality and Education in Nineteenth-Century America* (Milford, MI: Mott Media, 1978, 1982), 151-152.

22. Corrie ten Boom, *I Stand at the Door and Knock* (San Francisco, CA: HarperCollins, 2008), 95.

CHAPTER 10—RETURNING TO GOD AS LAWGIVER, NOT A VACILLATING RULER

1. "The Enabling Act," *Holocaust Encyclopedia*, https://encyclopedia.ushmm.org/content/en/article/the-enabling-act.

2. Gerald Suster, *Hitler, the Occult Messiah* (New York: St. Martin's Press, 1981), 134-135.

3. William L. Shirer, *The Rise and Fall of the Third Reich* (New York: Simon & Schuster, 1960), 234.

4. "Nazi Party Platform," *Holocaust Encyclopedia*, https://encyclopedia.ushmm.org/content/en/article/nazi-party-platform. See also Peter Matheson, ed., *The Third Reich and the Christian Churches* (Grand Rapids, MI: William B. Eerdmans, 1981), 1.

5. Peter Matheson, ed., *The Third Reich and the Christian Churches* (Grand Rapids, MI: William B. Eerdmans, 1981), 1. See also "Nazi Party Platform," *Holocaust Encyclopedia*, https://encyclopedia.ushmm.org/content/en/article/nazi-party-platform.

6. A. W. Tozer. *I Talk Back to the Devil: The Fighting Fervor of the Victorious Christian*, The Tozer Pulpit, 4, Wingspread, Kindle edition.

7. Quoted in *The Third Reich and the Christian Churches*, Peter Matheson, ed. (Grand Rapids, MI: William B. Eerdmans, 1981), 1-2.

8. Quoted in *The Third Reich and the Christian Churches*, 2.

9. Quoted in *The Third Reich and the Christian Churches*, 4.

10. *The Third Reich and the Christian Churches*, 9-10.

11. David G. Fountain, *Contending for the Faith: E.J. Poole-Connor, a Prophet Amidst the Sweeping Changes in English Evangelicalism* (London: Wakeman Trust, 1966), 37.

12. Shirer, *The Rise and Fall of the Third Reich*, 268.

13. Quoted in Joachim C. Fest, *Hitler* (New York: Harcourt, 1973), 212.

14. R.J. Rushdoony, *Law and Liberty* (Fairfax, VA: Thoburn, 1971), 33.

15. Shirer, *The Rise and Fall of the Third Reich*, 238.

16. Heinrich Himmler, October 4, 1943 speech to the SS Group leaders in Pozan, quoted in "Heinrich Himmler," *Jewish Virtual Library*, https://www.jewishvirtuallibrary.org/heinrich-himmler.

17. "Adolf Eichmann's Final Plea: 'In His Own Words,'" *Remember.org*, https://remember.org/eichmann/ownwords.

18. See PDF of mail message to Mark Lee Dickson, https://www.liveaction.org/news/wp-content/uploads/2020/06/Scan2020-06-10_092620-letter.pdf.

19. Benjamin Franklin, "Constitutional Address on Prayer," delivered Thursday, June 28, 1787, quoted in *The Records of the Federal Convention of 1787, Vol. 1*, Max Farrand, ed. (New Haven, CT: Yale University Press, 1966), 151.

20. "The Declaration of Independence," *National Archives*, https://www.archives.gov/founding-docs/declaration.

21. Charles Gregg Singer, *A Theological Interpretation of American History* (Phillipsburg, NJ: Presbyterian & Reformed, 1964), 285.

22. "Give me the man and I will give you the case against him," see *Wikipedia*, https://en.wikipedia.org/wiki/Give_me_the_man_and_I_will_give_you_the_case_against_him.

23. David Kallman, "The Hate Police Are Coming for You," *Detroit News*, June 8, 2023, https://www.detroitnews.com/story/opinion/2023/06/07/kallman-the-hate-police-are-coming-for-you/70298045007/.

24. "Bill C-4," *Parliament of Canada*, https://www.parl.ca/DocumentViewer/en/44-1/bill/C-4/royal-assent.

25. "Executive Order on Ensuring Responsible Development of Digital Assets," *The White House Briefing Room*, March 9, 2022, https://www.whitehouse.gov/briefing-room/presidential-actions/2022/03/09/executive-order-on-ensuring-responsible-development-of-digital-assets/.

26. John Knox, "The Appellation from the Sentence Pronounced by the Bishops and Clergy: Addressed to the Nobility and Estates of Scotland 1558," *Still Waters Revival Books*, https://swrb .com/newslett/actualnls/Appellat.htm.

27. Although some dispute that Göring said these exact words, the statement has historically been shown to be true.

CHAPTER 11—RETURNING TO THE GOD OF WRATH
AND GRACE, NOT UNCONDITIONAL LOVE

1. The original quote is "Without God and the future life? It means everything is permitted now, one can do anything." From Fyodor Dostoevsky, *The Brothers Karamazov*, trans. and annotated by Richard Pevear and Larissa Volokhonsky (New York: Farrar, Straus and Giroux, 2007), 589.

2. Dostoevsky, *The Brothers Karamazov*, 238.

3. Clay Jones, "We Don't Take Human Evil Seriously So We Don't Understand Why We Suffer," ClayJones.net, 2011, 1, https://www.clayjones.net/wp-content/uploads/2011/06/Human-Evil -and-Suffering.pdf.

4. Jones, "We Don't Take Human Evil Seriously so We Don't Understand Why We Suffer," 10.

5. See Aleksandr Solzhenitsyn, "Acceptance Address by Mr. Aleksandr Solzhenitsyn," *Templeton Prize*, May 10, 1983, https://www.templetonprize.org/laureate-sub/solzhenitsyn-acceptance-speech/.

6. Quoted in "What Does 'God Gave Them Over' Mean? A Study in Divine Retribution by Dr. S. Lewis Johnson," *LifeCoach4God*, June 2, 2012, https://lifecoach4god.life/tag/an-exegetical -study-of-romans-118-32/.

7. "What Does 'God Gave Them Over' Mean? A Study in Divine Retribution by Dr. S. Lewis Johnson."

8. Thomas Watson, *The Mischief of Sin* (Morgan, PA: Soli Deo Gloria, 1994), 8.

9. "What Does 'Gave Them Over' Mean? A Study in Divine Retribution by Dr. S. Lewis Johnson."

10. Rosaria Butterfied, *The Secret Thoughts of an Unlikely Convert* (Pittsburgh, PA: Crown and Covenant, 2012).

11. Jonathan Edwards, *The Sermons of Jonathan Edwards: A Reader*, eds. Wilson H. Kimnach, Kenneth P. Minkema, and Douglas A. Sweeney (New Haven, CT: Yale University Press, 1999), 50-51, 53.

12. Edwards, *The Sermons of Jonathan Edwards: A Reader*, 55.

13. Edwards, *The Sermons of Jonathan Edwards: A Reader*, 63.

14. Horace, *Horace's Satires and Epistles,* trans. Jacob Fuchs (New York: W.W. Norton, 1977), 89.

15. Tim Townsend, *Mission at Nuremberg—an American Army Chaplain and the Trial of the Nazis* (New York: HarperCollins, 2014), 271-272.

16. George Matheson, "O Love That Wilt Not Let Me Go," *Hymnary.org*, https://hymnary.org/ text/o_love_that_wilt_not_let_me_go.

EPILOGUE: A GLORIOUS DARKNESS

1. Adrian Rogers, "How can it be 'gloriously dark'?" *Love Worth Finding*, September 11, 2018, https://www.lwf.org/daily-devotions/how-can-it-be-gloriously-dark.

2. Martin Luther, "A Mighty Fortress," *Hymnary.org*, https://hymnary.org/text/a_mighty_fortress_is_our_god_a_bulwark.

OTHER RESOURCES FROM
ERWIN W. LUTZER

"If I could, I would put this book into the hands of every Christian in America."
—Dr. David Jeremiah

Responding Courageously to Our Culture's Assault on Christianity

We Will Not Be SILENCED

Erwin W. Lutzer

WE WILL NOT BE SILENCED

We Will Not Be Silenced prepares you to live out your convictions against a growing tide of hostility. Gain a better understanding of nonbelievers' legitimate hurts and concerns regarding issues like racism, sexism, and poverty—and identify the toxic responses secular culture disguises as solutions. In the process, you'll see how you can show compassion and gentleness to those outside of the faith without affirming their beliefs.

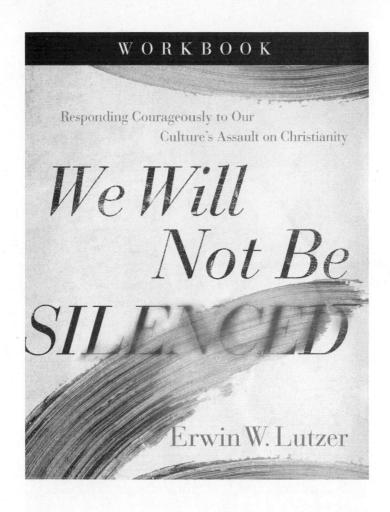

WE WILL NOT BE SILENCED WORKBOOK

This companion workbook to *We Will Not Be Silenced* gives you practical tools for responding to culture's hostility with Christlike strength and compassion. You'll be equipped to stand boldly for your faith and enriched in your understanding of how to do so effectively.

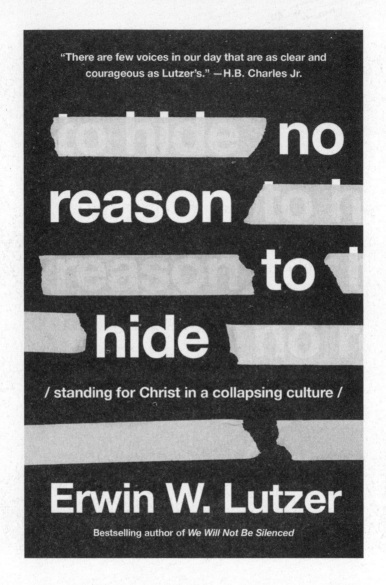

NO REASON TO HIDE

No Reason to Hide is a rallying reminder that Christians everywhere must have the courage to stand up and proclaim Scripture's truth to a culture in need of what only God can offer.

NO REASON TO HIDE WORKBOOK

In a culture where we as Christians can no longer afford to remain silent, the *No Reason to Hide Workbook* will encourage and equip you as you take a bold stand for faith in today's wayward world.

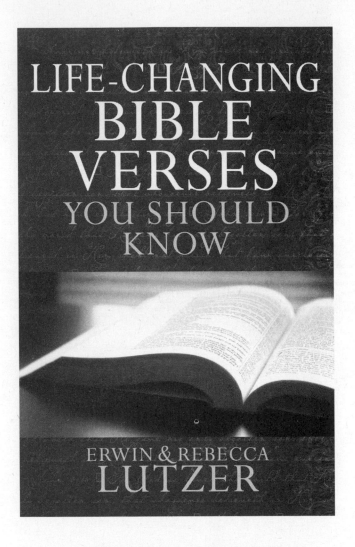

LIFE-CHANGING BIBLE VERSES
YOU SHOULD KNOW

With Rebecca Lutzer

In this book, Bible teacher Erwin Lutzer and his wife, Rebecca, have carefully selected more than 100 Bible verses that speak directly to the most important issues of life, and explained the very practical ways those verses can encourage and strengthen you.

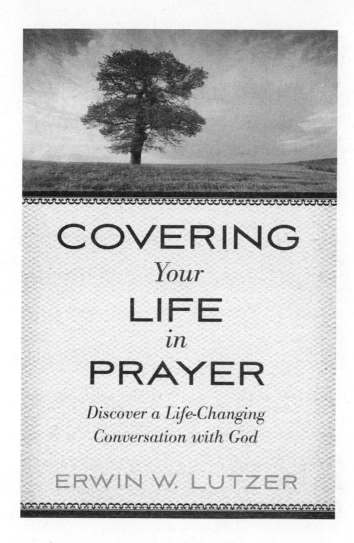

COVERING YOUR LIFE IN PRAYER

Every Christian longs for a better and more intimate prayer life. And one of the most effective ways you can grow more powerful in prayer is to learn from the prayers of others. In this book you'll discover new ways to pray. A wonderful resource for expanding your prayer horizons and enriching your relationship with God.

ERWIN W. LUTZER

THE POWER OF A CLEAR CONSCIENCE

Let God Free You from Your Past

THE POWER OF A CLEAR CONSCIENCE

Do you struggle with feelings of guilt about your past? This is not how God intends for you to live. Your conscience was not created to hold you prisoner, but to guide you and point you to freedom from guilt and bad habits. You'll learn that no failure is permanent and no life is beyond God's power to bring about change.

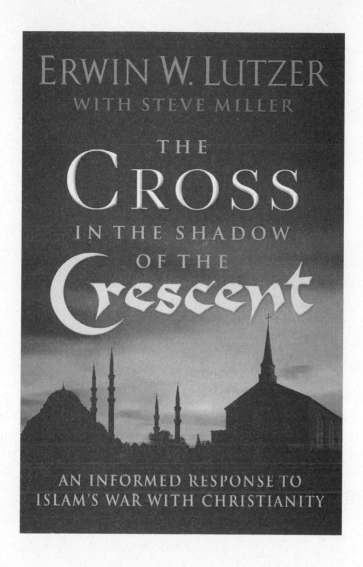

ERWIN W. LUTZER
WITH STEVE MILLER

THE
CROSS
IN THE SHADOW
OF THE
Crescent

AN INFORMED RESPONSE TO
ISLAM'S WAR WITH CHRISTIANITY

THE CROSS IN THE SHADOW
OF THE CRESCENT

Islam is on the rise all over the West, including in America. In this compelling book, Erwin Lutzer urges Christians to see this as both an opportunity to share the gospel and a reason for concern. A sensitive, responsible, and highly informative must-read!